DATE DUE

DE 8 '91			
FE 22 91			
MR 8 '91			
AP 1 0'92			
DE 4 '92			
JA 7 '94			
6-23			
5-2F-99			

A
Venom
in the Blood

A
Venom
in the Blood

by

Eric van Hoffmann

DIF

DONALD I. FINE, INC.
New York

Library of Congress Cataloging-in-Publication Data
Van Hoffmann, Eric.
  A venom in the blood / by Eric van Hoffmann.
    p. cm.
  ISBN 1-55611-206-8 (alk. paper)
  1. Gallego, Gerald Armand, 1946–   . 2. Williams, Charlene.
3. Serial murders—California—Case studies. 4. Sex crimes—
California—Case studies. 5. Murderers—California—Biography.
I. Title.
HV6533.C2V36 1990
364.1'523'092—dc20
[B]   89-46040
                                                          CIP

Manufactured in the United States of America

10 9 8 7 6 5 4 3 2 1

Designed by Irving Perkins Associates

To my sister, LCH, whose immeasurable help and advice made this book possible.

Acknowledgments

Thanks and appreciation to my agent, Joe DeRogatis, the very best, and of course to GCH, who was always there, and a big thank-you to UOS for all the encouragement, and to David Gibbons, an editor every writer should be lucky enough to have. And it is most certainly dedicated to all those hard-knuckled, thick-skinned partners in that Thin Blue Line out there on the streets with the fervent hope that our eleven ninety-nines will be answered soon.

THE GALLEGOS' KILLING GROUNDS

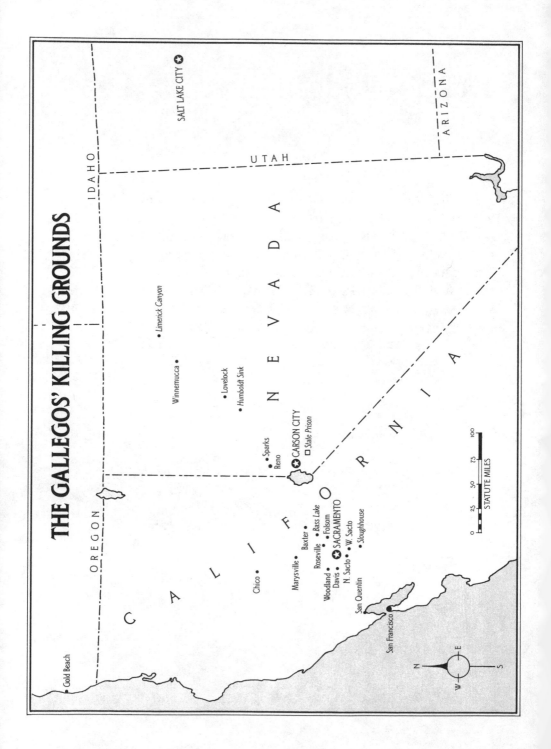

Foreword

In 1972, a totally new kind of multiple murderer suddenly appeared in America. The media, always anxious to create catchy new buzzwords, named them serial killers. According to the 1987 FBI Task Force statistics on multiple homicides in the United States, there are at least five thousand active serial killers operating around the country at any given time. The majority are sociopaths who prey upon any man, woman, or child who appears vulnerable or has something the sociopath wants or needs at that particular moment. Though their primary targets are women and sex, they must also make a living, so money and/or property is of equal importance to them.

As far as the experts can tell, serial killers are males who travel the freeways, streets, and country roads alone, looking for a hitchhiker, a disabled car, or almost any likely target. They stalk shopping malls, supermarket parking lots, isolated highway rest areas, and camping grounds. Their method of operation has been described by the FBI as a one-man guerrilla strike force: locate victim, strike, kill, retreat to safety.

And because they kill their victims, who are strangers and the only witnesses to the crimes, only one in a thousand serial killers is caught. The FBI report explains this, rightly or wrongly, by stating, "The average serial killer's victims are usually anonymous nonentities, who insist upon going in harm's way, and have no connection with their killer."

Nowhere in that mass of statistics is there a single reference to a husband-and-wife serial killer team. And not a single case has ever been officially documented by any law enforcement agency in the United States. As far as is known, the Gallego sex serial killer case is one of a kind. Due to its success, the Gallegos' method of operation has gone into the MO files of every major police department in the country, and is used as an example at the FBI training academy at Quantico, Virginia.

I became aware of the Gallego case sometime in late 1984 when I was contacted by a female relative of Gerald Gallego's mother, who had been an up-and-coming actress with the old MGM studios in the 1950s. At that time, my mother was a producer-writer-director at MGM, and the two women became friends while working on several films together. After listening to her story, I was intrigued by the fact that it was a husband-and-wife serial killer team rather than the usual, everyday variety of "I done it 'cause I hate my mother" or "God told me to do it" case, and I decided to find out if the story might be intriguing enough to write about.

I then discovered it was almost impossible to find a starting point because most court records were sealed. There was no real public information on Gerald or Charlene Gallego because of their several aliases; furthermore, the entire Gallego family was a closed entity. They had refused to talk to anyone about anything. Gerald's mother even claimed to be the housekeeper when questioned by police about her son and daughter-in-law. Gerald and Charlene never spoke a word to the press after their arrests or during their trials, and haven't to this day.

But after the former actress introduced me to Gerald's mother, Lorraine Davies, Lorraine agreed to give me the names and addresses of people who had known the killers for years, and literally ordered them to talk to me. Most of their stories, including Lorraine's, seemed so farfetched and outrageous, I knew that I would have to dig deeper into the case.

As a former police officer, I always imagined myself totally inured to the ferocious savagery one human being can and does inflict upon another. But in all my experience, I had never heard or read of a criminal case history so brutally bizarre and senseless as the ten kidnap-rape-murders committed by Gerald and Charlene Gallego.

I spent many weekends going over the twenty pounds of material I had now accumulated on the couple. The unprecedented and bizarre fact that a wife would not only actively condone, but would use herself as bait to lure the victims, then willingly and vigorously aid and abet her husband in a series of violent sex crimes was a first for me. I had never seen or heard of a documented sex-murder team comprised of a husband and wife—and certainly not one in which the wife was an equally active sexual aggressor.

Strangely enough, neither defendant ever claimed to be insane. In fact, they resented the implication that they might be, and never denied being anything other that what they were accused of being—two people who acted out their sexual fantasies, then killed their victims in order to avoid being identified.

I decided to locate as many of Gerald's ex-wives, mistresses, cellmates, and relatives as was possible with the intent of personally interviewing them. Thanks largely to my friend, the former actress, and to Lorraine, ninety-five percent of those interviews were successfully completed, and are interwoven throughout the story. I was fortunate enough to talk with Lorraine during more than thirty separate, secretly arranged interviews. She was terribly frightened of her own people, and like most of the Gallego clan, had refused to talk to anybody else about anything; I was also granted an exclusive interview with Gerald, who was by that time on death row.

This is the true narrative of the Gallego husband-and-wife serial killer team. It evolves entirely from their own words and actions, sworn statements from informants, information knowingly or unknowingly supplied by the killers, old court records, and statements by the people who knew them best.

It is not a detective story, a psychiatric textbook of opinions on serial killers, or an attempt at a psychological explanation or excuse as to *why* Gerald Armond Gallego and Charlene Adelle Gallego suddenly decided to commit ten kidnap-rape murders in less than three years. Their motivations became crystal clear after reading of their private lives and backgrounds and hearing statements such as this one from Charlene: "We had this sexual fantasy, see, and we just did it because it was so easy."

In most true crime stories, the names of *all* investigating officers even remotely connected with the case are mentioned prominently in exchange for their cooperation with the writer. That would have been the case with this story except for the fact that Sacramento County officers did not even come close to cracking the Gallego serial murders, and if Charlene hadn't solved it for them by confessing during a fit of jealous rage in order to get even with her husband, it is very likely that Gerald and Charlene would still be killing teenage girls.

Even though their names are withheld by request, many sincere thanks go to those half-dozen law enforcement burnouts in three states who gave this writer their true, inside, off-the-record accounts of this case, and for their many vignettes of dark cop humor.

In this narrative, many of the names, descriptions, and locations have been changed—some for sources who demanded anonymity before talking because they feared, and still do, retaliation from members of the Gallego family. In most cases, the names of the victims have been changed as well in order to spare their friends and families further agony beyond what they have already experienced due to the kidnapping and murder of their loved ones.

Chapter 1

Wayfaring Strangers in a Strange Land

Sloughouse is a dejected one-street town sitting in isolation to the southwest of Sacramento, California. But this corner of the Sacramento Valley has the richest farming land in the state, and produces two highly lucrative crops per year of onions, grapes, sugar beets, tomatoes, and various types of beans.

It is not a place where murder is even thought of, much less committed.

The Portuguese, Italian, Swiss, and Germans who own this land are descendants of California's first pioneer families. They are hard-working, wealthy, and powerful in state politics. They keep low profiles, never mention their enormous bank accounts and achieve their goals through federal and state politicians they've bought and paid for.

Because anything over a quarter-acre of land is a "ranch" in California, they are known as ranchers, not farmers, and would be somewhat insulted if they were called "farmers." They drive Mercedes rather than pickup trucks, wear business suits instead of overalls, and five-hundred-dollar Stetson hats in place of long-billed baseball caps with CAT printed on the front.

Marcello Silvero's family has owned such a ranch for the past 140 years. It fronts a two-lane highway called Sloughouse Road, and just at sundown on September 13, 1978, two of his farmhands were walking toward this road, hoping to hitch a ride into Sacramento, where they intended to cash their paychecks and buy money orders to send to their families in Jalisco, Mexico.

Julio Chavez and Cesar Aguilar had been close friends since boyhood; they had crossed the border illegally with the same Coyote who then surreptitiously shipped them via the trunk of a car to the Silvero ranch as irrigation hands.

"What's that?" Cesar Aguilar asked his companion, pointing to a white blob lying in the dry grass a hundred yards from the pathway.

"Looks like a bundle of old clothes," Chavez answered, peering through the gloom, "Or maybe some girl's panties and slip she left behind . . . you know how the gringos love to drive out here in the country and make love."

"Let's take a look. It might be something we can use," Aguilar said, leaping across the muddy irrigation ditch and walking toward the bundle.

"I'll wait here," Chavez called after him, adding that he didn't want to get his new cowboy boots dirty.

Aguilar walked to the object and stood looking at it in the dim twilight. He was motionless for a full two minutes, and Chavez shouted impatiently, "What is it? Something valuable?"

Aguilar whirled suddenly and came back at a dead run, cleared the irrigation ditch with a kangaroolike leap, and grabbed his friend by both shoulders.

"It's a dead body!" he panted, his dark Indian face pale with fear and surprise.

"Oh my God!" Julio whispered, crossing himself.

"A dead gringo woman . . . shot in the head!"

"Oh my *dear* God!" Julio murmured, crossing himself again.

The two men stood looking at each other, silently trying to decide what to do—should they be honest and report the body or be smart and run like hell?

The last thing they could afford was to become mixed up with a murdered gringo woman lying in a field less than five hundred yards from the shack they called home. At best, they would face questioning and miss valuable work time; at worst, they could be arrested and accused of the crime. Aguilar and Chavez were deeply religious, hardworking, unworldly country boys who hadn't seen a flush toilet until they arrived in California. But they were well enough acquainted with the pitfalls of everyday life to know that policemen are the same the world over—they like to solve crimes in the fastest and least complicated way possible.

Both men were weak in the knees with fear because they were well aware of the fact that two single male illegal aliens with no family, money, or even a working knowledge of the language who "discover" a murdered woman less than five hundred yards from their sleeping quarters would be ideal suspects in any country.

And they knew that gringo justice was not a last cigarette and a fast firing squad as it was in Mexico. They'd heard about the death house in San Francisco, where men were strangled with some kind of poison gas that caused them to cough up great chunks of their lungs as they died slowly . . .

"We could bury the body," Chavez whispered, "or throw it down that old well . . ."

"You stupid donkey ass!" Aguilar snarled at his boyhood friend, whom he'd always considered to be a nice fellow, though somewhat lacking in brains. "Suppose we get caught carrying the body . . . and everyone at the ranch knows we passed right by here . . . suppose Mr. Andersen is watching us right now, just to see what we'll do?"

Ollie Andersen was the ranch superintendent, and Chavez

glanced fearfully toward the small white tenant house where Andersen lived.

"What do you want to do, then?" Chavez asked, removing Aguilar's hands from their tight grip on his shoulders.

"We will go to Mr. Andersen. He speaks fluent Spanish, and, for a gringo, he is not a bad man. We'll put our trust in Mr. Andersen . . . and God."

"You may trust Mr. Andersen, and I will trust God," Julio Chavez said, crossing himself twice while praying that God was having a slow evening and had time to help two very frightened and totally innocent wetbacks out of what was shaping up to be a lot of trouble.

It was completely dark when Andersen, Chavez, and Aguilar returned to the area. They stood at the edge of the irrigation ditch and Ollie Andersen pointed the beam of his three-cell flashlight into the field.

"About there?" Andersen asked, just as he saw a small white blob on the brown grass.

"I don't think so, *Patron*," Aguilar answered, "it was further down . . ."

"Oh my *GOD!*" Julio Chavez gasped, feeling his knees start to buckle as he crossed himself with speed and vigor, "There's *two* bodies now!"

Forty-five minutes later, three units from the Sacramento County Sheriff's Department arrived, followed by an ambulance. The uniformed deputies found two dead white females lying exactly eighteen feet, ten inches apart. One body was in a slight depression, which accounted for Aguilar not seeing it the first time. Julio Chavez thanked God and crossed himself again because at least now he knew that the devil wasn't trying to get him and his boyhood friend by dropping another dead body on the ground every time they turned their backs.

Chapter 2

The Garbage Collectors

Six uniformed sheriff's deputies and an ambulance crew stomped all over the wet field, obliterating numerous footprints along with any other evidence that may have been lying around. When two plainclothes homicide cops from the Sacramento County Sheriff's Department arrived an hour later, both bodies were already in the ambulance. The older cop unzipped the body bags and found himself staring at two blood- and mud-covered corpora delicti, who looked more like wax dummies than former human beings.

They always do, the cop thought.

"A coupla teenage kids," the younger cop commented, more or less to himself.

"Yeah," his partner grunted, "ten to one they're runaways and we'll never ID 'em. When are these teenage babes-in-the-woods gonna learn that hitchhiking on the freeways and fucking around shopping malls is about as safe as a pocketful of white-lipped cobras?"

He bent down and unzipped both body bags completely, then shook his head.

"No pants. I don't need no coroner's report to tell me they been fucked—but raped or willing? Well, partner, from here it looks like after sex, they got a good smack in the head, then took three, maybe four small-caliber rounds in the skull. Nice lookin' kids . . ." He noticed stretch marks on the tall one's belly. Probably an unwed mother, he figured, so maybe welfare could come up with something if they found out where she was from. "Goddamit, when will they learn that staying home with mama ain't nowhere near as bad as ending up like this?"

"Mostly they'll learn just like these two did," his partner answered, "about ten seconds before they're chopped up. Some guy offers them a joint or snort of coke, they figure it's a simple trade for some pussy."

"Yeah. Well, I been familiar with the power of pussy since I was fifteen and it sure ain't as valuable as it used to be. Too much of it around, I guess. And now, we got a new generation of guys who ain't satisfied with a straight fuck and maybe a blowjob. These assholes gotta kill somebody or *know* they're gonna kill somebody before they can even get it up.

Both homicide men were law enforcement burnouts. They hated the victims they were forced to handle almost as much as the killers they seldom caught—not an unusual phenomenon. As the psychiatrists say, sooner or later we all come to hate the things that distress us the most, be it aging parents, children, lovers, bosses, or a car that won't start on a cold morning.

Between them, the two cops had just over forty years of law enforcement experience on the streets and country roads of Sacramento County. Stints as corrections officers, traffic officers, as members of the narcotics, vice, robbery, and burglary details were long behind them. For the past twelve years, they'd been first-string homicide investigators.

Both men were in their middle forties, both eligible for retirement. The older man intended to pull the pin next year and live on his two-acre peach ranch near Marysville, hopefully getting to know his wife of twenty years, who had stayed with him through all the neglect and lonely nights of being married to a hard-working cop.

The younger cop knew he'd have to be a thirty-year man because of three ex-wives and a total of nine children to support—and it was a mathematical certainty that a fifty-percent-of-salary pension wouldn't come close to covering it.

He had investigated and picked up the parts of close to a thousand homicide cases; he kept a record of them in a thick, curling, crumbling notebook carried in his left hip pocket. He had a vague idea of writing a book someday—what the hell, he often thought, Joseph Wambaugh did and got rich.

But he couldn't spell any word over five letters, and had no idea of how to start. Furthermore, he didn't *really* want to think too often about what was in his notebook, that twelve-year journal of horror in which he'd recorded such things as the long-term smoldering sparks of hatred between a man and woman that eventually ignite into bloody domestic murder, the kids he'd seen who'd been beaten to death by their mother or father—or by both at the same time—sex killings with tree limbs or jack handles sticking out of vaginas or stomachs or rectums, dead men, women, and children who'd been stomped, smothered, decapitated, shot, stabbed, burned to a crisp—all were listed in that old notebook.

But most of all, they were listed in his *head*. And he knew what he really was—not a homicide cop, but a glorified collector of human garbage. He, and the others like him, came along behind the fifty thousand reported murders each year and picked up the pieces, solved twenty percent of the crimes, forgot about the others, and tried to maintain their sanity until retirement.

"Well that's it," his partner said, slamming the ambulance door. "Let's get back to town and have a nice dinner. I feel like some liver and onions . . . I told those two wetbacks to get lost." They were scared shitless the cops would turn them over to the INS, but far as he was concerned, they didn't do anything but sneak into the country to find work. He figured he would have done the same thing if he was in their position. As far as Aguilar and Chavez' status, forget it. Let the feds hire a few more women and minorities to run down their illegal aliens. "That suit you?"

"Sure. What's a couple of more wetbacks? I don't have anything against the honest ones. Suppose we'll get anything worthwhile from the coroner's report tomorrow?"

"Naw. Nothin' we don't already know from eyeballin' the victims. Raped, knocked in the head and shot. Just two more fucked-up teenyboppers. We'll never catch the guy unless he shows up and confesses. Even if we get a possible blood type from his semen . . . a lot of fuckin' good that'll do unless he *does* come in and confess."

The other cop knew that his partner was somewhat behind the times in his colloquial description of teenage females, but probably accurate as to the rest of his statement. He lit a cigarette and walked slowly behind his partner across the muddy road to their car. He was overly tired tonight, and tried to think pleasant thoughts as he tiptoed through the mud, knowing that he was ruining a new pair of thirty-dollar made-in-Korea Shoes-Are-Us loafers.

He thought about going home to his filthy one-bedroom apartment, feeding his dog, and reading the latest Joe Wambaugh novel . . . old Joe, the favorite writer of every cop in America. Old Joe calls a cocksucker a cocksucker, a spade a spade, and a fucking thief a fucking thief. He speaks the language of the real world, hates everybody 'cause he's been there, just like us. He knows there ain't no good guys any more; it's just *us* and *them* . . .

Maybe I'll write that book when I retire, he thought, find me a literary agent in New York or maybe one in Hollywood who'll get the book made into a big movie, then get rich and buy me a two-million-dollar house next door to Wambaugh on Linda Isle in Newport Beach, get me a bugeye ketch and sail to Catalina Island on weekends, start getting my pussy and blowjobs from beautiful film starlets instead of plump waitresses with BO and hair that smells of bacon grease. What the hell, everybody's gotta have a daydream . . . even a garbage-collector of a cop like me.

Chapter **3**

The First Coroner's Report

Positions in the coroner's and pathology departments of large cities are known as lousy jobs because the pay and working conditions are poor, there's no prestige, no accolades, not even a pat on the back. Only a desperate doctor looking for short hours and a civil service pension would work in a place filled with dead derelicts, disease-rotted elderly bodies, and homicide victims who resemble something from *Return of the Living Dead.*

Most laymen believe that a coroner's report is a brilliant synthesis of forensic science and medical facts as to how the crime of murder took place, and that it will instantly pinpoint the bastard who done it. All the cops have to do is read the report, then arrest the murderer.

Contrary to TV shows, movies, and detective novels, all a coroner can do, depending upon his time, inclination, and the amount of skill he possesses, is attempt to determine how the victim died, what was done to the body before and/or after the death, and most important, the time death took place. Other than that, there's nothing magical about a coroner's report.

10

Placing the time of death is an educated guess at most, and depending upon temperature and position of the body, that guess can be off by more than forty-eight hours.

It was eleven o'clock when the two murdered females found on Silvero's ranch were delivered to the morgue-coroner's office. The one attendant on duty signed for the two DOAs at exactly 11:03 P.M.

The aide was a nice-looking man in his early thirties, with wavy black hair, soft brown eyes, and who spoke with a slight but noticeable stutter. He had been an aide in the coroner's office for five years and made nine dollars and fifty cents per hour.

The aide wheeled the bodies into a small, brightly lit, white, tile-covered room, where he followed normal operational procedures by stripping both victims naked and putting their clothes in separate plastic personal property bags.

One corpse was barefoot, but he was careful to inspect the shoes of the second victim for notes, money, or narcotics. If he found cash or dope, he kept it, and always made copies of any notes on the off-chance it might be worth something to a reporter.

This victim's shoes were empty, but the aide was always surprised at the number of DOAs who had a hundred-dollar bill or a bag of grass or coke in their shoes.

He looked at the dead teenagers for a few minutes as they lay under the bright light, then went down a hallway to his locker and came back with a Polaroid camera.

He photographed both bodies, at a distance and close up. Rigor mortis had left them and they were pliable as dough as he spread their legs for what is known in the porno business as a gape-shot of their genitalia.

The aide had many necrophilic customers eager for such photographs; they lived all over—from Sacramento to Los Angeles to San Francisco, among them writers for true detective magazines and big-name individuals in the film business. These particular gape-shots would be sold to a retired local judge, who happily paid one hundred dollars per photo of any dead teenage female with her genitalia exposed.

After locking his camera and pictures away, the aide covered both bodies with a dingy threadbare sheet and pushed them into the main cooler, where they would await their final indignity—an autopsy the following morning.

Every human being with an average IQ wishes to live with dignity and when they have the age and/or nerve to think about it, wish to die with dignity in their sleep. But most of all, they want their body treated with dignity until it's laid in its final resting place. They want to be remembered by tearful relatives and friends as one hell of a nice person.

Anyone with that reasonable desire in their heart should make sure they do not become a homicide victim.

To be on the sharp end of murder is not a dignified way to die—it almost *never* happens in your sleep, and from the moment your body is discovered, it belongs totally to the state or county in which it was found. In the autopsy room, where it must go first by force of law, the word "dignity" is about as rare as an uncensored editorial in *Pravda.*

At 3:30 P.M. on September 14, a coroner's deputy pathologist finished his autopsy on the two murdered teenagers found in the vacant field. He ordered his tape recording transcribed, then sent a typewritten official report over to the Sacramento County Sheriff's Homicide Bureau.

The coroner's autopsy reports, translated into plain language from the Latin code all medical people love to use, but still retaining all the qualifiers ("probably," "indication of," "appears," "is possible") which are more than enough to satisfy any Harvard law graduate, read as follows:

#91478–13–04: Jane Doe One is a well-nourished normally developed white female, 15–18 years of age, 5 feet 2 inches tall, weighing 135 lbs., long brownish hair that appears natural. No unusual marks, scars, or tattoos.

Clothing consists of a pink-and-blue-striped tank top–type blouse, blue jeans, a pair of jogging-type tan suede shoes with thick crepe soles. No underwear.

Following routine autopsy procedures, body was opened from esophagus to pubis. Vital organs appear to be normal. 12×12mm specimens of lungs, heart, liver, uterus, and tongue were removed and flash-frozen for poss. future patho. exam.

Victim was having menstrual cycle at time of death with a Tampax-type sanitary pad inserted in vagina.

No traces of semen were found in or around vagina, and there is no indication of vaginal trauma. Severe trauma around anus area is present and 1.2 ml of semen was found in rectum and mouth of victim.

As normal human male ejaculation, depending upon age, is 3 to 5.5 milliliters of semen, there is not sufficient quantity of semen here to indicate a normal ejaculation.

A preliminary Boron-X5 test of this semen indicates perpetrator's blood type to be 'O', the most common of all human blood types.

There is a deep human bite wound 1cm below victim's left breast and nipple of same has been almost severed, indicating another probable human bite. Perpetrator's teeth marks are 4×8mm, indicating normal-sized natural human front teeth (photos enclosed).

A sticky residue on both wrists and ankles indicates possible taping of victim's hands and feet before or after death.

There are pine needles, leaves, and tree bark entangled throughout victim's hair (samples enclosed).

There is a deep trauma wound on left side of victim's head near temple area indicating a blow from a solid rounded instrument, possibly a jack handle or tire iron.

There are three 6mm-sized (probably a .25 caliber) bullet wounds in victim's head, any one of which could have caused death. Slugs passed through skull area at a 40-degree angle, tearing right brain quadrant, and exited 3mm below left cheekbone, shattering 2 upper molars and dislocating jawbone.

CONCLUSION: Cause of death is probably due to one or all three bullet wounds to head. Victim was probably unconscious at time of death, possibly due to blow on head. Victim was sodomized and apparently performed fellatio on perpetrator sometime prior to death.

Time of death estimated to be within last 48 hours.

#91478–13–05: Jane Doe Two is a well-nourished normally developed white female, 16–24 years of age, 5 feet 7 inches tall, weighing 110 lbs. Clothing consists of a black-and-white tank top–type blouse, blue jeans. No underwear. No shoes or socks on feet.

No scars or tattoos. Stretch marks on abdomen and scarring of cervical neck indicate a past full-term pregnancy. Following routine autopsy procedures, body was opened from esophagus to pubis. Vital organs appear normal. 12 × 12mm specimens of lungs, heart, liver, uterus, and tongue removed and flash-frozen for poss. future patho. exam.

There is 3ml of semen in victim's vagina. There is 4.5 ml of semen in victim's rectum. Traces of seminal fluid also found in mouth and left ear. The 1.5 ml difference between amounts of semen in vagina and rectum would indicate the probability that victim was sodomized before vaginal penetration.

Judging from the grossly differing amounts of semen in rectum and mouth of Jane Doe One and Jane Doe Two, it is probably indicative that Jane Doe Two was sexually molested first. Semen samples from Jane Doe Two indicate the perpetrator's blood type to be 'O'.

There is a deep human bite wound on victim's left buttock, 2cm left of anus opening. Teeth marks are 6 × 7mm, indicating perpetrator has normal size natural front teeth. (THERE IS A MARKED DIFFERENCE IN TEETH SIZE IN COMPARISON TO BITE ON JANE DOE ONE AND POSSIBLY INDICATES THERE WERE TWO PERPETRATORS—Photos enclosed.)

There is massive trauma to victim's right breast nipple, indicating probable chewing from human teeth (photos enclosed).

There is a sticky residue on victim's wrists and ankles indicating her hands and feet were taped before or after death.

There is a "grazing" type, nonfatal bullet wound behind victim's left ear. There is a massive trauma wound on top of victim's head, indicating a blow from a rounded metal instrument, possibly a jack handle or tire iron.

There are three 6mm-size bullet wounds in victim's head, indicating Jane Doe One and Jane Doe Two were shot with same weapon, probably a .25 caliber handgun. (There are three surviving slugs, all in prime condition and are enclosed.) All three slugs penetrated victim's skull at a 60-degree angle, tearing brain tissue from a crosswise slant and stopping against left jawbone. Despite blow to head and "grazing" type bullet wound, victim was probably conscious when fatal shots fired.

CONCLUSION: Cause of death probably came from any or all of three bullet wounds to head. The massive trauma of the genitalia and anus area indicate victim was probably sodomized then raped via vaginal penetration with ejaculation occurring in both body cavities. Victim probably performed fellatio on perpetrator sometime prior to death and ejaculation may or may not have occurred in victim's mouth.

Time of death is estimated to have taken place within the last 48 hours.

At 8:30 P.M. September 14, while the coroner's autopsy report languished in the pile on a desk in homicide, occasionally being perused by several uninterested dead-body cops, none of them anxious to get involved with a new killing because they all had at least two dozen unsolved cases in their files, a detective from Sacramento Metro PD Missing Persons and a sergeant from sheriff's homicide met in the Sizzler restaurant on 16th and Broadway.

"What a lousy fucking day," the missing-persons detective

gasped, slurping boiling hot coffee. He lit a cigarette, then looked with perplexed surprise at the one he'd lit a moment before and dropped in an ashtray.

"Yeah? So what's different from yesterday? Or tomorrow, for that matter?" the homicide sergeant asked, firing up his fortieth Camel of the day, then extending a trembling hand toward his coffee cup.

"Some asshole's been driving me nuts since noon. He calls a dozen times, telling me his wife and her girlfriend's missing and I'd better find 'em for him. Then the prick comes in and braces me at my desk while I'm on the phone trying to convince the ex-wife not to go to the DA just because I'm a few months behind with child support payments . . ."

"Which ex is that?" said the sergeant, interrupting.

"Second one. Hell, my first and third ex wouldn't piss on me if I was on fire, much less give me a break. Anyway, I told the asshole to fuck off. Then his *mama* called Deputy Chief Norman Allen . . . you know him from when you were with Metro PD."

"Yeah. A paper-pusher. Never spent a day on the street, far as I know."

"Right. Well, he fell on me like a ton of elephant shit. Said I wasn't 'being responsive to the citizens' needs,' and I better get my ass over to the guy's house and talk to him. Soon's I'm done here I gotta go see this guy and his mama."

"Two splittails, you say? His wife *and* her girlfriend?"

"Yeah."

"Sounds mighty suspicious to me. Maybe the wife caught him dorking the girlfriend and he smoked both of 'em. How long they been gone?"

"*He* says two days."

"Oh. I thought a long time. Hell, they're probably at a motel catching up on their fucking and snorting free coke. How old?"

"Wife's seventeen, the other's sixteen. He says . . ."

"Wait a sec." The homicide sergeant interrupted again. "I got two brand-new teenage broads in the morgue that could fit. Whatta they look like?"

"He gave me a picture of the wife . . ."

"Lemme see it." The homicide cop held the photo in one hand and lit his forty-first Camel of the day with the other. He looked at the 5×7 color photo for a full minute, then nodded.

"Yep. This is one of mine. Looks like we gonna clear your missing-persons case and maybe I can pin this on the little smartmouthed fucker of a husband—or his mama."

"Hot dog!" The missing-persons cop smiled broadly. "Let's go treat sonny and mama to the sad news."

"I'm with you. I need a good easy collar . . . maybe get me on TV. Look great on the record . . . maybe get a leg up for that promotion to lieutenant. I'm looking forward to scaring the shit outta the grieving hubby when I ask for his alibi."

In the cop business, the finger of suspicion *always* points like a compass needle toward a male spouse when a wife is killed, even in an apparent auto accident—and for good reason.

That suspicion is based upon hundreds of years of experience; in eight out of ten cases in which the wife dies violently, she *was* killed by her husband. This automatic suspicion makes it almost impossible for a husband to commit a good, foolproof murder of his wife, no matter how much he feels she deserves it, or what her death might gain for him, be it money, property—or that cute little firecracker of a girlfriend he wants to marry without handing everything he owns over to the wife and her greedy lawyer.

Unfortunately for the homicide cop in this case, after he had the good luck of banging head-on into the husband of the murdered seventeen-year-old, the genuinely grieving hubby *did* have a cast-iron alibi, as did his belligerent mama.

Then, within a matter of minutes after the news of the two murders went on television, the finger of suspicion swung 180 degrees and pointed at two other good suspects who were equally innocent. The two would remain under suspicion for three years—mostly because of their race and their preference for women of a different color.

The meeting of the two cynical, highly experienced but over-worked cops for coffee, each of them with exactly the right information in head and pocket, accounted for the incredibly fast identification of the teenage victims found in that vacant field—not that it helped one bit in finding the real murderers.

Those two teenagers were to be the first in a long, convoluted string of serial kidnap-rape murders that would be carried out in three states over the next thirty months.

And not once during that time did a single police agency or individual officer connect the crimes, or even remotely suspect that they were all committed by a pair of shrike lovebirds who had their nest at 2067 Bluebird Lane in North Sacramento, California.

Chapter 4

The Predators

Gerald Armond Gallego, age 33, sat on the couch in his living room at 2067 Bluebird Lane watching an evening TV newscast. What he had just heard about a local double murder made him feel good.

He put his arm around the tiny, blond woman sitting next to him and said softly, "We're safe, baby."

"Do you think so, Daddy?" Charlene Adelle Williams Sonnenberg, age twenty, looked up at her common-law husband with adoring blue eyes.

"Of course. Didn't you just hear the news? The cops are zeroed in on a couple of niggers—and they'll never back off even if they know the niggers didn't do it. I tell you we don't have a thing to worry about."

"But that's *unfair!*" Charlene exclaimed. "It's just . . . just typical police racial prejudice!"

Gerald's wide, square head swivelled slowly on his thick muscular neck as he turned to glare at his pretty wife. He then drew back his arm and gave her a terrific thump in the ribs with his right elbow.

"You dumb cunt!" Gerald snarled sarcastically," You don't even understand what I'm talking about, do you?"

"Yes, I do!" Charlene protested, taking a deep breath and pressing a palm against her aching ribs, "it just seems so unfair."

"What do you care about a couple of niggers? You think they're all like those rich ones you used to fuck?"

"Of course not! You've told me how many blacks there are in prison and all, and how they intimidate and beat up the white guys, and how one tried to kill your sister." Charlene spoke in her most seductive voice as she snuggled against Daddy Gerald. As an extra precaution against another crack in the ribs, she put her hand between his legs and squeezed gently. When Daddy Gerald was annoyed—which was most of the time—he had a very disconcerting, but attention-grabbing habit of giving her an elbow smash to the ribs. It was very painful anytime, but when he did it in public, it was embarrassing *and* painful.

Charlene sometimes wished she hadn't told Daddy Gerald about her black ex-lover, Tyrone, because he insisted on bringing it up at the most inconvenient times. He would call her a nigger's whore or ask her in front of their friends if Tyrone had a twelve-inch cock. Gerald had been so open and honest with her when they first met and told her everything about himself, she, in turn, just couldn't resist whispering to him the deepest, darkest, most thrilling secret of her young, liberal, upper-middle-class white life—that she'd had a *black lover!*

Tyrone was a law student at Stanford when fifteen-year-old Charlene met him at a frat party she'd been invited to by his sister. He came from one of the wealthiest black families in northern California. Charlene told her best girlfriend about Tyrone, and the girlfriend promptly told everyone in school, noting that he was "all balls and shoulders." Tyrone was also tall, light-skinned and very handsome, so light that he could, and often did, pass for white.

Charlene Adelle Williams fell hard for Tyrone. Whether it was real love or just exotic sex, she never really knew or cared. At fifteen, Charlene was several men and boys past virginity, but as she told Gerald, only Tyrone had fulfilled each and every one of her sexual fantasies—until he, Daddy Gerald, came along, of course.

Charlene has been accused by almost everyone who knew her of having a chameleonlike personality in that she could, and did, adapt herself instantly to *any* situation. At seventeen, her IQ was determined to be 160. She played classical violin so well she'd been invited to study at the San Francisco Conservatory of Music.

Even though some so-called experts claim that such a thing doesn't exist, Charlene has a genuine photographic memory—an amazing ability for total recall that was to astonish some very skeptical cops and lawyers when she led them directly to some dead bodies she and Gerald had buried three years before in a remote-as-the-moon sector of Nevadan desert.

Charlene's father and mother, Charles and Mercedes Williams, never knew about Tyrone, though they were well aware that their beloved, petted, indulged, and pampered only child had used narcotics since she was twelve, and was a borderline alcoholic at fourteen.

They knew it in fact, but denied it in practice. As far as her parents were concerned, Charlene had not and never could do anything that would hurt *them.*

Like most parents who refuse to believe, Mr. and Mrs. Williams were in for one hell of a surprise. Later, even after Charlene admitted her part in ten barbaric sex murders, Charles and Mercedes never abandoned their daughter, and threw all their considerable wealth, knowledge, and influence into her defense, even risking prison by breaking several federal and state laws in order to protect Charlene *and* Gerald.

Gerald shifted his muscular body on the couch, pushed Charlene away, and said to her, "Get me a cup of coffee, and if you're gonna stay here, keep your mouth shut. I want to see that investigative reporter on channel eight. Maybe she'll have something new on the . . . uh, story."

And the reporter did, something that would infuriate Gerald, but give him even more confidence that he and Charlene had committed two perfect crimes. Charlene brought Gerald's coffee, and they sat watching a foxy blond reporter standing in the field where the murdered teenagers had been found.

". . . And over there," the reporter said, gesturing with her thumb, "the bodies of two young white females were discovered last night by farm laborers. Police have refused to release their names until next of kin have been interviewed.

"But this investigative reporter has reason to believe the victims are a sixteen-year-old runaway, and a seventeen-year-old married woman, both of whom lived in the Sacramento area. Sources indicate that police are seeking two young black males, who witnesses claim were seen riding in a car with the female victims early yesterday afternoon. However, this reporter has spoken with Dr. Emilie Hart, an eminent and well-known local television parapsychologist, and it is her opinion, and I concur, that this horrible crime was committed by a sick, lonely, frightened white male who is crying out for help, and did this terrible thing in order to get attention.

"I am now asking that sick man to call this station. If you will surrender to me, I will see that you get the help, treatment, care, and love you've always wanted and needed . . ."

Gallego came up off his couch with the primordial growl of a saber-toothed tiger who'd just fallen into the La Brea Tar Pits. He threw his cup and saucer against the wall and screamed, "That stupid, lying cunt! Frightened? Sick? Lonely? Crying out for help? Who the fuck is she talking about?

"She's just making it up, Daddy," Charlene soothed, moving a pillow in front to protect her ribs from an expected elbow smash, "You know how she's always lying . . . she couldn't know who you are. Just relax." Charlene knew that Daddy Gerald was going to be real cranky *all* night, and if she wasn't careful, he'd beat the crap out of her before morning.

But Gerald wasn't thinking about Charlene. He was walking the floor and thinking about that reporter's sob-sister, pseudo-psychiatric description of the killer—a description that threw Gerald into a rage he hadn't experienced since his daughter had squealed about their long-standing incestuous relationship. Gerald's first thought was to call the reporter and entice her into meeting him someplace, then kidnap the phony bitch, and give her a sample of exactly what the two teenagers had gotten. But he knew she would have a camera crew, and very likely, the police waiting in ambush for him. It was much safer to just forget it . . . for once, Charlene was right, the bitch didn't know him . . . didn't know him at all.

But then, no one ever *really* knows a sociopath.

If ever a man had marched to a different drummer all of his life, it was Gerald Armond Gallego. He flatly refused to change step and pick up the normal cadence of life no matter what society did to him.

At thirty-three years of age, Gerald would be considered a habitual criminal by any law enforcement agency in the world in that he'd been arrested twenty-seven times on high-grade felony charges starting with a felony juvenile fall for burglary and assault with a deadly weapon when he was ten.

Despite those arrests, and seven felony convictions, he'd spent less than six years in prison. Of course all that penitentiary time didn't include his reformatory and county jail time—those five years were considered by Gerald to be nothing more than a good prep school for the major crimes he intended to commit later.

Burglary, grand theft auto, assault with intent to commit murder, jail escape, assault and battery with intent to cause great bodily harm, felonious assault upon a person over sixty-five during a strong-arm robbery—the felonies went on and on with the state penal system doing nothing in the way of "reforming" Gerald, but still refusing to put him away for good despite the fact that California's "three-time-loser" law stipulates that a person convicted of three high-grade felonies in a row *can* be incarcerated for life without parole.

New York and several other states have similar statutes on their books, but like California, those states haven't sentenced anyone to that maximum penalty since the late 1930s.

Gerald had an above-average intelligence, could read, write, and do complicated math in his head even though he'd barely made it out of grade school with an F in all categories. Gerald Armond Gallego's one claim to fame in school was that his number of arrests for truancy had set an all-time record for Sacramento County that hasn't been equalled to this day.

He was a trivia buff and read everything from true confessions to a smattering of Greek classics—and he was one hell of a good jailhouse lawyer, having defended himself in three major felony trials and winning acquittals each time.

But other than his native intelligence, which was probably inherited, Gerald hadn't fared too well in the paternal or maternal ancestral departments. His father, Gerald *Albert* Gallego, had been executed in the gas chamber for the brutal, cold-blooded murders of two policemen when Gerald Armond was ten years old.

Gerald once told Charlene that he wasn't exactly sure how his father had died, and didn't *really* give a goddamn. But ever-the-opportunist Gerald would seek out and find the truth when he knew he'd need the sympathy an executed father might generate during a courtroom battle for his own life.

Gerald's uncle and three cousins on his mother's side were serving life in various California prisons for first- and second-degree murder. In fact, almost all of Gerald's male relatives had violent criminal records, and his half brother, David Hunt, was grinding out a fifteen-to-life sentence for shooting a liquor store clerk during an armed robbery.

Gerald's family was so contaminated by murderers, thieves,

and assorted other criminals, one of his former wives said that Gerald's blood was more poison than a cobra's venom, and that the unmanageable teenage daughter she'd had by him inherited that same venom in *her* blood, and would probably end up a multimurderess like Winnie Ruth Judd.

When he wanted to use it, Gerald Armond Gallego could project a Svengali-like charisma. He was friendly when he needed to be, and was said by some to be downright *charming*, with a born con man's ability to convince anyone to swallow whatever story he was laying on them.

Gerald was five feet eight or ten (depending upon whom you'd rather believe, Gerald or California penal records) and was built like a silver-backed gorilla, with a deep barrel chest, short muscular neck, and the massive legs of a running back.

To those people unlucky enough to have met Gerald Gallego, all said that the most impressive thing about him were his eyes. They were a deep, dark, brownish black, always cold, wide, staring, rarely blinking. His eyes, they said, bore a startling resemblance to those of the mad Russian monk and con man, Gregory Efimovich Rasputin.

Venom-blooded or not, Gerald leaked sex appeal like a rutting moose. And like Rasputin, Gerald didn't need to look for women—they flocked to him like buzzards to a dead carcass. So many that Gerald simply didn't have time to do justice to them all. So he used a very selective shotgun approach—whoever had the biggest welfare check, the best job, whoever acquiesced most gratefully to his sexual proclivities, and *showed* that appreciation by handing over their welfare money, paychecks, cars, and by taking total care of his domestic wants and needs—those were the women who received Gerald's *quality* attention. The others took leftovers, and if we believe what they now claim, were happy to get a few crumbs—barely enough to satisfy the sexual frenzy Gerald seemed to generate in all women.

One of his most unfriendly ex-wives said that Gerald was "terribly handsome—in a rugged, scary sort of way." And another ex who claimed to be still nuts about him would say that

"just *standing* next to Gerald made a woman wet in the crotch
. . . and even if she hated him, there wasn't a damn thing she
could do about that sexual attraction . . . I mean you wanted to
get him between your legs so badly it just *hurt,* and I actually
had wet dreams about Gerald until I got him in bed.

"Now, he didn't have a really *big* one, like some I've had, but
he sure knew how to use what he had . . . and I'd rather have
an hour with six inches of hard action than five minutes with ten
inches of a marshmallow."

Stories of Gerald's sexual abilities varied widely among the
many women who would later freely talk about him—some
swearing that he was a veritable virtuoso of sexual invention.
Only one complained that, ". . . he couldn't get it up at all unless
I sucked until my jaws ached, and even then, it wouldn't stay up
more'n a minute."

One of his ex-wives, a beautiful, blond, upper-middle-class
woman who readily admitted that she hated Gerald Gallego far
more than any ex-wife has a right to hate a former husband, said
that he was ". . . a perverted psychosexual maniac . . . it was like
being in bed with a rabid Tasmanian Devil. But his only inter-
ests in sex were sodomy, fellatio, and cunnilingus—in that
order. All of that was repugnant to me, but when I'd refuse to
go along, he'd beat me until I was a quivering, incoherent mass
of hysteria who'd do anything he wanted."

This ex-wife might have been somewhat dramatic in her description of the treatment she received at Gerald's hands, but
having the hell beaten out of them was the one consistent com-
plaint of every women who'd had a close relationship with Gerald Armond Gallego—wives, mistresses, girlfriends, all were
subjected to the one element Gerald used to keep his women
in line—force.

Like an old-time circus animal trainer, he'd learned how to
apply pain without serious injury; he usually administered with
dispassion and with the intent of forcing the subject to do exactly his will. In exchange they could avoid further pain and
receive a little reward now and then.

Surprisingly, only two of his women walked out because of the physical abuse. And one of them, who said she still missed him, took off only after Gerald tried to cut her throat during a hand-to-hand battle in their living room.

Some psychiatrists *claim* that women have a natural bent for masochism, which might account for all those women hanging in there with the likes of Gerald Armond Gallego. They claim that women have a higher tolerance for pain and accept subjugation far more readily than men, which might explain something about Gallego's women.

Sociopaths like Gerald Gallego are also masters of psychological manipulation, and again, if we believe psychiatrists who state unequivocally that the females of the species always subconsciously "want to do the right thing" in a love relationship, and are always willing to take first blame, that too might account for the loyalty of Gerald's women.

Whether or not those psychiatric hypotheses come close to the truth, Gerald Armond Gallego had somehow arrived at the same conclusions through trial and error. He had developed a scenario of mental harassment, physical abuse, and a system of rewards that unquestionably worked for him in controlling his women—and *control* is the name of the game with all sociopaths.

Simply put, Gerald had accidently discovered the exact same process used by the Marine Corps—to destroy a recruit's civilian personality, and then rebuild it to Marine specifications. The Corps truthfully states "Once a Marine, always a Marine"— any man who has passed through that mental tearing-down process will, at least subconsciously, belong to the Corps until the day he dies.

There is no way of knowing if that large covey of women who were closely involved with Gallego will always feel that at least a small part of them still belongs to Gerald. But again, according to the psychiatrists who studied this case for the defense, every one of those females will always be connected to Gerald Armond Gallego through their children with him, and by that rabid Tasmanian-Devil sex they'd experienced, but will never find again.

After all, there just aren't *that* many Gerald Gallegos around.

Even with such an aptitude for using his fists, Gerald had never been called a bully, not even by one of his long-suffering bruised women. In fact, Gerald had a minor reputation in grade school of defending any underdog kid who was the victim of a lunch-money shakedown, or was being mistreated in any way by the bigger kids. He was never accused of beating or mistreating his stepchildren. He'd never stayed around long enough to even *see* his own kids when they were small, not even his lover-daughter. One mistress said that Gerald was the kind of stepfather every woman hopes to find for her children.

Gerald loved all animals, particularly dogs, and was once arrested for knocking an elderly woman through a picket fence with his famous elbow smash to the ribs when he saw her beating her Pekingese with a stick because it had crapped in the wrong place. Not only did Gerald steal the dog, he scared the old lady so badly she refused to testify against him in court after her granddaughter had Gerald arrested.

But for all his sweetness toward stepchildren, championing of bullied schoolboys, and protection of animals, Gerald *was* a vicious streetfighter who could have taught the Hell's Angels a few things. He never looked for fights (like women, they just seemed to come to *him*) but when involved in one, Gerald fought to win—no sissy overhand jabs, no pussy slaps or scratches, he went in with dropkicks to his opponents balls, eye gouging, and all the other tricks experienced brawlers like to use. Even though he sometimes looked worse than the other man when it was over, Gerald was never known to lose a fight.

A Sacramento County parole officer who'd had him under supervision for a few months in 1968 said that Gerald had the strength and physical coordination of a champion boxer, the single-minded killer instinct of a mongoose when it sees a cobra, and an absolute disregard for the rights or safety of *anyone* who happened to be standing between him and something he wanted.

Gerald once told Charlene that because of his terrible parentage, he knew that he had been "touched" by the devil at the precise second he was born, and that curse would stay with him as long as he lived. Perhaps he had been. At least that's what one of the preachers who conducted funeral services for one of Gerald's victims was reported to have said.

It was after midnight when Gerald finally calmed down and stopped pacing the floor of his living room at 2067 Bluebird Lane. He forgot that the reporter had called him a frightened, sick, lonely white male who needed love and attention, and turned his cold, unblinking stare toward Charlene.

After a hard eighteen hours planning and carrying out the murders the day before, and no sleep for twenty-four hours, Charlene was all tired out. She'd fallen asleep, head back on the couch, snoring softly, mouth open so wide her chin was almost resting on her chest.

She still held the pillow protectively against her ribs in case Daddy Gerald decided to wake her with another thump in the slats.

Gerald Armond Gallego stared at his teenage-looking wife for a minute, shook his head in disgust, then walked over and gave Charlene's shinbone a vicious kick with the pointed toe of a wingtip Florsheim shoe.

"OOH-WHEE OW!" Charlene squealed as she leaped up and hopped around the room on one foot while rubbing her shinbone, cursing Gerald, and trying to light a cigarette, all at the same time.

"Uh! OWEE! Daddy, that *hurt!* You son of a bitch, I'm gonna tell my mama on you!"

"Aw, stop overreacting and shut up," Gerald said, unmoved by the threat, as he knew her mother loved him—almost as much as her daughter did, but in a different way, of course. "You're not hurt . . . I said, shut up, you cunt! Get that crap cleaned up!"

Gerald grabbed Charlene roughly and turned her to face the shattered cup and saucer he'd thrown against the wall.

"Get on it right now. You gotta get up early and clean the Olds and van—and I mean *clean.* You got that?"

"Okay, Daddy," Charlene whined, "just give me a minute . . . oh, that still hurts!"

Gerald took a handful of her long blond hair and gave it a painful jerk, whirling her dizzily around to face him.

"I told you what to do," he said, almost whispering. "Now get it done, or you're gonna get something that'll really hurt. Got it?"

Charlene knew that the moment had arrived to shut up and forget her shinbone because if she didn't do as Daddy Gerald ordered he would beat the crap out of her within the next few seconds. This certainty was based upon almost two years of experience in having the shit kicked out of her whenever Daddy Gerald thought she was a "bad girl."

Charlene picked up the broken cup and saucer, wiped the wall and carpet, then came over and stood more or less at attention while she waited for his next order.

"After you get the van and Olds clean, take these clothes and throw 'em in that dumpster back of the Lucky supermarket," Gerald told her as he started to undress. He was still wearing the clothes he'd had on the previous day when they'd done the murders—which was very strange, as Daddy Gerald changed clothes at least twice, sometimes three times each day—an idiosyncrasy that kept Charlene hopping between the laundromat and the ironing board.

Three and a half years later, Charlene would remember with her incredible ability for total recall the exact clothing he was wearing; she could repeat verbatim the conversation and action that had transpired that evening.

Gerald handed her a blue-and-white-striped shirt with blue cuffs and collar, dark blue cotton corduroy pants, and the brand-new black Florsheim wingtip shoes he'd used to turn her shinbone blue from knee to ankle.

"I'll get rid of the pistol tomorrow," Gerald said as she stood facing him, holding his clothes in her arms, waiting again for his next order.

"Let's take a shower and get some sleep," Gerald told her, "I want a good blowjob and a Greek fuck from you tonight, and no argument. Got that?"

"Yes, Daddy," Charlene answered obediently.

Just before Gerald went to sleep, Charlene put her arms around him tightly and whispered in his ear, "Daddy, yesterday was the most exciting day of my life . . . you were just marvelous out there . . . the way you handled everything, and showed those girls what I wanted. Thank you, daddy, and I'm sorry I ever doubted it when you said that I needed it as much as you . . . or even more than you . . . and I'm *glad* you killed them so we wouldn't have to worry about getting caught . . . so they can't *ever* identify us . . . when do you think we can do it again?"

"I don't know—when I feel it's time. Now get some sleep, goddamit. And leave me alone."

Charlene turned on her back and stared at the ceiling. She wouldn't be able to sleep of course, because she was reliving the events that had led up to the most exciting day of her life.

Gerald and Charlene had decided on the kidnap-rape-murder scheme some three months before their first hit. This decision was made sometime in late summer of 1978, a few weeks after Gerald came home from work early one afternoon and caught Charlene in bed with *his* sixteen-year-old runaway go-go dancer girlfriend. The go-go dancer was a cute little pug-nosed Irish amateur whore from Los Angeles who kept herself in pocket change and dope by doing a little nude dancing, and a lot of hitchhiking back and forth on the four-hundred-mile main route across the San Joaquin Valley between LA and Sacramento.

Her fees varied; a blowjob for a burly truck driver was five bucks or a two-nostril toot of good unstepped-on Colombian coke, or a bundle of fine California-grown grass from Mendocino County. At night she usually stopped at some ramshackle highway motel with a horny trucker in exchange for a hamburger, fries, milkshake, and the room rent. The go-go dancer always took in more dope than money, but that suited her just fine.

On numerous occasions she was picked up by a woman driver who was as horny as any trucker. But the women usually took her to a first-class motel for the night, bought her expensive dinner, sometimes a new pair of jeans or a tank top, and on rare occasions, a crisp one-hundred-dollar bill was slipped into her ragged backpack.

How the girl met Gerald isn't clear. But he brought the runaway home one day, introduced her to Charlene, and the three spent the night together in a sort of one-way ménage à trois. According to the runaway's recollections, both girls performed fellatio on Gerald, and he had anal sex with the go-go dancer, but he adamantly refused to allow the girls to have sex with each other. Like all *straight* ex-convicts, Gerald despised anything resembling gay sex, and once, while doing time at the California Correctional Facility at Chino, he stabbed and badly wounded an old jock who'd insisted upon sucking Gerald's cock while they were in the shower.

When Gerald came home early that fateful afternoon and caught his women in bed together, they were using a donkey-sized dildo and moaning and gasping and just enjoying the hell out of each other. Gerald was shocked absolutely speechless for a full minute, then flew into a murderous rage and tossed the go-go dancer through a window—which, luckily for the dancer, was open at the time—then proceeded to beat on Charlene until he was out of breath. When the go-go dancer went through the window, she hit the ground running and didn't stop until she was in LA. She didn't return to Sacramento until three years later when she read about Gerald and Charlene being arrested.

The purpose of her visit was an attempt to sell her "story" to the newspapers or television, her only recollection being that Gerald had tried to kill *her* when he'd caught the dancer and Charlene in bed together. Considering all the other weird aspects of the Gallego case, her additional angle was zilch newswise, and no one was interested.

So the pug-nosed Irish dancer ended up telling it to a bored cop in hopes of at least being called as a witness. The cop wrote down everything she said, then dropped it into Gerald's evidence-discovery file with one comment typed on: "bullshit."

Gerald's mother claimed Gerald told her that Charlene had said to him she'd never wondered about the fact that she was equally comfortable in bed with a man *or* woman. Lorraine also said that Charlene told Gerald she had never, at least consciously, remembered being sexually attracted to any woman in particular, and that she didn't look for lesbian relationships— they just sort of found *her*.

After Gerald discovered Charlene's propensity for other women, he was a total psychological wreck. He took the incident as a direct and degrading personal affront to his masculinity in that no woman of Gerald Armond Gallego's had ever started to swing both ways after she'd been to bed with him.

He beat Charlene at least once a day, and after each beating, would curse and call her every vile name he could think of—and considering Gerald's prison, cop, and jailhouse-lawyer vocabulary, Charlene probably got called a lot of bad names.

It was more than Gerald could stand. From that moment on, he had great difficulty in having an erection with Charlene as his sex partner unless she agreed to anal intercourse, which she didn't like, and all that made for big trouble in the love nest at 2067 Bluebird Lane. Their sexless sex life limped along for a month, a humiliating month for both of them. Charlene even left Gerald but came back after a week with her parents. Gerald spent the entire week Charlene was absent in bed with a shapely red-haired waitress—and had an iron-bar hard-on the entire time. For some reason, that made Charlene so jealous she stopped complaining about his limp dick and started trying to think of a way to cure it.

Charlene didn't care *who* Gerald fucked as long as he did it at home. Which seems a little bizarre even for Charlene and Gerald Gallego. What happened next was even more bizarre.

On July 17, 1978, Gerald's thirty-third birthday, Charlene suggested he invite his fourteen-year-old daughter, Mary Ellen, and her fourteen-year-old girlfriend to come down from Chico and visit them. It isn't clear whether or not Charlene knew at that time about Gerald's long-running molestation of his daughter, or if she hoped to have sex with the girl herself. It turned out to be a real party for Gerald, and a very enlightening experience for Charlene, who discovered that Gerald had no trouble at all in having an erection when he celebrated his birthday by sodomizing Mary Ellen—and very easily talking her fourteen-year-old girlfriend into orally copulating him. Lorraine said, and Mary Ellen confirmed in an affidavit, that Charlene joined in and/or watched the entire sexual episode with the two nubile girls, and decided she now knew how to cure Gerald's limp-dick problem with her. So after the four-way sex party, when the children had gone home, Charlene sat Gerald down for a long talk.

Charlene reasoned that if Gerald could turn into a raging sexual athlete with two fourteen year olds (the fact that one of them was his own daughter never seemed to bother Charlene at all) why not keep a pair handy at all times? To be shared with *her,* of course. Gerald countered that there was no way they could control two teenage girls every minute of the day and night, and sooner or later, they would leave or escape and blab the whole thing to someone.

"And *then,*" Gerald said morosely, "we'd be lip-deep in shit."

"That's very true, Daddy," Charlene agreed, "but we wouldn't need or want them underfoot all the time—we'd just need them when we're planning a party for the two of us."

Gerald's wide, unblinking Rasputin eyes became even more wide, staring, unblinking, and scary as his mind slowly absorbed the awesome, dangerous, and tremendously exciting possibilities.

"Our OWN love slaves? Gerald whispered hoarsely.

"Yes, Daddy. Our very own *disposable* love slaves!" Charlene answered happily.

ERGO, EUREKA, QUANTUM SUFFICIT!

The sinister scheme hatched by the two lovebirds was a classic exercise in simplicity. They would be the most brutal and bizarre string of murders in California history—and California is a state that's famous for outlandish, exotic, eccentric, and senseless homicides.

As soon as the plan was made, the Gallegos started a week-long training program. Gerald took Charlene out into the foot-hills near Roseville, and like an infantry firing-line instructor, taught her how to shoot their pistols: a .25 caliber Spitfire, a Smith & Wesson .357 Magnum, a .38 Colt revolver, and an AR-15 semiautomatic rifle, which is the civilian version of a military AR-16.

In two days, Charlene could put three out of six rounds smack in the center of a bulls-eye—which is better than most line policemen can do on their best day at the shooting range.

They spent hours perfecting the spiel Charlene would use to lure the potential love slaves. They put their hearts and souls into preparing themselves for those kidnap-rape murders, planning them like a precision guerrilla-style operation.

Charlene was still wide awake at 2:00 A.M., so she quietly reached under the bed for a joint she always kept handy when she couldn't sleep. Daddy Gerald didn't allow her to smoke in bed—and for a very good reason. Charlene had a dangerous habit of falling asleep while doing so, and once set the bed on fire, along with Gerald's hair.

He never forgave her for that, and would later say that she had tried to pull a "burning bed" scene in an attempt to kill him. Gerald didn't use narcotics, other than tobacco and alcohol, and was contemptuous of anyone who did. But he generously allowed Charlene to have a little coke and marijuana now and then, providing she only used it at home, where Gerald could keep an eye on his scatterbrained lovebird.

"Dope'll put you lip-deep in shit," Gerald told her knowingly, using his favorite expression for big trouble.

Gerald was a heavy sleeper, and now Charlene lit the joint, took three deep, satisfying puffs, and let her total-recall memory recorder start playing back the exciting events of the previous day.

Chapter 5

The Prey

On Tuesday, September 12, 1978, Gerald Armond Gallego was awake by 7:00 A.M. He brought Charlene to life with his usual elbow smash to her tender ribs.

"Wake up, cunt! Today we do it!"

Charlene didn't ask what they were going to do because she knew, and had been waiting impatiently for Daddy Gerald to decide when the time was right for their first adventure into the disposable love slave business.

She was excited and happy, but could have done without the elbow smash. It was the way Daddy always woke her up and even though she was used to it by now, Charlene wished he'd stop calling her cunt all the time. She liked it much better when he called her baby.

They had their usual breakfast of eggs, bacon, toast, and coffee, which Gerald cooked most of the time because he said that Charlene was the worst cook he'd ever seem outside of a prison mess hall, a charge Charlene couldn't deny, as cooking was something she'd never managed to get the hang of—mainly because she hated to do it.

After eating, Gerald went into the living room and began cleaning, oiling, and loading a .25 caliber semiautomatic pistol.

It was a tiny imported handgun, the type that was sometimes called a Saturday Night Special. It was cheap, functional, and a deadly accurate killing machine up to a distance of about twenty-five feet. Gerald had always loved those little .25 caliber pistols, and he'd carried one off and on ever since he was ten years old.

While Gerald got the weapon ready, Charlene was dressing in the bedroom. She put on blue jean cut-offs, a tight blue tank top, sans bra, which she didn't need anyway, combed her long blond hair straight down over her shoulders, then fluffed it out into a sort of windblown look. Charlene was to play the role of a teenager that day, and anyone looking at her would have agreed that she fit the part. She didn't look a day over fifteen, and her tiny, slim, five-foot-tall body resembled that of a just-developing young girl. Even the dialogue was perfect because Charlene kept up on all the teenage gibberish that passed for English.

In fact, Charlene bore an uncanny resemblance to fourteen-year-old Mary Ellen, the one he always thought of as his one-and-only true love, the daughter he'd had sexual relations with since she was six. And Gerald Armond Gallego was the first to agree that *all* of his females looked like that daughter-lover in one way or another.

Gerald was waiting impatiently in the 1973 white-and-gold Dodge van with green-and-white pinstriping—a very expensive prop Charlene had bought in her name a few days after they'd decided on the disposable-love-slave scheme. They had furnished it with a surplus army cot, and Gerald curtained off the driver's compartment and blacked out the rear window with a one-way-view dark plastic film. Charlene added a blue ice chest, a small propane stove, and a macramé cover for the cot that she'd made with her own little hands.

Vans are the most popular vehicle among teenagers and young adults for the simple reason that they can be used as a portable motel or a rolling drug den, and are easy to hide in when the cops come cruising down a dark street. The van sat gleaming in the hot morning sun, apparently an inviting, private sanctuary for adventurous teenagers but in reality a death trap on wheels, waiting for the bait to be placed. When Charlene ran down the driveway and got in beside Gerald, the bait was in place, the trap ready to snap closed on a couple of unsuspecting victims. Gerald and Charlene thought it was very exciting and erotic *not* to know at that moment just who those girls might be. It was almost like a classic porn movie they'd seen about a Victorian whorehouse, where dozens of naked girls paraded in front of a young prince until he picked the two he wanted for the night.

In the parking lot at the enormous Sacramento Country Club Plaza shopping center, Gerald switched off the van engine and turned to look at Charlene. His unblinking, Rasputin eyes glittered as he spoke carefully and distinctly.

"I'll walk with you until we spot the two we want. Then I'll come back to the van and hide in the driving compartment. You bring them to the back door, unlock it, and let them in. When you're all seated, I'll open the curtain, put my gun on them, then we'll tape 'em tight and drive to the mountains. From then on, we'll wing it. Got it?"

Charlene nodded. "Yes, Daddy. But let's get started before I lose my nerve."

Gerald smiled slightly. "You won't lose your nerve, baby. Cause you need this more than *I* do."

Even though it was a weekday, the huge mall was packed with a panting crowd that shopped and sweated under a 105-degree sun. Schools were still closed for summer vacation, and sixty percent of those shoppers were teenage girls—just as Gerald Armond Gallego knew they would be. As Gerald's hungry gaze surveyed the crowd, he whispered in Charlene's ear, "Goddamn, there's so much good-looking teenage pussy here, it looks like a fucking smorgasbord!"

For what Gerald and Charlene had in mind, it was just that—with thousands of young girls swarming around the mall like tropical butterflies, dressed in everything from skin-tight cut-off jeans to tiny bikini tops.

The young people were on one last shopping spree before school started, spending old dad and mom's money on everything from popsicles to porn magazines.

Suddenly Gerald stopped and stood rigid as a bird dog on point.

"There they are," he said.

Charlene followed his gaze and saw two girls standing in front of a hotdog stand. They wore jeans so tight they must have had to lie down to pull them on, and equally tight tank tops. Both were pretty, but Charlene couldn't see any difference between them and all the other teenage girls on the mall.

"Are you sure, Daddy?" Charlene whispered.

"Shut up. I'm psyching 'em out," Gerald said, covering both potential victims with that icy stare.

Charlene had no idea what he meant by that, but she rarely questioned Daddy Gerald about anything. He always knew what he was doing, and had an uncanny, intuitive power about what people would or would not do in almost any given situation.

But after a few minutes of standing with the stovetop-hot pavement burning through her thin-soled sandals, Charlene glanced up at Gerald, took a deep breath to protect her ribs, and touched his arm—*very* gently. Gerald seemed to struggle out of a trance, his body shivering as if an icy wind had swept down the mall. Then he nodded once.

"Yep. They're the ones. They'll do anything. Go get 'em."

Gerald turned abruptly and vanished into the crowd.

Charlene didn't dare to take her eyes off the two potential love slaves, knowing that if she lost them, Daddy Gerald would be really cranky and give her a very painful beating for being a bad girl again.

Charlene walked slowly toward her unsuspecting potential victims, and that amazing little recorder in her mind's eye took in everything, so that three years later she would be able to tell exactly what happened during the next eighteen hours—that is to say, she'd tell exactly what she wanted her listeners to know.

Charlene now stood with an elbow resting on the high counter of the hotdog stand, pretending to read the posted menu.

"The corndogs are good," the tallest of the potential victims said to Charlene, smiling a wide smile that showed a set of good, solid white teeth.

Charlene felt a little weak in the knees. Daddy Gerald had been right again in his judgment of people. It was going to be so easy that for a fleeting moment, Charlene felt a dizzy, hot flash of shame and guilt spread over her body like a sudden, unexpected wave of nausea. But in a moment her sense of purpose and duty to Daddy Gerald replaced the nausea, guilt, fear, and apprehension. She took a deep breath and made her pitch.

"Thanks, but I'm not very hungry. I need some . . . are you guys carrying any Barbies you'd like to trade? I gotta get down . . . I mean, like I was really up a pole last night."

The tall friendly victim nodded and clucked sympathetically.

"Really. I got a coupla 'ludes and one Seven-Twelve. You happen to have a speck of toot?"

Charlene grinned and winked. "Yeah. A little bit of good Cecil and even a drop of shit . . . but I don't wanna go up, I gotta get down."

"Awright," the tall victim said, "my 'ludes and the Seven-Twelve for a line of your coke. For me and my friend. Okay?"

"Really! The stuff's in my van. Wanna go check it out?"

Charlene was proud of herself. Shame and guilt were replaced by an euphoric sense of absolute power and control over the two girls. She had a flash of sexual desire so overwhelming it made her vision blur, her flesh tingle, her hands tremble, and her entire body ached with such an unbearable tension, Charlene thought she was about to have an orgasm right there in front of the hotdog stand.

But the sexual wave passed as they walked to the mall exit, chattering away like happy mockingbirds. The shorter victim, who hadn't said a word during the initial contact, joined in with a brief story of how she was a runaway from Nevada, and was staying with her good friend, and how they'd sneaked away from her friend's husband for a day of private shopping at the mall.

"Then you aren't expected home all day?" Charlene asked.

"Not till dark. You married or got an old man?" Asked the tall girl. "I'm a widow. He was wasted in 'Nam." Charlene was shocked that she'd told such a bald-faced, unnecessary lie.

"Bummer," the tall victim said. "Was he nice?"

"He was okay. I didn't know him very well."

"Uh-huh. There's lots of young widows around nowadays. Any kids?"

"Naw. You?"

"I had one when I was thirteen, but my mom gave it away."

"Really. Too bad, I guess," Charlene mumbled, eyes alert for anyone who might be watching them in the huge parking lot.

"Uh-huh. But I never saw it, so it don't really matter much . . . where's your van?" The tall victim seemed to get impatient for the first time.

"Right over there. The white-and-gold one." Charlene pointed to the gleaming death trap.

"Really! Nice. Bet it cost a lot."

Charlene didn't answer as they walked up to the rear door. Her fingers were numb as she carefully unlocked the double swing-out doors, opened one side and nodded for them to get in.

The inside of the van was at least 130 degrees and unbearably humid. Huge drops of sweat instantly popped out on their bodies, and Charlene fleetingly wondered how Daddy Gerald had stood such heat for the twenty minutes it took her to return with the disposable love slaves.

Charlene closed the door and pointed at the cot. "Sit down there, and I'll get my coke. You got the Barbies?"

"Uh-huh," the tall victim said, nodding and watching intently as Charlene sat on the blue ice chest and fumbled in her large purse.

Both victims were watching Charlene so closely, they didn't really see Gerald as he snapped back the curtain and emerged from the driver's compartment. When their eyes picked him up, they saw Gerald standing in the half-light, crouched over like a huge bear, his clothes soaking wet and black from perspiration, a pair of wide, staring eyes, and a large hand holding a tiny pistol that was pointed in their direction.

"You're a cop," the short victim stated almost sadly.

"Wrong, honey," Gerald said, then smiled. "I'm gonna be your new daddy for the next twenty-four hours."

Both victims stared at Gerald warily. There was no fright in them yet because the whole thing could be a big joke—or what passed for a joke among teenagers. Had the girls leaped up, broke through the back door and hit the ground running and screaming, they probably would have escaped without a scratch. Only a fool would have fired into the crowded parking lot or chased them on foot—and Gerald was no fool. But unfortunately, like most of the human race, the girls had lost their primordial survival instincts, and like most homicide victims, were willing to accept a violent death at the hands of another with barely a whimper of protest.

From where Charlene was sitting on the ice chest, the whole thing reminded her of the shower scene in Hitchcock's *Psycho*— the curtain flapping open, Gerald standing in the half-dark with his hand raised, crouched over awkwardly with a sort of embarrassed smile on his face, like Norman Bates had when he was talking to the sheriff. But the thing that *really* startled Charlene was the massive drops of sweat covering Gerald's face and forehead—they had the iodine-red color of diluted blood.

Gerald had a roll of gray duct tape in his left hand which he passed to Charlene with a curt order: "Tape their mouths shut first. Then do the same with their wrists and ankles. And do it right, got it?" Just as Charlene was about to clamp tape over the short victim's mouth, the girl looked soberly into her eyes for an instant and said, "This is really real, isn't it?"

"Don't worry, honey," Charlene assured the victim, "just do as we say and nothing will happen to you."

"That's right, Shorty," Gerald told her, "just be a good girl and everything will be marvelous for you and your friend . . . this is gonna be a day you'll remember as long as you live."

At that moment, the victims understood what was going to happen, and for the first time, the tiny, silvery mica-like flecks of terror appeared in their eyes. Gerald saw the terror and had an instant erection. Charlene saw the terror and her entire body tensed as it always did during that delicious instant just before an orgasm. Gerald handed Charlene the little pistol. "Watch 'em while I drive, baby. We're heading for the high country."

Chapter 6

Up Jumped The Devil

Baxter, California is fifty miles north of Sacramento, a small village more or less totally supported by the Southern Pacific Railroad, the only employer in town, other than a cluster of gas stations and a couple of greasy-spoon cafes that make a fortune off the steady, day-and-night stream of gamblers heading up US Highway 80 to Reno, Nevada.

Baxter has been nestled in the Sierra Nevada foothills since around 1840, and other than a dozen or so new houses at the north edge of town, hasn't changed at all. It is old, tired, dirty, and depressing. Baxter was a stage stop in the gold rush days, and the hills and rivers around it are still worked by desert rat–type prospectors who are so tough they could probably survive a hydrogen bomb blast if it exploded in the neighborhood.

For years, the main nighttime attraction was a ramshackle two-story whorehouse some thirty feet from the spur SP tracks, staffed by a half-dozen ramshackle whores, who, the locals claimed, were young when Christ was a carpenter. The boss was a creaking old madam who wore more makeup than a Kabuki actor, and often bragged to customers that over the past sixty years, she'd worked as girl and madam in *every* whorehouse from Bangor, Maine, to Point Barrow, Alaska. According to the local sporting gentry who patronized the house, the tariff was five dollars for as long as it took to get satisfied.

There was, however, a certain Manhattan/Beverly Hills snob appeal to the place because it conducted business only on railroad paydays—and if a gentleman wished to visit some other night, he must call and make a reservation. After all, the senior-citizen whores needed their rest, and couldn't be expected to stay up after ten o'clock on the off chance that a local brakeman might have five dollars left out of his grocery money to spend on well-seasoned pussy.

On the face of it, Baxter doesn't seem to be the kind of place that would attract the likes of Gerald Armond Gallego. But Gerald was as familiar with the entire area as he had been with his cell at the Big Q. In fact, he had been to that local whorehouse many times, not to buy sex, but to visit with the creaking old madam because he loved to talk to her about the old days and the famous people she'd known as customers.

Surprisingly, for a city-bred and prison-raised lad, Gerald was an enthusiastic outdoorsman who loved camping and fishing in the most remote and rugged areas of the Sierra Nevada mountains around Baxter. He'd even tried his luck at panning gold in the high-altitude lakes and streams for a few weeks while hiding from a parole officer. During the gold-panning period of Gerald's life, he claimed proudly that he'd lived off the land, and in a manner of speaking he had—by coldcocking an ancient prospector with a rock and stealing his entire summer grubstake. The eighty-five-year-old survived and reported the crime, but by then Gerald was back in jail, and the warrant for attempted murder-robbery was allowed to die for lack of interest by a local DA.

At around four in the afternoon, Gerald and Charlene arrived at Baxter with their terrified cargo. It has never been satisfactorily explained why it took Gerald over four hours to drive fifty miles. They spent another hour driving over a dozen narrow, rutted logging trails before the van stopped and Gerald crisply announced to his passengers, "This is the place."

Charlene got out and looked around, remembering every detail. They were in a clearing about fifteen feet long and twenty feet wide. To Charlene, the clearing looked like a miniature meadow, with short green grass, and even a few white Shasta daisys. Mockingbirds sang happily in the tall pines, and an excited gray squirrel flashed its bushy tail at Charlene then disappeared. The air was warm, clean, and smelled of pine trees. It was like a *Bambi* movie set without the deer.

What a lovely place for a picnic, Charlene thought . . . Gerald was standing beside her now and they heard one of their victims moan through her nose.

Charlene suddenly felt as if her blood temperature had jumped about twenty degrees, heating her up with a pleasant, exciting feeling, as if something good was about to happen to her. Then she noticed that Daddy Gerald's trousers were bulging with an enormous erection, and Charlene knew her theory about disposable love slaves had been right on the money. Gerald hadn't had a hard-on like this one since their foursome with his daughter way back in July. Gerald took her hand, and she felt him trembling. But Charlene was trembling even more.

Darkness falls early in the High Sierras, and their shadows were lengthy blurs on the grass when they opened the van and got in with their victims. Gerald went to where the girls were lying side-by-side on the narrow cot, and knelt down facing them.

"I'm going to remove the tape now," he said, "and then you will have sex with us—separately and together. If you do exactly what we tell you, you'll be sleeping in your own bed by morning.

If you scream, fight, or refuse to cooperate, we'll kill you. Got it?"

Charlene's total recall was operative as she listened to Daddy Gerald. She was proud of his no-nonsense, precise, calm orders to the girls. And he was speaking with his best grammar. He'd explained to her that he always spoke that way to prison psychiatrists and the parole board so they'd respect him, and let him out of jail as soon as possible. Daddy Gerald was *so* intelligent . . .

"Get your clothes off," Gerald was saying to the victims.

Charlene watched as Gerald removed his clothing, amused that he seemed to be having some trouble getting his shorts off over the enormous erection. She stared at it with admiration, knowing that the amazing hard-on was due entirely to *her* plan . . . it just *had* to be, because he'd never managed one of that size before—at least not with her. And she was so proud that the victims were staring at it too. Charlene wasn't going to mind sharing it with them at all.

Gerald pinned Charlene with those huge Rasputin eyes. "Get undressed, baby," he said in his nicest tone of voice, calling her by that sweet name she liked so much.

As Charlene took off her clothes, she was surprised to see that Gerald was sweating those huge iodine-red drops again . . . the color that reminded her of diluted blood. She knew the color was an optical illusion—or was it? Didn't the Bible say something about the devil being able to sweat blood when he was at his most sinful work? And hadn't Gerald once told her he'd been touched by the devil when he was born? Daddy Gerald had many strange powers. Squatting there on his muscular haunches, with his black hair standing up in front like little horns, it seemed all Gerald needed to complete the old biblical picture of Lucifer himself was a spiked tail . . .

The victims had stripped down to their panties when Gerald reached out impatiently and tore them off both girls. Gerald sat down hard on the floor, the enormous erection standing up past his navel like an ancient Greek pornographic tile mosaic. Then

Gerald's eyes rolled back in his head, and Charlene thought he was about to faint. She reached out to steady him, then saw that he was ejaculating with such force the semen was falling in his hair, and mixing with the great drops of sweat on his face.

It was after 10:00 P.M. by the time the kidnapper-rapists were finished with their dirty work.

Two days later, the victims' autopsies would describe what had been done to them during that four-hour ordeal in the van with Gerald and Charlene. Each victim had been sodomized, had been forced to perform fellatio cunnilingus on the perpetrator and had been bitten about the breasts, nipples, and buttocks.

Of course the autopsies only revealed the physical indignities—the stark terror they'd experienced from the moment they were kidnapped until that brief second before their grossly ignoble murders couldn't be perceived in such a simple procedure as an autopsy.

Gerald and Charlene were standing outside the van, shivering in the High Sierra night breeze. Their knees were rubbery from innumerable orgasms, and their faces had that beatific, sensual expression that every porno film actress tries to project but never quite manages in that obligatory full-face close-up while her male partner is pounding away.

Charlene would later describe those first few minutes outside the van in an entirely different context to a county jail cellmate, who was reporting every word Charlene spoke to the DA's office because they believed Charlene and Gerald had committed numerous other crimes, and hoped Charlene would eventually brag about them to their informant as most cons do. Charlene told the informant she had once seen an old-fashioned holy-roller-revival tent meeting on television, and that she felt exactly as those women looked who'd been caught up in that rapture-filled, ecstatic, screaming, gimme-that-old-time-religion fervor.

The wind moaned loudly in the dark pine trees, reminding

Gerald and Charlene of the sounds their victims had made during the last four hours. There had been some real screams, but only when Gerald and Charlene were biting the girls' breasts and buttocks.

The kidnappers looked at each other and smiled nervously. They knew it was now time for the "disposable" part of their plan. Gerald ordered Charlene to leave the girls with him while she drove the van back to Sacramento, made sure she and the van were seen, then drove back in her new Oldsmobile to pick up Gerald and the girls. Charlene failed to understand Gerald's strategy this time, but as usual, she didn't voice an opinion for fear of being smacked around some more. After Gerald ordered the girls out, she simply got in the van and drove away. Indeed, to any reasonable person, it would be impossible to understand why Gerald delayed his escape and remained there in the woods with both victims while Charlene drove over a hundred miles round-trip to Sacramento, changed vehicles, then came back. Other than the actual kidnapping in a crowded parking lot, it was the most dangerous thing Gerald had done all day. Anything could happen—Charlene might have a change of heart and call the police. She was perfectly free to do so during the next two hours. She might be involved in an accident, or stopped for a traffic violation and tell the whole story. Or she might just not come back at all, leaving Gerald in the wilderness with his two kidnap-rape victims to dispose of, then get back to town the best way he could. And there wouldn't have been a damn thing Gerald Armond Gallego could have done about it.

Was Gerald the sociopath increasing the risk of being caught? Perhaps. But the most logical explanation is that Gerald just wanted some time alone in the wilderness with the two girls. After all, he didn't have to share *everything* with Charlene.

Charlene told her cellmate that she figured Daddy Gerald intended to kill the girls while she was gone. But when she returned, all three were standing in the clearing. The girls were dressed, but looked as if they'd just finished a tag-team wrestling match. Their clothes were dirty, their hair filled with bark, pine needles, mud, and dried grass. Gerald didn't explain, and Charlene didn't care to ask any questions. If Daddy had had sex with the girls while she was gone, Charlene didn't want to know about it. Gerald got in the backseat between the two girls, and told Charlene to head for Sacramento. During that hour-long trip, Gerald was joking, friendly, and constantly reassuring the teenagers that he intended to keep his word and they would be sleeping in their own beds by daylight. When they were out of the mountains and nearing Sacramento, Gerald leaned over the seat and whispered to Charlene, "Take the Old Jackson Road toward Sloughouse." Fifteen minutes later, Gerald directed her into a narrow dirt road that was used by tractors to move farm equipment around the planted fields.

"Stop here," Gerald said abruptly, then leaped out and opened the car trunk, using a duplicate set of keys he always carried in his pocket. When he came up to the left front window, Charlene saw a jack handle in his right hand and the little .25 in the other.

She turned the engine off, and Gerald whispered hoarsely, "Keep it running, you stupid cunt! What the fuck's wrong with you?"

When he called her "cunt" again, Charlene almost burst into tears. She'd hoped Gerald would be grateful enough to at least call her "baby." After all, it had been her plan, and Daddy Gerald had had a whole lot of fun tonight. He's never grateful for anything *anyone* does for him, Charlene thought resentfully.

"Okay, girls, out of the car," Gerald told the victims cheerfully, "there's an old barn just behind those eucalyptus trees. I'm taking you over there and taping you up again. You'll be able to work loose in an hour and hitchhike home."

The victims got out and stood in front of Gerald, looking intently and hopefully at his wide, scary eyes. For the first time, the teenagers were probably beginning to believe they would survive the worst eighteen hours of their lives. In that first relieved, heart-pounding, ecstatic moment of release from imminent danger, it is likely they didn't even see the jack handle that gleamed in the pale moonlight.

"Jump over the irrigation ditch," Gerald said, "and don't try to run. I'm right behind you."

He was. They were barely across the ditch when Gerald brought the jack handle down on the shorter victim's head. There was a loud pop as her skull cracked. Before she hit the ground, Gerald had whirled around and hit the taller girl across her left temple. She staggered away like an out-of-step ballet dancer, then stumbled and fell into a slight earth depression.

Gerald went to her, bent over, and fired one round from the little .25 auto. He walked slowly back to his first kill and fired three rounds into her already-shattered skull. The exploding gunpowder echoed around the empty fields like an unexpected thunderclap. Gerald hadn't really heard the shots, but Charlene did, and called out, "Come on, Daddy, we'd better go!" Gerald was walking toward the car when he looked back and shouted to Charlene, "Goddamit, she's still wiggling!"

He ran to the victim lying in the small ditch, leaned over and shot her four times in the forehead. "That oughta do it," he said to no one in particular.

But Charlene heard and was relieved. For a moment, she'd been afraid that Gerald had panicked and *she* might have to finish the job herself. I'm too quick at judging him, Charlene thought lovingly, watching Daddy Gerald walk casually back to the car, it's just that I always seem to expect him to do exactly what he *doesn't* do . . . Charlene wasn't alone in that. Gerald Armond Gallego had been doing the exact opposite of what was expected of him all his life.

Gerald got in beside her and sat stiffly, taking long, deep breaths of cool night air. Charlene would say later that he looked terribly sad.

"Are you okay?" she asked.

"Yeah. Let's go." Gerald lit two cigarettes and passed one to Charlene. They smoked in silence while Charlene drove very carefully toward Sacramento. Daddy Gerald was awfully critical of her driving and she didn't want an elbow smash to spoil this beautiful moment.

"You were very good, baby," Gerald said, breaking the long silence and patting her hand that rested on the wheel. "Real, *real* good. I was damned proud of you today. From start to finish, you did everything exactly right."

Charlene was so happy, she had to squeeze her thighs together to keep from wetting her pants. It was the most unexpected, most completely satisfying compliment of her life. Even if Daddy Gerald had called her a cunt now instead of baby, she wouldn't have minded one bit.

"And *you* were just marvelous, Daddy. You know, I have to tell you something. You remember that story you told me, about you being touched by the devil when you were born?"

"Yeah," Gerald said, leaning back and yawning, his hands clasped over his head.

"Well, when we were in the van with the, you know, and I looked at you in that dim light, your hair was standing up in front with that cute little cowlick, like horns, you know, and you really *did* look like a devil. Isn't that strange?"

"There's nothing strange about it, baby. I had that devil in me *before* I was born. I inherited it from my parents—especially my father."

Even if one only *halfway* believes in such things, it's a lot easier to accept that Gerald had been touched by the devil than that a just and merciful God would simply release someone like Gerald and his disciple, Charlene, into an unsuspecting world.

Chapter *1*

Dad And The Southern Boys

Gerald Armond Gallego was born in the Sacramento County Hospital at 9:00 A.M., Wednesday, July 17, 1946. Gerald often claims to be Italian, but his mother is French-Irish, and the California and Mississippi penal authorities list his father as being of Portuguese ancestry.

In facial and bodily appearance, Gerald is a startling reproduction of his mother, Lorraine Pullen Bennet Hunt Gallego Bulgar Davies. Gerald bears absolutely no resemblance to his father, Gerald Albert Gallego. In fact, whether the late Mr. Gallego is actually Gerald's father, only Lorraine probably knows for sure. Official records indicate he was, and if one believes the old adage that the sins of the fathers are vested in the son, then certainly there are numerous hereditary character-istics that match. Gerald Albert Gallego was also a career crimi-nal, a common thief and burglar, and at least a three-time mur-derer whose career ended suddenly in 1955 when he was executed in the new gas chamber at Parchman, Mississippi, for two of those killings.

Gerald Albert Gallego did not influence his son's life by setting an example at home. In fact, he never saw him. The senior Gallego had left his pregnant wife and was back in San Quentin prison long before their son was born.

Even Lorraine didn't see her husband again. She never told the boy how his father died, and Gerald wouldn't know for sure that his father was an executed murderer until twenty-five years later, when he was preparing his own defense for a capital crime and needed all the sympathy he could get.

According to statements made by both Lorraine and Gerald Albert, they met on September 11, 1945, two weeks after Gallego was released on parole from San Quentin prison, where he'd just completed five years of a five-to-fourteen-year term for auto theft and check forgery. The twenty-seven-year-old Gallego had been ordered to report to his parole officer in Hawthorne, a suburb of Los Angeles, where he would live with his sister who'd found a job for him. But instead of checking in with the PO, Gallego met another ex-con in the bus station who helped him steal a car. They drove ninety-eight miles north to Sacramento, where the other convict claimed to have contacts with a first-class bank robbery gang. Of course the "gang" was just another ex-con's daydream, because there isn't a successful bank robbery team in the world who'd let Gallego and his scruffy partner hold their coats, much less go on a job with them.

Lorraine and a female companion were having breakfast in a small ptomaine palace called the Ten-Ten Cafe at Tenth and J Street when Gallego and his partner walked in and saw the two pretty girls sitting in a booth. Lorraine had just been released from the Sacramento County hospital after a partial recovery from hepatitis. She was weak, exhausted, sick, and flat broke.

Some thirty minutes after their meeting in the Ten-Ten Cafe, Gerald Albert Gallego and eighteen-year-old Lorraine Pullen Bennet Hunt were on their way to Reno, Nevada, to be married. Two months later, Lorraine was pregnant, back in the hospital with hepatitis, and Gerald Albert was back in San Quentin prison on a parole violation.

When Gallego paid a sneak visit to his sister in Hawthorne, two beat cops spotted him on the street, and after a five-block footrace, he was caught and managed to punch one of the harness bulls in the eye. The two officers beat hell out of Gallego with lead saps, then took him to the Los Angeles County jail in irons, where they beat him some more until their arms were tired.

While on death row in Mississippi, Gallego wrote in his diary that he'd made up his mind while being beaten that he was going to kill a cop before he died. And he did just that—in fact, he killed two cops, to be exact.

Gerald Albert Gallego served eight more years in San Quentin, then was released from California custody for the last time in 1953. Being born and raised in Southern California, it is anybody's guess how he ended up in Ocean Springs, Mississippi, on the night of May 27, 1954. Whatever the reason, it can be logically assumed that Gallego was unfamiliar with the Southern justice system of the 1950s, which was equivalent to that of modern-day Iran. When he made good his vow to kill some cops, however, he was quick to find out.

At dawn on the morning he arrived in Ocean Springs, Gerald Albert kicked in a glass window of what he thought was a liquor store. Mississippi was a dry state, however, and Gallego came away with six bottles of Coca-Cola. He was arrested within seconds by the thirty-one-year-old town night marshal, Ernest (Red) Beauquez, who attempted to handcuff his apparently docile prisoner. But there is no such thing as a *docile* Gallego, and Gerald Albert kicked the marshal in the nuts, disarmed him, and shot Beauquez dead with his own revolver—after allowing the cop to beg for his life for fifteen minutes.

Gerald Albert wrote in his death-row diary about that murder:

"I don't think I ever felt so good in my life as when that cop was telling me how much his wife and kids needed him. When he asked for five minutes to pray, I gave him thirty seconds, then let him have it right in the head."

Gallego was captured two days later in Gulfport, still carrying the dead cop's gun. He was taken to Pascagoula and put in the Jackson County jail to await trial for murder in the first degree. Two weeks later, Gerald Albert Gallego, accompanied by another murderer with the unlikely name of Minor Sorber, escaped when Gallego threw a bucket filled with an acidlike disinfectant into the face of the lone guard, Jack C. Landrum. Gallego proceeded to beat Landrum with his fists almost to the point of death, then took his keys. The pair of murderers escaped into the night; Landrum died a few hours later.

Gallego and Sorber were captured the next day after a typical Southern manhunt through the swamps, complete with bloodhounds and a posse on horseback. Mississippi's capital justice system was, as usual, swift and permanent. Gallego was tried, convicted of two murders, and sentenced to death. There were no lengthy appeals, no last-minute delays, no psychiatrists who took the stand and told the jury that if Gerald Albert hadn't been deprived of a bicycle in his youth, he wouldn't have killed anyone.

Gallego's court-appointed attorney, Frank J. Hammond Jr., had never tried a capital case before, and never tried one again after losing his client via a death sentence.

At 2:00 P.M., on March 3, 1955, almost ten months to the day after killing the two cops, Gerald Albert had the honor of being the first man executed in Mississippi's brand-new gas chamber.

He walked to his death with courage and dignity, accepting all blame for his actions, and told the warden, among many other things, that he deserved to die for taking the lives of two honest men who'd never harmed him in any way.

(Twenty-five years later, Frank J. Hammond Jr. was called to California as a witness in the double-murder trial of the son of the man he'd defended unsuccessfully in Mississippi. Mr. Hammond stated that prior to the trial in Jackson County, he'd been practicing law for just two years.

"I was scared, naive, and really shook up at the thought of holding a man's life in my hands. Every time I read about an execution now, I remember that trial. I haven't practiced criminal law since . . . I learned my lesson the hard way."

Mr. Hammond is a true Southern gentleman from the old school, and unlike most attorneys, has a conscience, which caused him to recognize his limitations with the law early in his career—and luckily, unlike his French counterparts, he was not required by law to witness the execution of his client.)

"I didn't tell him the truth about his father," Lorraine Davies said in a taped interview," because I didn't want to add to poor Gerald's burden—he'd had so much trouble in his life.

"I just told him his dad was killed in a car wreck . . . or in the war, I forget which. Someone else told him the truth later on, but he didn't believe them. Would you? No kid wants a triple murderer for a father."

According to Lorraine and a female cousin, Gail Farmer, who'd been her constant companion since childhood, that "someone" was the wife of Gerald Albert's brother. The aunt supposedly seduced Gerald when he was around fourteen—most likely on one of the rare occasions when he wasn't in jail—and told him the true story of his father's untimely demise at the hands of the Southern boys in Ole Miss. Gerald didn't believe her. In fact, he beat the hell out of his aunt after telling her that she was a goddamned liar and troublemaker, and that his mother would never lie to him.

If Lorraine had really wanted to be truthful, she could have said that poor Gerald hadn't fared very well on his maternal side either. Lorraine's first cousin, Frank D. Sloan III, a son of Gail Farmer, and Lorraine's nephew, Clifford L. David, a son of her sister, Ramona, and a close family friend, Robert G. McMahon, murdered Sandra Christine Tremper on April 12, 1974.

Tremper was a local barfly who was known to sleep with anyone for the price of a bed or drink—and sometimes just for fun.

The three young men picked her up off the street one night, gave her a bottle of good gin, then after she'd agreed to have sex with all three, drove her into the country area outside of North Sacramento. When it was over, the men became concerned that she might accuse them of rape—at least that's what they claimed later. After talking it over, they returned to where Tremper was still lying on the ground and each man fired one round into her head from a .32 semiautomatic pistol. That murder was so unnecessary and senseless it bordered on lunacy. An autopsy revealed that Tremper's alcohol blood level was .25, *fifteen* points above common drunkenness. With that much alcohol in her system, it was nothing short of miraculous that Tremper could even *move,* much less have the mental capacity to identify or file charges of rape against anyone, had she been so inclined.

There is no question that the men knew this, and it can only be assumed that they killed her just for the hell of it, then used the possible rape charge as an excuse to the police when they were arrested.

One day after the murder, Frank D. Sloan III said he had a vision—a vision of that apple-green gas chamber in San Quentin at San Francisco by the Bay. It was so vivid and scared him so much, he rolled over on his friends and cousin, went to the cops and blabbed the whole story. The police, as he hoped they would, offered him total immunity in exchange for testifying in open court. But apparently Sloan didn't know some members of his own family. While waiting to testify, someone arranged for a hit man to be booked into his cell. The hit man, a former close friend of Sloan's, managed to come within ten seconds of choking Frank to death before a guard came to his rescue.

After the trial, Frank was released into the California Valuable Witness program, married, and seemed to have settled down.

Gerald Armond Gallego had been close friends with the three

young killers most of his life, and perhaps he and Charlene would remember that murder and how easy it had been. Without a squealer, and with a little common sense, the boys would have gotten away with it.

Gerald's relatives are spread across California, Nevada, Oregon, and Washington State. They are a close-mouthed, vengeful group from which the Mafia might take some valuable pointers on *Omerta,* the code of silence. Though the entire family seems to hate each other's guts individually, they band together like the Hatfields or the McCoys against any outsider, and even refuse to admit their own names.

There is no doubt that Gerald's mother was the *one* female he trusted, that she had a profound influence upon his life. She never chastised him for his thieving ways, and in fact, encouraged her son to rob and steal if he wanted something he didn't have. Gerald probably loved her in his fashion, and she was always totally loyal to her favorite son, no matter what he did. As far as love went, Lorraine was never accused of that emotion by anyone—husbands, lovers, tricks, or family members.

Gerald had been a common thief almost from the day he could walk. His mother stated that at four years of age, little Gerald would toddle down to the supermarket a half-block away, sneak in and eat five or ten dollars' worth of cookies, Butterfinger candy bars, and a pound of his favorite bologna before he was spotted and tossed out of the store. Lorraine said, "He was just the cutest little thing I ever saw when he'd come huffing and puffing into the house with his little belly stick out like an overfed puppy, and tell me proudly what he'd been doing."

Gerald was "state-raised" in that he had been under the control of the California justice system most of his life. Gerald is not a stupid man, nor had he been an unintelligent boy. The question was, why did he resist *all* efforts of the state to make him into a law-abiding citizen?

Was it his past experiences as a mistreated, unloved, neglected child? The beatings he'd taken from Lorraine, her many boyfriends and husbands almost from the day he was born? Was it because his mother admittedly condoned every act of criminal and antisocial behavior he'd committed? Was it childhood poverty? Was he *really* touched by the devil? Or was it simply what any experienced street cop would say—that Gerald Armond Gallego was a born thief, a robber and a burglar, and a mean son-of-a-bitch to boot? And there wasn't anything this side of the graveyard that could change him, because that was what he *wanted* to be.

Chapter **8**

Mom And The Tall Truthful Texican

In murder trials nowadays, it is mandatory that the defendant submit to a court-ordered psychiatric evaluation. If the defense expects to win acquittal, it must accumulate plenty of psychiatric excuses for the defendant's actions. Of course, the oldest of those theories, and Freud's favorite, is that dear old mom was the cause of it all. As much as a DA or defense lawyer would hate to admit it, in Gerald's case, there just may have been a tiny grain of truth in that threadbare theory. After Gerald was arrested and charged with murder, five highly paid private investigators were ordered by the defense to look under every rock in Gerald's past—and in keeping with that classic theory, the very first rocks to be turned over would be those left behind by Gerald's dear old mum.

Most people who have lived by their wits and guile hide their personal lives with fabrications and excuses for every given situation. This description fits Lorraine Davies like an old shoe. During the initial meeting between Lorraine and the defense investigator, she freely accepted all blame for Gerald's crimes against society, saying that if she'd treated him better, he wouldn't have done the things he did. But the investigator sensed that she didn't really care what Gerald had done or what happened to him, and was simply mouthing the usual words expected from any mother with a son in trouble since the beginning of time.

After their first meeting, the investigator said that he was very uneasy with Lorraine Davies. He felt a sinister aura about the woman to the effect that with her as his mother, Gerald was destined for the gas chamber on the day he was born. He added that he would hate to have Lorraine as an enemy, especially sneaking up behind him in a dark alley.

In order to establish a good "mom-caused-it-all" argument, the defense needed to know much more about Lorraine Davies. No one believed her "I've-had a lot of bad-luck" spiel. They particularly wanted to know why mother and son claimed to be so close despite her admitted neglect and sadistic behavior toward him as a child. There were dark rumors in the family that Lorraine had sexual contacts with Gerald. They needed to know if her childhood had been worse than his, and if she'd simply passed more of the same along to her son. The one person who might be willing and able to tell the truth about Lorraine would be Harold Hunt, her second husband, whom Lorraine sometimes claimed was the father of her oldest son, David. Hunt hadn't been heard from in years, but if he could be located and was willing to talk, he might just have one hell of a story to tell, and very likely it would be the truth. It is an old maxim in the cop business that if you can get hold of an ex-spouse, there won't be any secrets anymore.

Through a complicated series of subterfuges, careful talks with cautious relatives, a tiresome search for veteran and state records, Hunt was finally located. He was almost as tough to find as Jimmy Hoffa. If anyone ever wishes to flat disappear from the face of the earth, they should talk to this man—because he managed to do it.

When contacted, Hunt readily agreed to an interview on the

condition that his whereabouts be kept secret. Most of those interviewed for this book requested that their privacy be guaranteed and Hunt was no exception. The investigator flew to Dallas, then rented a car for the long drive to Hunt's farm in the remote foothills of East Texas. He found Hunt to be a lean, tall, good-looking man in his mid-fifties, and he wore the East Texas uniform of neatly pressed jeans, white cotton shirt, expensive cowboy boots, and Stetson hat.

Hunt "farms" by raising giant lobsterlike red crayfish in numerous shallow ponds scattered over his remote two-hundred-acre spread. When the investigator parked, he could see in the distance a dozen or so Mexican farm laborers unloading crayfish from a huge tank truck and carting them into a long building. There, the crayfish would be flash-frozen, then shipped via jet to France and Italy, where they sold for forty dollars per pound. Obviously, Hunt earned a good living.

"Every man remembers his first love, so of course I remember Lorraine," Hunt said as he sat with the investigator on the front porch of his neat, two-story, Mexican-style hacienda. "I remember her whole damn family . . . and a meaner bunch of sunsuhbitches never drawed breath or walked the face of the earth. Sure, I recall that kid, Gerald, when he was about three."

Unable to believe his good luck, the investigator asked Hunt to tell him about Lorraine first.

"I met her on a blind date," he said. "I was fifteen and she was a year older—nineteen forty-three, I think it was. Lorraine was a sweet, naive kid, or so I thought, and we fell in love. At least what passes for love at that age, and we decided to get married.

"I was just an Okie kid myself, didn't know my ass from a pork chop. There were things about Lorraine I should have guessed, but until she came right out and told me, it all went over my dumb head. I just thought she was the typical, innocent, movie version of the All-American girl-next-door. But she sure wasn't.

"She had a sister named Ramona, who was a year younger

than her, a very pretty little gal, and she was with us on that blind date.

"Anyway, we ran off to another state to get married, but we didn't really do it. After we'd taken out the license and all, Lorraine took me over to the car and said there was something she'd better tell me. Said that when she was twelve, her mother *sold* her to an old guy who wanted a young kid for a wife . . . you know what I'm saying?"

The investigator nodded. What followed was no surprise.

"The man's name was Bennet, and he bought Lorraine for five-hundred dollars from her mother, Hazel. They got married in Portland, Oregon, where Lorriane was born, and old Hazel and Ramona attended the ceremony. Now, Lorraine was only twelve, but she could pass for twenty if she put her hair in an upsweep . . . you know what that is? Good. And she was a dead ringer for that actress, Joan Crawford—when Crawford was young, I mean.

"Well, when Hazel spent the five hundred, she welched on the deal, stole Lorraine from Bennet, and took off for Sacramento, where Hazel's parents lived.

"The day we were supposed to marry, Lorraine told me that she was still married to Bennet, and wanted me to go along with a scam . . . just pretend we'd married so she could get away from Hazel, who, according to Lorraine, intended to sell her again to some half-fag in San Francisco. Hell, I was happy to go along with her. Lorraine said that her mother would know damn well she wasn't divorced from Bennet and couldn't have married me, but Hazel wouldn't dare say anything because if Hazel's parents found out she'd sold her own daughter like some slave nigger, they'd have killed her.

"And from what I learned later on, that wasn't just a figure of speech! And let me give you a little advice, fellow . . . you fool with *that* bunch very much, you'd better be damned careful of yourself."

Hunt offered the investigator a beer. There were no signs of the man's family anywhere, though the investigator knew that he was married to a European aristocrat from a wealthy family, and had two grown sons who were both MDs.

The only evidence in the way of family was a pair of German shepherds big enough to take a man's leg off with one bite. They fixed the stranger with a hostile glare and an occasional show of fangs, clearly indicating they'd be more than happy to sample *his* leg. Neither Hunt nor the dogs seemed bothered by the 110-degree temperature, which was compounded by a 100-percent humidity, which left the visitor drenched with perspiration.

Hunt brought the beers and sat down. The Texican slowly continued his story:

"Lorraine and Ramona were the only children Hazel had, as far as I know. I saw a picture of their father, Robert Pullen, who was a very good-looking man, almost handsome, with dark, wavy hair and black eyes. Had a dimple in his chin, just like Lorraine. Matter of fact, that Gerald looks like the guy, at least from what I saw of him on TV and in the papers.

"Well, here's the real sad part of the story . . . when the girls were about seven or eight years old, their father, Robert Pullen, started molesting them both . . . goddamit, you never heard of anything like that then. Nowadays, it's common as a gas station holdup. Maybe there was a lot of it, and no one knew it, or maybe it has something to do with the way we live now . . . doesn't matter, I guess.

"Anyway, the girls told me about it, and I know it's true. I got to know that Ramona as well as I did Lorraine. You following me? And both of them told me the same thing dozens of times—separately or together, their stories always matched. Now I know how easy it is for kids to lie about their parents, especially girls who get pissed off at their dad and want to nail his ass to the wall, but you're in the law business and know that better'n me. I swear those gals told the truth.

"In addition to the sexual stuff, Pullen was a sort of sadist. On Saturday afternoons, the girls would ask him if they could go to the movies. He'd always say yes, if they'd let him bite them on

their behinds, where it wouldn't show. Not a nip, you understand, but a *bite.*"

By that time, bells were ringing in the investigator's head like
Big Ben at midnight. The bite marks on Gerald and Charlene's
victims and on Gerald's lover-daughter flashed across his
mind's eye as if it was a VCR on fast-forward. Had Gerald taken
up biting asses and molesting his daughter where his Grandpa
Pullen had left off? Was the whole damn family descended from
the Marquis de Sade? Was every single one of them a disori-
ented sex offender? Jesus H. Christ on a crutch, talk about
venom in the blood! This family had blood like the river alongside Three Mile Island!

An insanity plea for Gerald looked as sure as daylight . . . a
year or two in the comfortable state psychiatric prison at Vacaville, a few group-therapy sessions, a psychiatrist who needed
some "cures" on his civil service record in order to get that
promotion to E-15 and a fat pay raise . . . and Gerald Armond
Gallego would be back on the street. Yep, the investigator
thought, old Gerald has kicked the system's ass again.

"Did I lose you somewhere?" Hunt asked.

"No, no. Just thinking. Please go on."

"Well, Ramona told me, 'Hell, the pain only lasted five minutes, and the movie lasted all afternoon, so we'd always let him
do it.' I'm sure Hazel knew what the father was doing, because
just before she arranged the sale of Lorraine, she turned Pullen
in. He went to the pen for ten years, and got killed there,
according to Lorraine and Ramona. But I was never sure of that.

"Lorraine and I just pretended to be married, and lived together off and on about eighteen months. Then we just went
our separate ways with no hard feelings. In fact we always liked
each other for years. I'd see her occasionally in Sacramento, and
we'd fool around . . . you understand what I mean? But we never
got back together again.

"Then I met a girl and took up with her. I didn't see Lorraine
again until the latter part of nineteen forty-eight. By that time,
I was just out of the army and divorced. I walked into a skid row

bar on Second Street in Sacramento one night looking for some easy pussy—and there was Lorraine, working as a barmaid.

"We took up right where we'd left off, didn't live together or anything like that, but we'd meet when she got off work at two in the morning, maybe a couple of times each week, usually on Friday and Saturday nights. She told me all about this nice Portuguese guy she'd been married to, even claimed he'd taught her to speak that language—spoke it to me, in fact. But hell, at the time, I didn't know Portuguese from Chinese.

"Lorraine said she'd had a boy by him—and *that* would be Gerald Gallego, this serial killer who was on TV . . . the guy you're so curious about.

"Lorraine was living in a little Okie shack out in West Sacramento. Had some goofy-looking blond gal taking care of the kid, and I recall Gerald as being a whiny little bastard, always tagging after his mother, begging her to pick him up and hold him on her lap.

"Lorraine told me that she was doing some whoring on the side, and had a taxi driver named Chubby as her pimp . . . huh, strange how I remember that name after all those years. Anyway, I went over to her shack one afternoon, and Lorraine was screwing a trick on the bed, and that Gerald was sitting in the middle of the floor, screaming his goddamned head off."

"Mr. Hunt, did Lorraine ever indicate to you, during all those years you knew her and were close to her, whether the sexual molestation by her father caused her any mental problems later on?"

"No, she didn't," Hunt answered, "and thinking back on it, I'm surprised at the way both girls handled it. I got the impression they took advantage of his molesting them, rather than getting upset about it.

"In fact, they would laugh and brag about how easy it was to get money and candy from the guy after he started messing with them, and how they were in control of their own father and could make him do anything they wanted."

"Did you know any of Lorraine's husbands?"

"Not Gallego, if that's what you're getting at. But I met that George Bulgar several times. He either owned or leased a skid row bar, I'm not sure which. Anyway, Lorraine worked and lived with him a long time before they married. I had the impression that he was a tough son of a bitch and one mean fucking Greek.

"Lorraine had a couple of kids by him—seems like every time she got married, she got knocked up. Had a boy and a girl, and I understand the boy was killed by a car when he was pretty young. I think the girl is married and lives somewhere in Northern California, Chico or Redding possibly.

"Lorraine's grandfather, old man Sloan—that would be Gerald's great-granddad, told a friend of mine that Bulgar beat the shit out of Gerald every time he could catch him, and Bulgar not only hated Gerald, but was jealous of him and Lorraine—even accused her of having sex with Gerald."

"Do you believe that?"

"Fellow, I just don't know. They were the most fucked-up family I ever ran into, and with that bunch, anything is possible. But goddamn! I'd hate to think old Lorraine had fallen *that* low . . . but she was one mean fucking broad. In all the years I knew her, I never found a tender spot on that woman's body, especially her heart. She was the meanest, most calculating, manipulative cunt I ever had the misfortune to meet. And she deserved most everything she got.

"I'm really surprised that she's stayed married to that Davies guy so long. Maybe he didn't beat her too much, and brought in a steady paycheck—or maybe she just got old and decided it was the best deal she was going to get. As I said, Lorraine always did what she thought was best for her.

"Listen, fellow, it's almost sundown and I gotta feed my livestock . . . You can come along or stay here, whichever you want."

The investigator looked at the dogs, and decided his best bet would be to go with Hunt.

That interview was a defense lawyer's dream come true. Presented at the right moment in a charged-up courtroom, it would have had every one of those little blue-haired ladies on the jury bawling their eyes out, hating Lorraine and feeling sorry for poor dear Gerald Armond Gallego.

But it wasn't to be. Even if the defense had been aware of this information before his trial, Gerald probably would have refused to allow it in the record because it would lead to the impression that he was crazy—and no self-respecting sociopath would stand for that kind of misinformation to go public, not even to save his own life.

An interesting sidelight to the information provided by Hunt was that Lorraine Davies later corroborated his story 100 percent, saying, with a smile and a nod, "He was the only guy I ever loved. But it's too bad he has such a good memory. I thought he was dead."

Chapter 9

The Entrepreneur

Sacramento has been the capital of California since 1850, when the great gold rush originated nearby after a Swiss alcoholic named Captain Johann Sutter discovered a few nuggets while working on his sawmill at Placerville, some thirty miles east of Sacramento.

The area is a sizzling 112 degrees in summer and falls below freezing in winter. And whoever wrote the song "It Never Rains in California" couldn't have been in Sacramento when he did it. The rain starts in October and continues almost daily until April—a cold, pouring rain accompanied by freezing winds and a chilling, impenetrable, ground-hugging black fog.

The capital is an agricultural, business, and political community, and until the late 1970s, was a staid old town filled with beautiful Victorian houses and Victorian morals combined with an Old West spirit of rough-and-ready justice. When Ronald Reagan became governor of California, Nancy refused to live in the ancient three-story governor's mansion at Sixteenth and L Street, calling it (rightly so) a crumbling firetrap.

Sacramento is not a wealthy town because, like much of the rest of California, it never attracted major industries. The huge Southern Pacific Railroad, which once owned all of California and its politicians, hires most of the area's skilled work force today. And of course, there are thousands of minor political and bureaucratic jobs for those who are looking for a steady paycheck and their pension after twenty years of coffee breaks.

Compared to its counterparts in Los Angeles and San Francisco, the police and sheriff's departments of Sacramento have been considered fairly free of corruption. But its record of solving homicide cases is considered considerably less than average. There have always been plenty of instantly solvable domestic killings, and lots of murders done by two-bit holdup men while robbing liquor stores and gas stations who were caught before they'd gone two blocks.

These easy capital cases, with an appointed hanging judge sitting on every superior court bench, gave Sacramento County an enviable law enforcement reputation. Until the 1960s, one out of three death row inmates was from Sacramento County, and in fact, the last man executed in San Quentin, in 1967, was a cop-killer from Sacramento named Aaron Mitchell.

When World War II ended in 1945, California's economy fell right on its ass—and Sacramento fell the hardest. By 1954, the capital's skid row could compete with the worst of Los Angeles, Chicago, or New York City. The skid row area was five blocks wide and ten miles long, filled with human derelicts of every age and race, including almost as many women as men. There were fat, swollen, ugly squaws from the Digger tribe in the Sierras; snake-skinny, toothless white hags with running sores on their puffy, hairless legs; ancient blacks with faces like swollen balloons, barely able to creep along on calloused, sore, scab-covered feet. Night and day found them prowling, snuffling, and pawing through the trash in alleys, in ramshackle, slime-encrusted hotel lobbies, and outside the back doors of filthy cafes.

You can't bum from a bum, so whoring was the only way the women could get enough money for a short dog of Sweet Lucy wine. Being old and decrepit, they were happy that oral copulation was usually the only sex that interested the male derelicts. It was much easier and faster. Some of the more enterprising old gals would line up a half-dozen weaving, alcoholic men in an alley during broad daylight, and suck their way down the line in fifteen minutes, sometimes making as much as a dollar.

It was an acutely dangerous place to live, filled with vicious predators of all kinds: pimps, whores, bootleggers, dope ped-dlers, thieves, con men, muggers, psychopaths, and armed rob-bers. In 1954, it was a place that Gerald Armond Gallego loved and fit into as snugly and happily as Cinderella's foot in the glass slipper.

It is 1954, and at five in the morning, an eight-year-old boy is walking home after a hard night's work. He is skinny, has black hair, wide, staring black eyes, and a pale, sallow face with light freckles, which look as if they are painted on. He wears a grown man's khaki shirt tucked into faded, threadbare jeans. Neither shirt nor pants have seen water nor iron since they were handed down to him the year before from his half brother. Three sockless toes peep out from his half-laced, ninety-eight-cent tennis shoes.

The boy is Gerald Armond Gallego, a tough, smart, hard-working young lad. Gerald holds no social security card, pays no federal or state taxes, has no employee number, and punches no time clock. But he always has a pocketful of spending money, and even though he's never heard the word, Gerald would be proud to know that he is an entrepreneur.

His zone of entrepreneurship was the main skid row of Sac-ramento, from both sides of Fourth and K Street, all the way west to the river. His offices varied; an old beer storage room back of the Panama Bar, or a six-by-eight-feet whore's crib over the Hubba-Hubba Club, and sometimes two seats against the back wall in the "Open All Night Jewel Burlesque House." No burlesque anymore, just ancient cowboy movies no one watched. The customers paid fifty cents to come in out of the cold and sleep, not to be entertained. There was nothing left in the world that could entertain the walking dead of skid row. But Gerald was a very busy boy, and didn't use those offices very often, except during the winter, when rain and temperatures in the 30s ruined business on the street and drove his skinny, thinly clad body inside.

Gerald was a shoeshine boy, runner for pimps and whores, gofer for bartenders, panhandler on Thanksgiving and Christmas when the beat harness-bulls would look the other way; thief, car clouter, pickpocket, drunkroller and skid row hotel burglar. In 1954, whores didn't stand on street corners wearing crotch-high shorts, thigh-length plastic boots, or gold lamé skintight pants—and they didn't solicit passing motorists. Prostitution and loitering laws were strictly enforced, so street whores would have been arrested within about thirty seconds. Instead, the whores worked as barmaids or waitresses in hole-in-the-wall, three-stool cafes, or dozed in fifty-cent movie houses and dark bars until their pimp sent word that he had a trick lined up and waiting in a car or crib—or, if he was low-class, standing up in a dark alley. Carrying the message to whores that their services were required was Gerald's best-paying job. A taxi driver would pull to the curb, motion him over and say, "Go tell Joanne it's the back seat of my Cad parked in the Union Garage. Trick's already paid." A bartender or barmaid would come out and whisper in his ear," Tell Sandy it's room ten, Waldorf Hotel. She should collect six bucks." And Gerald would be off and running to find Joanne or Sandy at the movie house or hotdog stand and deliver the message. Those trips were good for a quarter, sometimes a half-dollar, and on most occasions, the whore he woke up at the movies or whispered to in the cafe would give him an extra dime.

A shoeshine was also good for a quarter, but Gerald didn't like kneeling on the sidewalk in front of *anyone,* and he despised the numerous sneaky, stinking pedophiles, who would furtively rub their penes in his hair while he bent over the little wooden shoeshine stand he always carried with him. That shine box was his diplomatic passport to roam the streets at night. Even a mean, iron-knuckled beat cop wasn't likely to order a hardworking shine boy to move on. In 1954, a common beat cop carried the will of the people in his nightstick, and when he growled, "Get your ass moving, and keep it moving", that order was obeyed without question.

Gerald was a boy who kept his mouth shut, handled his own problems, asked no quarter and gave none. And the citizens of skid row knew it and respected him for it. He was well liked and trusted, rarely stole from a friend (unless the temptation was just *too* great) and only snitched on his enemies. Bartenders would send him to their parked cars for gallon jugs of bootleg whiskey, from which they filled empty bottles of Jack Daniels or good Scotch. They couldn't keep the rotgut inside for fear an Alcohol Beverage Control officer might find it and jerk their license. Those trips were always good for a dollar, and Gerald liked them because they afforded him an excellent opportunity to scout his territory, spot a rollable drunk down in an alley, or perhaps a likely car he could break into when things were slow on the lighted streets. He'd taken some good things from glove compartments, under seats, and in car trunks. One item he remembered in particular—a heavy 14k gold man's Gruen wristwatch. He'd loved that watch, and cried like a baby when his mother took it away and gave it to a boyfriend.

On cold, rainy winter nights, eight-year-old Gerald would prowl the dark, slimy, stinking hallways of skid row hotels, shimming flimsy door locks and picking the ragged pockets of sleeping drunks. Gerald was a fair-to-middling burglar, so even if it was too cold and wet to work the streets, he still made a nice piece of change.

There was no question that, at eight years of age, Gerald Armond Gallego was a very astute, All-American entrepreneur.

Gerald had now walked to the end of K Street, and could smell the Sacramento River and see early morning mist rising from the dark water. The change stuffed into his right front pocket made a comfortable weight and jingled pleasantly when he broke into a trot. In the left front pocket Gerald carried his door shim and a razor-sharp one-bladed snap-open knife. A knife was the only weapon an eight-year-old could safely carry, but Gerald intended to buy himself a pistol, if he wasn't lucky enough to find one in a car he was clouting. If he bought a pistol, it had to be a .25 caliber semiautomatic. Not only was the tiny weapon easy to conceal and deadly at close range, Gerald *loved* that particular little handgun. His mother had one, but always carried it in her purse or bra, and Gerald never had a chance to steal it.

At this point, except for his school attendance, everything was on balance in Gerald's young life. He went where he wanted, stayed as long as he wanted, and did what he wanted. He made good money and was respected on the streets—even feared by some who called him a crazy, dangerous little bastard, an eight-year-old conniving hustler with the mind and soul of a hard-line, hard-time, thirty-year-old convict.

That description didn't bother Gerald at all. In fact, he was secretly proud of it.

Eight-year-old Gerald had to pay his mother for room and board, even though she never cooked a meal, and his room consisted of a sagging cot in the kitchen. But he had money leftover, and as he was under orders from his mom to stay away from the house when her boyfriends and tricks were there, he had plenty of time to work at the job he loved.

The school authorities, who were unaware that Gerald worked until four most mornings, just didn't understand why the boy couldn't get to school every day. One teacher repeatedly called him an illegitmate, stupid Okie because he dozed off in class and couldn't concentrate. Gerald deeply resented the accusation, and plotted revenge. He didn't mind being called what he *was,* but in the first place, he wasn't an Okie *or* a bastard. And in the second place, he was far from stupid. He could read, write, and do arithmetic—which was considerably more than his third-grade classmates could do.

As much as Gerald hated the system, he couldn't beat it. So he went along and called the teacher "ma'am," the principal "sir" and was tearfully contrite about all his shortcomings. They all felt sorry for him and his miserable life—just as he knew they would. The truant officer, however, was not so easily conned. He chased Gerald all over town and arrested him at every opportunity because he knew the eight-year-old for what he was, and hated him. He also leaned heavily on Gerald's mother when he could catch her at home, and once threatened to get a court order and take Gerald away from her.

"I wish you would do that," she had replied, "then maybe I could get rid of the little bastard and have some peace."

Gerald turned right along the river bank toward his mother's shack in West Sacramento. He cut across a large vacant field overgrown with weeds and ancient, rusting hulks of abandoned cars. It was here, in the middle of this dark, junk-filled open space, that he met his friend every morning. He loved her more than anything. She was, in fact, his *only* love. She was always ecstatic to see him, lavishing all her affection and caresses on the love-starved, totally neglected eight-year-old boy. Gerald bent low, looking for her silhouetted outlined against the dark sky . . . and there she was, in the exact spot where she always waited for him.

"Queenie?" Gerald whispered. "Is that you?" He knew it was, but always asked her the same question. He trotted up to where she sat on the ground and knelt in front of her, taking the dog in his arms and hugging her against his chest. She responded happily by licking his face, neck, and forehead. The dog trembled with all the canine love she felt for the only human who had ever been kind to her.

"Time for breakfast," Gerald whispered, taking a large greasy sack from inside his shirt and letting Queenie smell it.

"Are you hungry, Queenie? I sure am!" Gerald removed two cold hamburgers, one a giant meal for Queenie, and a smaller one for himself. He also had french fries and a pint of milk for the dog. Using his knife, Gerald cut off the milk carton top, and sliced the Giant Meal hamburger into four pieces. Gerald shivered with happiness as he watched the skin-and-bones, flea- and filth-covered dog lap her cool milk and gobble the huge hamburger—catsup, mustard, onions, tomatoes, lettuce and all. Gerald loved dogs—all animals, in fact. He'd found them to be trustworthy, loyal, and loving—which was a lot more than he expected, or got, from the humans he knew. As Gerald ate his smaller burger, he fed Queenie the fries, one by one, petting and caressing her scared, smelly, mangy body. She responded by licking his face after each french fry, and wagging her flea-bitten, half-hairless tail.

"I wish I could take you home," the boy whispered, "but like I told you when we first met, my mother would have her boyfriend shoot you, or do it herself, or maybe give you rat poison.

"But listen, Queenie, I got my eye on an old abandoned garage at First and J Street. If I can get it, we'll move in and fix it up just for you and me. You can guard our home while I work nights, and I'll take you to a dog doctor, and feed you real good, as much as you want.

"We'll go to the river most every day, and I'll fish while you watch for the truant officer . . . I know how to fry fish real good, and I'll take the bones out of yours, and if you have pups, we gonna keep them all and have a nice, happy family. We won't fight or hit each other, and everybody'll have plenty to eat, and you can sleep in my bed if you want to."

The dog looked at the boy with bright, intelligent eyes, seeming to nod at the appropriate places.

"I gotta go, Queenie," the boy whispered, hugging the dog and standing up, "but I'll see you same time, same place tomorrow—'an I'll bring you *two* hamburgers. They cost a dollar each, but *you're* worth it, Queenie, 'cause I love you and you love me.''

The scruffy, lonely, abandoned dog watched wistfully as the only person she loved trotted away—and the scruffy, abandoned boy looked back and waved at the only living thing he loved.

Chapter 10

The Perennial Bridegroom

About a week after the murders, Gerald started to worry. The reason was, he had a dream in the middle of the night about the Sandra Christine Tremper murder, and his cousin and friend who were doing life in the hard-time joint at Folsom Prison because a lowlife squealer had put them there. Folsom is the oldest and most feared penitentiary in California. The cells are chiselled out of a solid granite prehistoric riverbank, and the thirty-foot-high walls are giant blocks of solid granite shaped by convict labor. It is freezing in winter, boiling hot in summer, and the granite cell walls are always slimy, damp, and stink like rotten eggs.

Unlike most of California's other prisons, Folsom has no heat, no air-conditioning, no swimming pool, no tennis courts, no gym, no cable TV, no catered meals, no conjugal visits. The guards haven't read the latest psychiatric recommendations as to treatment of prisoners, and their answer to just about any problem is an ax handle upside a con's head—or so the inmates claim.

80

Folsom Prison has been sitting there on the banks of the American River for 140 years, and other than electricity and flush toilets, hasn't changed one bit. The prison, located about 35 miles north of Sacramento, just up the road from the one-street town whose name it bears, is home for California's most dangerous felons—the career criminals, the nuts, the escape artists, and the criminally insane, who are transferred there from other institutions if they are deemed too dangerous to handle. Despite over a thousand attempts, in 140 years only three men have escaped from Folsom alive. The inmates claim that when the cry "Man running!" is heard, the next sound is a rifle shot, and after that a shout of "Man dead!" It is a hard place to do time, and it worries career criminals and ex-cons like Gerald Armond Gallego. He was thinking about it now, in conjunction with the cold, hard fact that he might end up there if Charlene decided to turn on him. It never entered his head that he could just as easily end up in the gas chamber.

Gerald came to the conclusion that he had two options that would keep Charlene's mouth shut: marry her or kill her. Gerald was afraid to kill Charlene. If anything happened to her, Mr. and Mrs. Williams would be after him just like the in-laws of Jeffery McDonald, the Green Beret doctor who was accused of killing his wife and two children, and Gerald knew the Williams would hound him right into the gas chamber. As an immediate precaution, marriage seemed to be the answer. After all, one spouse can't testify against the other, right? Wrong!

Gerald was a good jailhouse lawyer, but he'd always "specialized" in criminal law, and wasn't up on some of the more intricate civil codes. Like most laymen, he relied on hearsay and didn't bother to research that law, which states, in essence, that a spouse can't be *ordered* to testify against spouse, but may do so if they so choose. And that choice was the key element that would eventually get Gerald two death sentences.

On Saturday, September 30, 1978, some eighteen days after their first two kidnap-rape murders, a very happy Charlene, a rather dubious Charles and Mercedes Williams, and a conniving

Gerald Gallego drove to Reno, Nevada. The Reno marriage license bureau is open seven days a week in order to accommodate the hundreds of customers who flock there daily for a no-wait, no-blood-test, cheap, uncomplicated wedding ceremony. Gambling, marriage, divorce, and legal whorehouses furnish the income that keeps Nevada afloat in a sea of worthless sand and rocks.

Charlene was no stranger to marriage. She'd tried it twice before, first to a mama's boy heroin addict who couldn't get it up and spent most of their married life hiding in a closet, drooling and playing with his dick. When asked by her mother if she hadn't known what she was getting into by marrying the wimpy little bastard, Charlene said no, she had thought he was one of that new breed of men the libbers said were sensitive, caring, loving and nonchauvinistic. She then married a soldier who, in a matter of weeks, told her to get lost when he discovered that when he married her he got not only a WASP princess but her king and queen parents as well.

As for Gerald, he'd been married more often than an old-time Mormon. In fact, from age sixteen on, he had been a perennial bridegroom.

Charlene wore a short, demure white lace sleeveless dress, white shoes, and had violets and orange blossoms interwoven in her hair. Everyone agreed that she was very pretty, and looked like the All-American bride in *Good Housekeeping* or *Redbook.* Gerald wore a C&R three-piece pin-striped blue suit, new black Florsheim wingtips, a white shirt, and a red tie. Everyone agreed he was very handsome, and looked like the All-American bridegroom in *Gentlemen's Quarterly.* Mercedes took lots of pictures of the happy couple, and hugged Gerald and kissed him. Charlene was pleased her mother and husband got along so well.

After marrying Charlene, Gerald's intention was to live the way he always had—steal when he found something valuable, deal a little dope, bartend part-time, and, even though he was lousy at it, cardshark now and then. Of course, he expected his woman to pay her own way. Through her father, Charlene found a job at ten dollars an hour cutting and packing meat in a packing plant, and Gerald made sure she kept it by forcefully explaining to her that he needed the money. It was either Charlene or her parents who bought Gerald a keen-looking 1974 candy-red Triumph sport coupe, and Gerald was so pleased he decided to show his appreciation by getting a job at the Windward Club on Del Paso Boulevard in North Sacramento as a bartender from 4:00 P.M. to 2:00 A.M. He was an excellent bartender and his boss later said that he attracted many women customers into the place.

When Charlene left work at five, she went home, cleaned house, made sandwiches for lunch the next day, then either took a nap or visited her parents. Around midnight, she'd drive to the Windward Club, where Gerald was on duty, sit in a dark booth in the back gulping straight shots of gin, and fantasize about being raped by sweaty-looking construction workers and the most feminine women.

Gerald would close the bar at two o'clock, and they would go out for a late dinner. On the surface, it seemed that they were just another hardworking couple trying to make ends meet in a depressed economy. But of course, nothing was as it appeared to be with the Gallegos.

During the next four months, Gerald and Charlene made a dozen trips to Chico to visit his mother and her husband, Ed Davies. Gerald's mother and stepfather lived in a half-converted old barn that resembled an Okie farm-labor camp in *The Grapes of Wrath.* A talkative Charlene would later tell her cellmate that the house was equally filthy inside as out, and she almost puked every time she walked in the door. She wouldn't eat there, and would make Gerald take her out for a hamburger when she got hungry.

Gerald's daughter Mary Ellen was living with her grandmother, Lorraine, and the real purpose of those visits to Chico was for Gerald to have sex with Mary Ellen and her girlfriend, with Charlene joining in whenever possible.

Considering Mary Ellen Gallego's testimony at Gerald's murder trial five years later, in which she would assert that she loved her father dearly, it is doubtful she would have ever squealed on dear old dad if it hadn't been for her girlfriend urging her on by saying they could get lots of sympathy, some new clothes for TV interviews, money from the state as abused children, and best of all, probably wouldn't have to go to school anymore.

During Gerald and Charlene's last visit to Chico, Mary Ellen decided the time was right to tell her step-grandfather, Ed Davies, that Gerald had sexually molested her the first time when she was six—that over the years, he forced her to orally copulate him, that he sodomized her, that he had sexual intercourse with her, and when she objected, he beat her with his fists, slapped and kicked her, and once chipped a tooth by kneeing her in the mouth.

Whether the beating actually occurred is anyone's guess, but they would certainly be in keeping with Gerald's usual treatment of females. Gerald and Charlene had gone to the store for beer and cigarettes, and Mary Ellen took the opportunity to tell her step-grandfather about the way her father had treated her. Ed Davies is a solid, working-class man, and when he heard Mary Ellen's story, he simply went nuts. He had raised the girl and loved her, and he decided to kill Gerald Armond Gallego.

When the newlyweds came back, Ed Davies was waiting with a 30-.06 deer rifle, fully intending to blow Gerald's head right off his shoulders.

Lorraine prevented Ed from killing Gerald by locking her husband in a bedroom long enough for Gerald and Charlene to get away. But while Gerald was talking to his mother in the front yard, Ed Davies called the police from his locked bedroom. They promised him they'd get there in time to arrest Gerald. Standing in the yard, with Charlene in the van screaming for him to hurry, Lorraine told Gerald that he was a dumb bastard for not telling her about his sexual relationship with Mary Ellen, and that it was too late for Lorraine to stop her big mouth.

"I can keep Ed from killing you or going after you, but not the cops. How could you let a kid get something like this on you by doing such a thing?" Lorraine was scared and shouting at her son.

"I was just trying to show Mary Ellen how much I loved her," Gerald tearfully replied. "She said she understood . . . maybe it wasn't legal, but I did it out of love."

"It's all right, sweetheart," his mother assured him, perhaps remembering *her* father, "just try not to do it again. And no matter what happens, always know that I love you."

The cops arrived long after Gerald was gone. They talked to Ed Davies, Mary Ellen, and her girlfriend, then called the Butte County district attorney at home. By 8:00 A.M. the next morning, Gerald was, to use his favorite expression, lip-deep in shit. A warrant was issued, charging Gerald Armond Gallego with numerous sex offenses against his fourteen-year-old daughter and her girlfriend, including incest with Mary Ellen—a charge that carried a minimum fifty-year prison term in California. By that time, however, Gerald and Charlene were back in their love nest on Bluebird Lane. No one, not Mary Ellen, not her girlfriend, and certainly not Lorraine, ever told the Butte County authorities where Gallego was living. And in order to keep the peace in his house, Ed Davies also decided to remain silent. (Even if someone had informed Butte County of Gerald's whereabouts, the Butte County authorities would have had to contact Sacramento County, which in turn would have had to track him down and arrest him. The local police forces simply did not have the resources to pursue such investigations, overwhelmed as they were with many more seemingly urgent matters at hand. Furthermore, Gallego was about to assume an alias, which was yet another impediment to any local force's ability to capture a fugitive quickly and efficiently.)

Charlene was worried sick about that outstanding warrant, and she convinced Daddy Gerald to let her tell Mr. and Mrs. Williams that the love of her life was in big trouble. When she did tell them, the first thing her mother wanted to know was whether Gerald had *really* been framed by his daughter and stepfather, as both Charlene and Gerald swore he had.

Mercedes drove to Chico alone, and managed to get an in-depth look at the charges against Gerald, along with part of his rap sheet. She had a long talk with the deputy DA handling the case, who told her that they had Gerald bang-on, and he was definitely headed for hard time at Folsom just as soon as they could lay the irons on him and force him to stand trial. Mercedes was boiling mad when she got home, and told her daughter that she and Gerald were goddamned liars, that she now *knew* Gerald was not only a child molester, but a habitual criminal as well, and as far as she was concerned, they could hang Gerald from the nearest tree. To which Charlene replied: "None of that matters. I love Gerald, and intend to stay married to him." That statement settled matters as far as Mercedes Williams was concerned. If her beloved daughter wanted Gerald Armond Gallego, then she could have him—incestuous bastard and habitual criminal that he was.

On the face of it, it would seem that *any* doting mother like Mercedes would have secretly turned Gerald in to get her child out of harm's way. Why she didn't remains a mystery. But Mr. and Mrs. Williams *did* lay down a few rules—no more bartending and no more women on the side for Gerald. He would get a good, steady job and support their daughter like any other decent husband. Charles and Mercedes put their money, influence, and a lot of good advice where their mouth was. The first thing they did was to slip some good, foolproof cover over Gerald. Charlene was ordered to visit her cousin, Steven Robert Feil, a man who strongly resembled Gerald in physical appearance, and steal Feil's birth certificate.

Charlene was told exactly where to look for the document, and had no trouble stealing it—after all, who the hell would suspect Charlene, the darling of the family, of stealing anything? Charlene gave the birth certificate to Gerald, who immediately used it to obtain a California driver's license and other verifying IDs under Feil's name, and used the Williams' address as his own. Feil's resemblance to Gerald Gallego ended abruptly with physical appearance in that, ironically, Steven Robert Feil was a highly respected member of the California Highway Patrol, the most elite and prestigious law enforcement agency in the state.

Gerald also transferred the Triumph into his new name, and quit the Windward Club, saying he was headed for Texas. Charles Williams used his influence and got Gerald a job with a supermarket chain as a truck driver, at eleven dollars an hour, the most money Gerald had ever earned honestly in his life. The Williams also told the couple that they would furnish the down payment for a house just as soon as Gerald had been on the job long enough to qualify for a mortgage.

It would seem that Gerald Armond Gallego would have been a happy young man. Everything had been arranged. Even the Mafia couldn't have done better for a favorite soldier. All he had to do was keep a low profile, work hard, and stay at home. But damn it, Gerald hated getting up at six in the morning and going to work, hated being told what to do, where to go, and how long he could stay. It reminded him of prison. Worse than prison, because he had to pay his own way, do his own planning and thinking, and he didn't have time to steal anything, or to deal dope or play poker all night. And because of the Williams' standing order, Gerald was afraid to take on another girlfriend even if he had the time. He was just a bit nervous about doing that anyway. He wasn't altogether positive that Charlene wouldn't take her away from him. Gerald's home life was once again in a total shambles. With his daughter and her girlfriend out of reach, he couldn't get it up at all now; Charlene was already hinting that they should do another disposable-love-slave number.

Gerald wanted to oblige her in the worst way, but he still didn't trust her totally. Until that outstanding warrant cooled down, he wasn't real eager to go in harm's way. Furthermore, Charlene's parents were watching him like a pair of hungry

buzzards and he knew they wouldn't hesitate a second in starting him on that short road to Folsom if Charlene showed any
significant amount of unhappiness.

Gerald wasn't accustomed to being backed into a corner, and
he didn't like it one bit. He wondered how it was possible that
the Williams family could have sneaked up behind him and
taken such a very firm grip on his balls.

According to a conversation between Charlene and her cellmate, things came to a head one afternoon in the fall of 1978
when Gerald and Charlene got into a knock-down-drag-out
fight because she'd sucked until her eyes bugged out, and Gerald couldn't even get close to a hard-on. Both had been drinking
gin all day. Charlene was one of those little people who get
belligerent when they're drunk. She was *very* drunk and needed
some good sex.

"Are you a fucking fag or what?" Charlene screamed at her
husband. "I can deep-throat better'n Linda Lovelace, and a *real*
man would've been hard as a rock by now!"

It was the wrong thing to say of course, and Gerald hit her
on the forehead so hard he fractured his little finger. But Charlene didn't do her usual "Oh, Daddy, I'm sorry" routine this
time. Instead, she ran to the bedroom closet, picked up a three-
foot-long steel vacuum cleaner hose, and used it to start pounding a very surprised Gerald about his head and body. Gerald
grabbed a broom, and they fought back and forth across the
living room like two saber-wielding, stark naked swashbucklers
in an Errol Flynn pirate movie, shouting curses and insults at
each other. He gave her a vicious crack on the skull, and she
went flying headfirst over the couch.

"You fucking Okie hardhat redneck bastard!" Charlene
screeched from behind the sofa while trying to untangle herself
from the curtains, "Only an uneducated, chauvinistic prick like
you would hit a WOMAN!" She popped up like a jack-in-the-
box, leaped the couch, and came at Gerald with her steel club,

fully intending to knock his brains out—then stopped so suddenly her bare feet actually slid on the carpet. She was stone-cold sober in an instant.

Gerald was pointing a .357 Magnum at her head, and she could see the little copper tips of the bullets in the chambers. First he held the big revolver in a typical TV cop stance, then he shifted to a *real* shooting position by turning sideways and holding the pistol at arm's length. His wide Rasputin eyes were more ominous than the barrel opening, and Charlene said later that she'd never been so frightened in her life because she knew he was about to shoot her in the forehead, just like the love slaves.

For the first time, Charlenen later told her cellmate, she realized that Daddy Gerald was afraid of *her*. And that really scared her.

Then, like a stage play cue, the unlocked front door opened, and in walked the diminutive, five-foot-two, one hundred-ten-pound Mercedes Williams.

"Put that gun down, Gerry," Mercedes commanded, walking right up to Gerald and slapping his face so hard his eyes crossed and he dropped the pistol.

She picked it up, glared at Gerald, then smacked him across the temple with the gun butt, causing blood to start pouring down the side of his head. Gerald covered his face with both hands and started crying.

"Stop that," Mercedes told him roughly, "I don't know what this is all about . . . but I can guess. Gerry, go wash that blood off and I'll bandage your head. Charlene, get some clothes on . . . you too, Gerry."

Twenty minutes later, Gerald was calm, cleaned up, dry-eyed, dressed, and bandaged.

"I'm splitting you two up for the rest of the day," Mercedes said in her no-nonsense way," Gerry, you're coming home with me. Charlene, you'll stay here until I send him back. Hear me?"

"Yes, Mama," Charlene said obediently.

At three-thirty in the morning on June 24, 1979, Gerald woke Charlene with his usual elbow smash to her ribs.

"Wake up, cunt! Today we do it again!"

At last! Charlene thought, rubbing her side, but feeling the tension and overwhelming sexual anticipation start building in her body like thick, hot bubbling lava from a volcano that was ready to explode. She didn't even mind being called cunt, because Charlene knew Daddy Gerald would be whispering "baby" before nightfall.

"The same place, Daddy?" Charlene asked.

"You ignorant cunt! *Never* in the same place! We're going to the Nevada State Fair in Reno. There'll be so much cute little teenage pussy running around, we might just grab four of them instead of two!"

"Oh, Daddy!" Charlene squealed, "That would be wonderful . . . but do you think we can handle that many at one time?"

"Of course we can. Once we get 'em tied and gagged, what can they do?"

Charlene jumped out of bed and started putting her teenage costume together.

Chapter 11

Shootout At Humboldt Sink

From Sacramento to Reno is approximately 102 miles of hard, sphincter-tightening driving over a treacherous, serpentine two- and three-lane highway that crosses the Sierra Nevada Mountains, following almost exactly in the tracks of the old wagon train route the pioneers took from St. Louis to Sacramento. The road leaps from sea level to over seven thousand feet, then plunges down at a forty-degree pitch to four thousand feet, levels out, then, with a sigh of relief, the driver passes under a huge neon sign arched over the road that reads, "Reno, The Biggest Little City in the World".

The Nevada State Fair is like most state fairs, complete with horse racing, prize livestock shows, cooking and canning competitions, cake and pie contests, and of course, a carnival midway. Gerald and Charlene arrived at the fairgrounds around ten on Sunday morning, June 24, 1979—Father's Day.

They parked the van in a huge lot, then went to a restaurant and had a good, nourishing breakfast of ham and eggs, toast,

hashbrowns, oatmeal, coffee, and a large fruit cup of water-
melon, cantaloupe, and seedless grapes.

Gerald was so hungry, he had a side order of pancakes and
maple syrup while Charlene smiled and nodded approvingly at
his huge appetite. She felt that Daddy Gerald didn't eat properly, what with all the hamburgers and other junk food he had
while they were on the go. She always thought of him as a big
man who needed lots of food. He wasn't really, but compared
to her, Daddy Gerald was gigantic. They left the restaurant,
walked hand-in-hand to the top of a grassy knoll, then sat down
to have a smoke and watch the crowd building up on the fairgrounds.

Charlene had her blond hair in bangs and pigtails, wore white
shorts, a white T-shirt, and open-toed white sandals. She didn't
look a day over sixteen. But she was carrying a small .44 over-
and-under two-shot Derringer in her purse, and Gerald was
armed with a .357 Magnum—the same pistol he'd scared the
hell out of Charlene with when he'd pointed it at her head that
day the past fall.

They sat on the little hilltop for an hour, watching like two
patient lions surveying a herd of antelope for potential targets
in the crowd below. Charlene was relaxed, filled with anticipation, and pleased as punch that Daddy Gerald hadn't called her
a cunt since they'd left home.

Suddenly Gerald stiffened and went into his rigid bird-dog
point. Charlene followed his gaze and saw a lone female at the
bottom of the knoll, walking slowly toward the main midway.
The woman was about sixty feet away, and looked not over
twenty. Tall, with long, silver-blond hair, dressed in tight-fitting
white cowboy-style pants, a wide tightly clinched red belt, white
silk shirt, and red cowboy boots.

She was a head-turning beauty who walked with a proud,
sensual, bouncing gait, a woman who was obviously aware of
the image she projected.

"Goddamn," Gerald gasped, "looks like she's walking and
fucking at the same time!"

"Uh huh," Charlene said, wishing that *she* was five feet seven and weighed one-twenty like the blond beauty boogeying on by.

"Go get her," Gerald said, turning the full force of his hypnotic stare on Charlene.

"But Daddy, I thought we were going to try for four . . ."

"Shut up. We'll take her, then come back for the rest. Get going, baby."

Charlene got up without another word, went down the slope and fell in behind the beautiful blond with the wiggling rear. Knowing that Daddy Gerald was watching from the knoll, Charlene felt very nervous and tense, not able to keep her mind on the job at hand, to psych herself up the way she had in Sacramento. The blond stopped suddenly in front of a home-canned jam and jelly display table, and Charlene walked up to stand beside her.

"Wish I could make stuff like this," Charlene said to the blond, waving her hand at the shiny, multicolored jars of jams and jellies spread over the tabletop.

"Uh-huh," the blond mumbled without interest, not even turning her head to look at Charlene. Then she abruptly moved on, headed for the livestock barn across the dusty fairgrounds. Charlene waited for the woman to stop before approaching her again. Now she had a very bad feeling about the whole thing; Daddy Gerald was watching, and Charlene was frightened of what he'd do if this one got away from her.

Charlene followed the woman into the long, cool, high-roofed livestock barn, which smelled of animal manure and urine. When her eyes adjusted to the dimness, she saw the blond standing with her arms folded on the top rail of a wooden fence, one red cowboy boot–clad foot resting on the bottom rail, looking at four miniature Scottish ponies who were dozing in the midday heat.

Charlene made her final approach by walking up and looking down at the tiny horses. "They're beautiful, aren't they?" Charlene said, glancing sideways at the intended prey.

This time, the woman turned her head and stared Charlene

right in the eye. Up close, she wasn't nearly as young as they'd thought. Her face whispered thirty, but her hands shouted around forty. Whatever her actual age, the woman's face showed she'd been there and back *several* times, and probably hadn't felt or thought like a teenager, even when she was one. Then she spoke in an icy voice that had probably cooled down many a hard-breathing male pickup artist.

"Don't fuck with *me,* kid. If you're looking for a dyke and a few bucks, you ain't found them yet. Now get the hell away from me, cause I'm gonna yell for a cop in exactly five seconds."

"Oh, I didn't mean . . . ," Charlene stammered, actually feeling her faced turning red with embarrassment, "I didn't mean anything like that!"

"Uh huh," the blond said nonchalantly, "you got two seconds left, kid."

"Oh!" Charlene squealed. "Oh, you're just *horrible!*" Then she turned and ran from the manure-and-urine-scented barn.

Whoever that voluptuous blond with the bouncy rear end may have been, and even though she'd never know it, there's no question that Sunday, June 24, 1979 was the luckiest day of her life.

Meanwhile, it was turning out to be a bad day at the fair for Gerald and Charlene. She'd tried to pick up two separate pairs of potential teenage victims, but backed away each time because they'd said their parents were somewhere on the fairgrounds. By five o'clock Gerald was livid with anger and frustration, calling Charlene every vile name he could think of, claiming she wasn't really trying, and that he intended to beat the crap out of her the minute they got home. At six, it was getting dark and they decided to have dinner in Reno, then come back about eight and try their luck with the evening crowd.

They trudged wearily and dejectedly toward the exit gate in the gathering twilight, stoop-shouldered, dragging their heels in the dust, both down in the dumps, feeling frustrated and mean, temporarily hating each other's guts, with Gerald muttering, "ignorant bitch" under his breath, and Charlene hissing, "Okie prick" through clenched teeth.

Suddenly Gerald's shoulders snapped back, his head went up, eyes wide and shining. "There they are," he whispered. Charlene looked at two girls who'd just walked through the gate and stopped, talking to each other. Both were young, pretty, dressed in denim jeans and shirts, and Charlene noticed that one had beautiful, honey-colored hair that hung to her waist.

Charlene had been having problems with her brain camera all day, but now it clicked in, putting the girls and events on a film that would remain in her memory for years.

"Use the windshield flyer scam," Gerald said, referring to another entrapment plan they'd discussed several times. "Now go get 'em, baby. Don't fail me this time."

"I won't, Daddy," Charlene answered, already approaching the potential victims.

"Hey, you guys," Charlene said, flashing her best smile, "how'd you like to make a quick twenty bucks each?"

Both girls looked startled, and eyed her warily. But Charlene could see they were interested. She watched Gerald peripherally as he faded away toward the parking lot like Dracula at sunrise.

"Twenty for doin' what?" asked the one with waist-length honey-colored hair.

"Helping me put advertising flyers on car windshields in the parking lot," Charlene answered, now face-to-face with the teenagers. "Won't take more'n an hour. How about it?"

The victims glanced at each other, then nodded. "Okay," the long-haired girl said, then smiled. "We thought you were hustling us for your boyfriend."

"Oh, that was my boss, not a boyfriend." Charlene laughed and touched the girl's arm, realizing that now they'd seen Daddy Gerald, she couldn't let them get away, no matter what she might have to do. Charlene put a hand into her purse, gripping the .44 Derringer.

"Okay, we'll do it. Where're your flyers?"

"In my van way over at the back of the parking lot. What're you girls doing here—I mean, are you alone or with someone?"

"Naw, we're alone. What's your name?"

"Millie . . . short for Mildred. And I hate both of 'em. You guys got a name?"

"I'm Brenda," the long-haired victim said, "and she's Sandra."

"How old are you girls?" Charlene asked, realizing that something didn't match between their voices and those curvaceous bodies.

"I'm thirteen," Brenda said, "and Sandra's fourteen."

"Uh-huh," Charlene mumbled. She was shocked. Christ, she thought, they could easily pass for twenty if they didn't open their mouths. These girls matured awfully fast, and they'd been living in the fast lane a long time, judging by that "hustling us for your boyfriend" remark.

During the two-block walk across the parking lot, Charlene learned that the victims were from broken homes in Montana and Arizona, that they were chronic runaways, that Brenda would run away with Sandra, then Sandra would take off and stay with Brenda.

Charlene got the impression that both girls were rather proud of their problem because it gave them the necessary excuse to cut out whenever it suited them. But exchanging one lousy environment for another didn't make much sense to Charlene until the girls explained that they did a lot of hitchhiking between houses, and always had a real good time with the guys who picked them up. They got some great grass and coke, which they couldn't afford to buy themselves, what with one mother being on cheap Montana welfare and the other an Arizona alcoholic who spent her alimony, child support, and welfare on booze and boyfriends.

Typical lowlifes, Charlene thought, and the world won't lose a thing when they're gone. We're actually doing everyone a favor by getting rid of two lifetime welfare recipients and troublemakers like these.

Pseudoelitist that she was, Charlene tried hard to believe that, but she knew that *her* past life hadn't been any better than Sandra and Brenda's—worse, really, because her parents had maintained a good home and given her anything she wanted. She never had to hustle for clothes or dope, or maybe food, like these two girls—at least not until she met Daddy Gerald. Charlene was so troubled and deep in thought, she actually ran into the side of her van. She had the keys ready to unlock the back door when a voice roared out behind her.

"Hi, there, girls!"

The totally unexpected outburst frightened Charlene so badly she fell to the ground like a shotgunned dove, positive that a cop had walked up behind her. When she jumped to her feet, Charlene couldn't believe her eyes. Gerald stood there, a wide grin on his face. He was supposed to be hiding in the van. What the hell was he doing outside, scaring her half to death? The Okie prick was *always* doing the opposite of what he was expected to do . . .

"Lost my keys," Gerald said, glancing meaningfully at Charlene. "Open the door and let's start getting those flyers on windshields."

Charlene opened the back door and both victims entered the trap like two eager mice smelling food. They had barely sat down on the cot when Gerald slammed the door and drew his .357 Magnum.

"All right, girls, it's a kidnap. Don't make a sound."

This time, the shock, fear, and terror came immediately. Both victims burst into tears, mouths wide open, throats swollen with tension and suppressed screams. Neither Gerald or Charlene were prepared for that instant terror; this time, there was no thrill in it as there was with the first two victims. Both recognized the uncontrollable hysteria about to explode, and without being told, Charlene ripped off two strips of duct tape and clamped them over the girl's mouths.

"Tape their wrists and feet," Gerald ordered nervously. The victims' reactions had thrown him off stride, and he was wondering if he should strangle both girls on the spot, drop their bodies in the desert, and write the whole day off as an exercise in futility and bad luck.

"No," Charlene said firmly, seeming to read his mind, "I . . . we worked too hard for them, and they're probably our last chance for today. We can't afford to be seen around here tomorrow."

"Okay." Gerald nodded in agreement, then knelt on his knees in front of the victim with the long hair. "Sweetheart, I'm gonna take the tape off your mouth. If you holler, I'll kill you. Got it?"

The girl's head bobbed slightly, eyes big as quarters. When Gerald removed the tape, vomit gushed from her mouth in a yellow, stinking flood, covering Gerald's shirtfront and knees.

"You fucking little whore!" Charlene screeched, "how dare you do that to my Daddy?" Then Charlene slapped her so hard, the victim's head spun halfway around.

Gerald removed his shirt and threw it into the girl's face. "All right, cunt, get on your knees and wipe that puke off my pants—untape her hands, baby."

The victim did as she was told, and Gerald replaced his shirt with a gray lightweight nylon zippered jacket he kept in the driving compartment. The other victim sat on the cot watching, crying silently, huge tears pouring down her face. Gerald retaped the long-haired girl's mouth and wrists, then ordered Charlene to get behind the wheel.

"Head toward Lovelock, you know the place, where we camped last year. And keep it under fifty-five. Got it?"

"Yes, Daddy," Charlene answered dutifully, sliding into the driver's seat. As she drove out of the parking lot, Charlene was jolted right down to her toes when she saw her beautiful blond friend getting into a pickup truck, and angrily thought it was too bad the old bitch wasn't in the back of the van with Daddy Gerald.

"I'd love to bite off *both* your nipples," Charlene whispered as she drove out the exit gate.

At nine o'clock that evening, Charlene, Gerald and the two victims were halfway between Reno and Lovelock. She would remember the exact time even though her brain camera was clicking off and on as if something was causing it to short-circuit. Highway 80 was dark, almost deserted on a Sunday evening, with only an occasional tourist whizzing by in the hot, sticky desert heat. Daddy Gerald was dozing on the cot, and the two victims were lying on the floor. Charlene couldn't see them and was a little worried that they might get loose and attack her. But Daddy Gerald said he'd do the worrying and told her to shut up and drive.

Charlene was shakey and trembling inside from a nerve-rattling eight hours of trying to kidnap the two stupid teenagers. It had been like a Laurel and Hardy comedy, like Murphy's Law, with everything going wrong that *could* go wrong. And that beautiful blond cutting her dead and calling her a dyke had caused Charlene more humiliation than anything that had happened to her since Tyrone waved bye-bye.

My God, Charlene wondered, is it really worth all this? I mean, we could have a couple of little amateur whores in our bed almost anytime we want, in our own safe little apartment on Bluebird Lane, willing and eager to play all the games. Then Charlene knew she had answered her own question. *Play* was the key word. Those girls would be barely one step above street whores, willing and eager, sure, but there wasn't anything exciting about phony whore sex or doing it in a safe place. No, to be really satisfying, it had to be illegal, like with his daughter and her girlfriend. It had to be breathtakingly dangerous, it had to be done so that only our wits and brilliant planning prevent us from being caught. The biting and the raping has to be *real,* not pretend, not love bites and play-rape like between a man and woman who love each other. When I show the girl how I want it done to me, and then Daddy Gerald makes her do it, that fear has to be there . . . it has to be real to satisfy us now. I know that Daddy Gerald doesn't like to make love to me. He's said so plenty of times, and it hurts. But he said it even *before* he caught me in bed with his go-go dancer . . . I've never been real crazy about any man's dick except possibly Tyrone's. When I want sex from a man, Daddy Gerald has the looks and body I like, and if he could get it up without all that anal stuff, and could do it like Tyrone, I think I might be satisfied . . . no, I'd probably still want a girl now and then . . . but Daddy Gerald wouldn't ever let me have a girl of my own, and I'm not sure I'd want one just for myself. I think that we really do love each other in a strange way, and this love-slave thing is something we both *need*. It holds us together when nothing else does, and now that we've tried it, we can't let go. If it has to end in the gas chamber, at least we'll still be together . . .

All that was quite a realization for Charlene, way out there in the middle of a dark Nevada desert. It was too much for her to think about and made her head hurt. So she tucked it neatly onto a back shelf, the same place where she'd put to rest that old realization of the fact that she was equally at ease in bed with men or women. She tried to think positive thoughts about her life with Gerald Armond Gallego.

. . . I'm not all that bad no matter what Daddy Gerald says, even if he does make fun of my lovemaking and calls me Lucy in front of people because he claims I'm real loose down there. Maybe I am, because a woman can't tell, but then, no other man except Daddy Gerald ever complained, and *he* isn't all that big unless it's with his daughter or the love slaves, so he must be complaining about something that's his own fault rather than mine . . . I'm going to remember that from now on when Daddy Gerald insults my lovemaking because I'm not really all that bad at it. I *know* I'm not, but I wish I could love sucking dicks like some of the women I've talked to. Even Daddy Gerald says I'm good at it, but I never *liked* to do it. Daddy Gerald must know I don't really like to . . . I wonder why I can't enjoy it the way those other girls do?

The van was barely illuminated, and Charlene glanced in the rearview mirror. She could see that Gerald had the love slaves up and untapped. He was stripping off the last of his clothes when Charlene turned her head and screamed at him, *"What the hell are you doing?"*

"What's it look like?" Gerald said, panting, "I'm gonna fuck . . ."

"No you're not!" Charlene screamed again, "you're supposed to wait for me, you son of a bitch!"

"Fuck you, cunt. You don't deserve *none* of this. If I hadn't found these two, we'd be in a motel watching TV. So *you* don't get none!" Gerald had both girls on the floor now, and he shouted at them, "Get naked, you little bitches!"

Charlene could see the victims taking off their clothes, and Daddy Gerald helping by pulling on the legs of their tight jeans.

"I'm going to stop!" She screamed.

"Go ahead. But if you do, I'll knock your brains out." Gerald was kneeling over the nude victims with a knee between each of their spread legs, totally ignoring Charlene.

Without the threat, Charlene knew better than to park on the freeway. If a Highway Patrol or tourist car passed, they were sure to stop and ask if she was having car trouble—an old courtesy of the desert road. She had to keep driving until they reached the Humboldt Sink turnoff that headed out into the desert.

Charlene spent the next fifteen minutes alternately watching the road and darting frantic glances back at Gerald and the victims in the rearview mirror. It was like a kaleidoscope—one second she'd see the arrow-straight road, then Gerald and the girls in a tangle of naked arms, legs and bodies, then the dark road again. Charlene was shaking, and her body felt as if she was freezing in the 110-degree desert night.

Charlene heard Gerald laugh, and looked in the mirror. He was now having sex with the long-haired girl, holding his torso up on outstretched arms, looking down into her face.

"You sure you're only thirteen?" Gerald said, panting, "I mean, you got a pussy like a grown woman."

Charlene slammed on the brakes and the van screeched to a stop—and as Gerald went sliding over the victim, his stiff member caught under her chin, bending it *back* up between his legs, then his head cracked into the blue ice chest. Charlene reached down and grabbed Gerald's hair, jerking his head painfully around until she could look him in the eyes.

"You dirty Okie prick! You two-timing bastard!" Charlene was screaming again, spraying saliva into Gerald's grimacing face, "You leave those girls alone . . ."

"Get off the highway!" Gerald shouted back, "Go to the turnoff . . . I can't do anything . . . I hurt my dick! Get off this highway, goddamit! Get going before a cop comes by!"

Charlene, mad as she was, knew it was good advice. She dropped Gerald's head, turned in the seat, and shot the van forward, its tires smoking and squealing on the hot pavement. Twenty miles before Lovelock, she saw the sign pointing to a dirt road that read: HUMBOLDT SINK 15 MILES. Charlene turned into the road at fifty, causing the van to slew around, the victims to scream, and Gerald to moan and curse.

Charlene drove until the van couldn't be seen from the highway, then turned off the lights and braked to another sliding stop. She couldn't remember ever being as angry as she was now. Charlene would later tell her undercover cellmate that for the first time, she hated Gerald enough to kill him. As she opened the door, Charlene lost her balance and fell out of the van, flat on her face in the dirt road. She lay there panting, trying to open her purse, calling Gerald most of the vile names he usually called her. Gerald hit the ground right behind her, stark naked, holding his injured member in his left hand and the .357 Magnum in the other. He stumbled over Charlene's prone body, staggered ten feet, then turned, the pistol pointed at Charlene, who was getting up.

An enraged Charlene came up shooting. The .44 Derringer

slug burned across Gerald's left bicep as he fired point-blank at her. Charlene felt hot wind as the bullet whizzed past her ear, and she let go with the other barrel—her last shot.

Gerald staggered backward and fell.

"Oh Daddy!" Charlene screamed at the top of her voice, "Oh, my God, I've killed Daddy!"

As she ran toward the fallen gunfighter, Gerald lifted his arm and fired at her again. Charlene was so close, the blue-green flame from the muzzle blast seemed to touch her hip, and blinded her for a moment—and she knew that his next shot would kill her. How could Gerald miss from two feet?

But Daddy Gerald didn't shoot again. Instead, he dropped the Magnum and groaned piteously, "I'm hurt, baby! I'm hurt bad!"

Charlene threw down her Derringer and fell on Gerald's prone body, crying and moaning, kissing him and cradling his damp, sweaty head in her lap, all hate evaporating from her heart like a black cloud.

"Oh, God, where are you hit? Where, Daddy, where are you hit?"

"My left arm, baby. You shot me in the arm." Gerald answered weakly.

Charlene couldn't see blood, but could feel a tiny swollen ridge where the bullet had blistered Gerald's skin as it passed.

"It isn't bad, Daddy, just a scratch," Charlene whispered soothingly, sounding like a heroine in a Roy Rogers movie.

"My dick, baby . . . my dick is broke!" Gerald gasped.

"Your dick . . . oh, but I didn't shoot . . . oh, Daddy, what happened to your poor dick?"

"I broke it when you put on the brakes . . . I went sailing right over the girl . . . and it caught on her chin . . . bent it right back to my asshole . . . oh my dick!"

Charlene would tell her undercover cellmate this scenario a dozen times, complete with gestures, pantomime, and hilarious giggles. That night, Charlene was grateful she hadn't killed

Daddy Gerald, but his mentioning the girls brought back the fact that he was cheating her out of her well-earned share of the spoils. And she got mad again.

But first, at Gerald's request, she did inspect his injured member and told him that it seemed okay to her, but she couldn't really tell.

"Oooh . . . it hurts so bad . . . maybe I can't get it hard no more!" Gerald wailed.

"Serves you right," Charlene said sharply. "Now Daddy, I want at least a few minutes with those girls . . ."

"Girls?" Gerald shouted, "My God, the girls . . ."

Both leaped to their feet and stared at the open van door.

"Gone!" Gerald whispered, "They're gone!"

Charlene ran to the Dodge and looked in—then almost fainted when she saw the victims were still lying on the floor under the dim light, untaped, naked, eyes wide with fear. Again, primordial instinct failed and the two victims hadn't even tried to escape.

Charlene went back to Gerald and put her arms around his waist, saying, "They're still in there. But we should get going—and you'd better dress."

"Okay, baby," Gerald said, "we'll drive to the other side of Humboldt Sink, where that underground creek comes out, where we camped, remember?"

"Of course I do." It was where they sat under the stars and Gerald played his guitar and sang to Charlene. She would always remember that place. Charlene kissed Gerald, then got in the driver's seat while he entered from the rear door and began dressing. She didn't hate him now, but she didn't love him either.

Humboldt Sink is a dried-up prehistoric lake that sank below sea level into the desert sand several million years ago. The area is filled with huge black volcanic rocks stacked neatly one upon the other, as if some ancient Herculean tribe had attempted to build a wall around the lake. Cholla cactus and sagebrush grow year-round, and millions of red, gold, and blue flowers blanket the sand after every three-minute rainfall. To some, it is breathtakingly beautiful. To most, it is a 130-degree waterless hellhole filled with sudden sandstorms, thousands of aggressive sidewinder rattlesnakes, spiders, beautiful but deadly Gila Monster lizards, and poisonous scorpions that love to crawl up a leg or into a pocket, then stab their victims with a quarter-inch stinger, injecting a cobralike venom that can kill a full-grown man.

It is a place where almost every living creature stings or bites—asks no quarter, and gives none. At 11:00 P.M., Sunday, June 24, 1979, two equally dangerous creatures arrived in the middle of this desolate spot with their intended victims.

Gerald and Charlene sat in the van for twenty minutes, listening and watching, in the unlikely event another human being was around. Huge silver stars sparkled in the dark sky like diamonds thrown across a black fur cape, and a bright yellow moon appeared to be no more that a few hundred feet above them. To their right, a few anemic willows and cottonwood trees grew along a sandy creek bank, sinking their roots hopefully toward the life-giving water. Far beneath the desert floor an underground river reluctantly furnished pure, clean water for the small creek, and they could hear it gurgling as it came up, flowed thirty feet, then was swallowed by the sand.

Somewhere to their left, in the foothills of the high, blue-black mountains, a coyote let loose with an agonizing lonesome howl that was immediately answered by a dozen others. The hair stood up on Charlene's neck as the canine screams echoed eerily around the van, and she gripped Gerald's arm and whispered, "Oh, Daddy, maybe we'd better not do this anymore. We're going to get caught, you know."

"Maybe . . . but if we do, I'll take all the blame. I'll say that I forced you to go with me. Anyway, it's too late to worry about that now. I don't think I could stop even if I *knew* we were going to be busted tomorrow. Understand?"

"Yes. Because I feel the same way, Daddy. It's just too good
. . . do you think there's other people like us, I mean, who do
like what we've been doing?"

"I don't know," Gerald answered softly, "there must be
. . . I don't think we could be the only couple in the whole world
who like to . . . uh . . . do stuff . . ."

"I guess not," Charlene said, feeling better but wondering
why they would never say out loud to each other the exact words
that described what they were doing with their innocent prey.
"I'm sorry I didn't get the blond," Charlene murmured, resting
her head on his shoulder. "I know how much you wanted her."

"Forget it, baby. You did fine. I'm sorry I got mad and
wouldn't let . . ." Gerald turned suddenly and spoke to the silent
girls on the floor. "You, with the long hair, you ever make love
to a woman?"

The victim shook her head, then said eagerly, "But *she* has!
If she does it, will you let us go?"

"Sure, kid. No problem," Gerald said cheerfully, somewhat
amused that the victims could believe there was an "if" involved.

"All right, baby," he whispered to Charlene, "she's all yours.
I'll wait here because of my sore dick. Get back there and enjoy
yourself."

"Thanks, Daddy." Charlene smiled and patted his cheek. She
was starting to love Daddy Gerald again—not much, but a little
bit. She slid out of the seat and hurried to the girls, removing
her clothes as she went.

Gerald poured himself a cup of coffee from a thermos bottle,
lit a cigarette, and stared out the windshield as he listened to
Charlene and the fourteen-year-old victim having sex on the
floor behind him. Charlene's moans and gasps just made his
sore dick ache; he had no interest in watching them or joining
in.

He was amazed that instead of the overwhelming sexual desire he usually felt when they had love slaves, he now felt a
gut-deep regret at what they had done to the four girls—and

knew that Charlene was correct. It *was* too good a thing to let go of. He knew he couldn't stop, not now, not ever. He also knew that sooner or later, he would kill Charlene, or she would kill him. They were both frightened of each other, for different reasons, and the only thing they now had in common were their depraved acts. The love they shared was held together by their sexual fantasies, without substance or trust. Like all fantasies, it could come and go, it was as fragile as a spiderweb. Gerald Armond Gallego was not a deep thinker, but he was as sure of that as he was of the fact he would kill the two victims within the hour.

Gerald smiled as he listened to the sharp, prolonged squeals Charlene always gave when she was having an orgasm, and he thought, that makes three—one more, then I'll break it up. I want to get this over with . . .

Charlene's next squeal made his ears ring, and then one of the victims screamed, and he knew Charlene had bitten her nipple. He waited another five minutes, then turned to look in the back. Charlene was getting up, roughly shoving the fourteen-year-old from between her legs. Gerald glanced at the thirteen-year-old, who lay on her back with Charlene's head on her chest. Blood was running from the right nipple of her apple-size breasts. Yep, Gerald thought, I was right on—she really chomped on the kid . . . wonder why she loves to bite *nipples* when she comes? Well, long as she don't do it to me, I won't worry . . .

"All finished, baby?" Gerald asked, lighting a cigarette for her.

"Yes, Daddy," Charlene answered in the little-girl voice she always used just after sex. "Give me a minute to dress."

Gerald got out of the van, then reached under the seat and removed an army surplus folding infantry shovel, opened it out to its three-foot length, then locked it into place.

Charlene was beside him now, looked at the shovel, then took his hand. "This is it, isn't it, Daddy?"

"Yeah. You want to do it?"

"No . . . I . . . I don't think I could . . . I mean, I could if I had to. I wouldn't like to, but I could."

Gerald smiled. "It's okay, baby. I'll take care of them this time. Get back in and hold the Magnum on 'em. I'll take 'em one at a time down to the creek bank . . . they won't be coming back," he added, then smiled again.

Charlene got in as Gerald went around and opened the back door, holding the shovel behind his back.

"All right, you with the long hair—come on out. We're just going for a walk. Not to worry."

The thirteen-year-old victim climbed out of the van without a word, and Gerald took a handful of her honey-colored hair, turned and led her toward the creek bank. Charlene sat on the blue ice chest, staring at the fourteen-year-old girl, who stared back, a faint glimmer of survival now showing in her wide blue eyes.

"Let me go," the victim whispered, "while he's gone . . . let me go. I'll run and hide . . . you can say I got away . . . please! Let me go!"

Charlene appeared to consider the girl's plea seriously, nodding slightly as she talked. Then she suddenly lunged forward, gave the victim a hard slap, grabbed her hair, then put the muzzle of the Magnum against her forehead and cocked it.

"You little bitch-whore! You little welfare witch! Why, do you think I'd let you go just because Daddy Gerald's back is turned—I want you dead, too! Just as dead as your friend is about to be right *now!*" Charlene glared at the terrorized victim, who seemed to shrink before her eyes, then sat back down on the ice chest, still glaring at the victim. There was a small pinkish circle on the girl's forehead, caused by pressure from the gun muzzle. The back door opened suddenly and Gerald stood there, looking at them with those wide, unblinking eyes. "What's going on?" He asked suspiciously.

"She's just trying to talk me into letting her go because you're not here," Charlene said, giving the victim another hard slap in the face.

"Take it easy, baby," Gerald said, chuckling. "You're turning into a real mean bitch. My goodness, what *would* your parents say?" he added sarcastically.

Suddenly, he was all business, his Rasputin eyes taking on a malevolent gleam." Get her out. You'll walk behind us. I'm gonna show you how it's done, baby. About time you learned what the other end of this disposable-love-slave game is."

"*NONONO!*" The victim's sudden, totally unexpected, ear-piercing scream scared the crap out of Gerald and Charlene Gallego. Gerald dropped his shovel and leaped back from the open door. Charlene jumped up off the ice chest and banged her head solidly against the van roof.

"JES-US Christ!" Gerald gasped shakily, "Get some tape on her fucking mouth. They could hear her back in Reno!"

Three minutes later, they were walking toward the creek bank, Gerald in front, leading the victim by her wrist and carrying the shovel, Charlene walking behind, the .357 Magnum in her right hand. When they got to the creek bank, Charlene saw the thirteen-year-old lying on the sand, eyes wide open, seeming to stare up at the golden moon directly over her, face streaked with dark blood, her once honey hair now the color of rust.

Charlene looked curiously at the girl and thought, I didn't know dead people kept their eyes open . . . that's really strange . . . but I've never seen a dead body up close before . . . she looks so *surprised.*

Without saying a word, Gerald turned the fourteen-year-old around, facing away from him, lifted the shovel high over his head, and brought the flat side down with all the strength in his powerful arms and shoulders. When the shovel hit, Charlene thought it sounded like a flat object striking against thick mud, a loud splat. The girl fell slowly, knees buckling first, then bending at the waist, going down as if her body was a melting, hot, wax candle. She hit the sand on her face, both arms folded in under her stomach, legs sprawled apart, blood coming from her splintered skull.

Charlene looked down at the victim with a sort of clinical interest. "Does she feel anything, Daddy? I mean, did it hurt?"

"Naw. When that shovel landed, it was all over. Her brain just shut down. Hell, I wouldn't hurt nobody just for fun. I'm no fucking sadist, you know."

"I know you wouldn't . . . she didn't know what hit her, did she?"

"Nope. Did you know that the skull is the hardest bone in the human body?"

"No," Charlene said, squatting down in order to get a good look at that hard skull, "Wow!" Charlene murmured, "squashed like a stepped-on eggshell! Why are their eyes open, Daddy?"

Gerald was digging a grave in the sandy creek bank, and grunted an answer. "Cause a dead brain can't send no signal to close the eyes—now shut the fuck up and let me work."

After a few minutes, Charlene got bored and wandered over to the thirteen-year-old. She knelt on her knees, inspecting the corpse with great interest. My goodness, Charlene thought, she hardly has any pubic hair at all. I guess it's because she's only thirteen. I've got to remember that, and surprise Daddy Gerald.

Charlene dipped her index finger in the blood on the victim's head, then drew a heart on the girl's stomach with the navel in the exact center. Then she drew an arrow through it and printed GG, then CG. She inspected her artistic work for a few moments, then the coyote began howling again and she moved over close to Daddy Gerald.

Gerald was making the sand fly, his sweaty, naked torso bulged with muscles that rippled and gleamed in the moonlight.

Damn, Charlene thought, he's so handsome and strong. That's the kind of male I like. I'd love to fuck him right now, right here on the sand. He's smart too . . . bet there's not many people who know a skull's the hardest bone or why dead people can't close their eyes.

It took Gerald almost an hour to dig a three-foot wide, four-foot long, three-foot deep grave. When it was finished, he put both victims in on their left sides, stomach to back, knees bent, fitted neatly together like spoons in a drawer. They were buried as they had lived in the womb—naked and in a fetal position. Gerald covered them with sand, stomped it down, then rolled a large black rock onto the grave.

"That should do it," Gerald Armond Gallego said to no one in particular, then sat down on the rock and lit a cigarette.

Then Charlene came over and sat beside him, her arms around his waist. "How do you feel, Daddy?"

"Sad."

"Me, too. We should go, don't you think?"

"Yeah, might as well. It's a long drive home."

As they walked arm-in-arm back to the van, Gerald said, "We'll throw all the clothes—theirs and ours—in that supermarket dumpster tomorrow afternoon. When we cross the Sixteenth Street Bridge on the way home, I'll throw the shovel and their purses in the river . . . baby, that pot you took out of the kid's purse . . . you can roll yourself a joint if you want to. Maybe I'll have a toke. I'm real beat."

Gerald and Charlene stopped in Baxter the next morning and bought a dozen donuts and two cups of coffee to go. Gerald paid for it with three dollar bills they'd taken from the purse belonging to the girl with the long, honey-colored hair.

At 4:00 P.M., Monday, June 25th, 1979, Gerald and Charlene finally went to bed in their apartment on Bluebird Lane for the first time in almost forty-eight hours. The clothes, purses, and shovel had been disposed of, the van washed and vacuumed. All evidence of the two kidnap-rape-murders had vanished—and Gerald Armond Gallego was sleeping like a hibernating bear beside a restless Charlene, who was exhausted, but couldn't sleep. She needed some male sex in order to relax. She eased the covers down, intending to wake Daddy Gerald with one of her special blowjobs. But when her mouth fastened onto his sore member, Gerald howled like that coyote out in the desert, and Charlene caught an elbow smash in the ribs that knocked her right out of bed.

"Leave me alone, you skinny-assed cunt!" Gerald shouted. "I gotta get some sleep cause I'm going fishing tomorrow. And you have to get up early to go to work."

Well, Charlene thought, lying there on the floor and not bothering to get back into bed, everything is the same again, and Daddy Gerald is his mean old self . . .

Chapter 12

The Boy Bandit

Gerald Armond Gallego's first recorded felony arrest occurred on Wednesday, March 7, 1956, when he was ten years old. Gerald, his mother Lorraine, and one or two assorted boyfriends lived in a rented house in what was then a middle-class Sacramento neighborhood known as Oak Park.

At nine that morning Gerald broke into the house of a woman who lived directly behind his mother. Gerald had been watching the lady's house through a hole in her backyard fence for two weeks, carefully noting that she went grocery shopping each morning at exactly 9:00 A.M. on the dot, and was gone for at least an hour. When he saw her walk out the back door toward the garage, Gerald ran around the block to her front door, shimmied the lock, and sneaked in. Gerald had no idea that the woman was still in the garage because her car wouldn't start, or that after five minutes, she would return via the back door to call the Auto Club.

The irritated housewife was mumbling to herself and absentmindedly heading toward the living room to make her phone call as Gerald was sneaking on tiptoe out of her bedroom, carrying a portable TV set and a half-carat diamond ring.

The surprised victim and burglar ran smack into each other in the dining room, scaring the hell out of each other and both staggering backward due to their unexpected bodily contact. Gerald dropped the TV and ring, burst into tears, then fell on the floor and started beating his head against the carpet, screaming, "You tricked me, you old bitch! You're supposed to be at the store!"

Then, according to the police report of the incident, Gerald jumped up, drew his switchblade knife, and advanced on the burglary victim, making slashing motions with the weapon, expecting her to run screaming from the house. But instead, the lady grabbed his wrist, spun Gerald around, threw a chokehold on his skinny neck, and held it until a surprised Gallego passed out. When he came to, three policemen were standing over him and Gerald was hustled off to jail in handcuffs.

The woman said later that she didn't know a chokehold from a dishrag, she'd just held on, not knowing what else to do, and was afraid to let Gerald go even when he went limp in her arms. So she'd just dragged the skinny ten-year-old burglar over to the telephone and called the cops.

Probably the greatest irony in Gerald Armond Gallego's life is that even though women loved him obsessively, they were also the cause of ninety percent of his arrests in one way or another, and they would eventually be his total downfall. Gerald *never* forgot his first humiliation at the hands of a woman, and swore he'd get even with her.

If he hadn't pulled the knife, Gerald would have been sent home to his mother. Instead, he was charged with first-degree burglary, carrying a dangerous weapon, and assault with intent to kill. A juvenile court judge sent him to a reform school at Whittier, in Southern California, tagged with an indeterminate sentence. Gerald escaped the next day, but turned himself in that same afternoon because he couldn't find his way home.

"They drove me up here in the middle of the night," ten-year-old Gerald said to the superintendent, "and I slept all the way. When I busted out, I didn't have no money, and being in a strange town, didn't know where I could steal any. Also, I don't know the way to Sacramento and was scared to ask directions, me being ten and all."

At the Whittier School for Boys, each inmate was required to say a prayer before meals; if they refused to do so out loud, they weren't allowed to eat. Within a month, Gerald was chanting prayers like an Indian witch doctor, calling everyone sir, and driving the staff nuts by trying to be "helpful."

And just as a conniving Gerald figured, he was released in ninety days by convincing the staff psychiatrist that he was just what he appeared to be—a ten-year-old boy far from home who missed his loving mother, her cooking, hugs and kisses, and being tucked into bed each night.

Of course none of that was necessarily true, but in ninety days Gerald was back in Sacramento, and within twenty-four hours, the woman who'd shamed and captured him had her house set on fire. The fire department said it was arson, but neither they nor the homeowner knew that Gerald was back in town.

Over the next two years, Gerald was in and out of juvenile halls and jails a dozen times, charged with everything from auto theft to shoplifting. Gerald was already an expert at manipulating the system, and like all sociopaths, could control any psychiatrist and sometimes even the most cynical kiddie-cop. He would just deny everything, cry and scream, beg to see his mother, threaten to commit suicide—and as some long-forgotten juvenile cop noted in his record ". . . this little bastard could cry and lie his way out of hell . . ."

When he was twelve, Gerald Armond Gallego was charged with raping a six-year-old girl—the only sexual offense he was ever accused of, until the incest charge by his daughter. How that crime occured and Gerald's ignoble capture was related by by Ellen Weed, Gerald's first wife and the mother of Mary Ellen Gallego, Gerald's one-and-only true love daughter. Weed said that Gerald told her the story numerous times during their stormy, eighteen-month marriage, which featured constant hand-to-hand combat, and that four years after it happened, Gerald was *still* furious at the humiliating chase and capture by a two-hundred-pound woman.

Gerald's mother had moved again, and rented a ramshackle old Victorian house at 2120 M Street in Sacramento, where Gerald became know as the terror of that quiet, genteel but rundown neighborhood almost overnight. He ripped hubcaps off the neighbor's cars, cut garden hoses into bits just for the hell of it, sneaked into garages and stole tools, lawnmowers, fishing gear, or any salable item not welded, screwed, or bolted to the floor or walls, then sold them to second-hand stores around town. (Gerald was still the All-American entrepreneur.)

On October 12, 1958, a cold Monday afternoon, Gerald was playing in the basement of a house ten blocks from home. The owner knew he was down there, and sent her six-year-old daughter to keep an eye on the thieving Gerald, with orders to call her if he tried to walk off with something. The woman knew there wasn't anything in the basement to steal except the water heater and furnace, but knowing Gerald's reputation, was still cautious about the little neighborhood thief who could just walk across your property, and by the time you looked out the window, it was stripped bare as a cornfield after a plague of locusts had passed through. The lady was busy preparing dinner for her husband and forgot about Gerald until her six-year-old daughter walked in the back door stark naked, and calmly told her that she and Gerald had been playing "Mama and Daddy in bed" down in the dusty basement.

The horrified mother, who weighed about two hundred pounds, simply went nuts. She ran out the back door, picked up a double-bladed ax used for splitting fireplace wood, and headed for the basement. The disheveled woman was standing in the basement door before Gerald looked up and saw her. Then she came at him with raised ax, screeching like a police siren. A terrified Gerald Gallego ducked right between her legs, ran out the door, and headed down the street, screaming for *his* mother.

Gerald's knees almost reached his nose with each running step, and when he glanced back over his shoulder every other second, he could see the specter of a vengeful mother narrowing the distance between them with amazing speed.

Mouth open, ears red, panting for breath, and flushed with adrenaline, the two-hundred-pound mother came after Gerald like a charging rhinoceros. Each time her size-ten foot slapped the pavement, she screamed a bloodchilling "EEE-YOW!" like an angry Indian warrior after an enemy scalp.

Gerald managed eight blocks before he was totally exhausted. He stopped and leaned against a sixty-foot-high oak tree, panting, gasping, and retching. Then he glanced to his left and saw the hideous ax-wielding aberration almost on top of him. Gerald gave an earsplitting shriek and went up that oak tree like a squirrel with its tail on fire.

The murderous mom didn't even look up at Gerald clinging to the branches thirty feet above her. She just started chopping, and each time her ax struck, the old tree trembled and the woman let loose another awesome "EEE-YOW!" which Gerald was now answering with his own high-pitched plea of "MAMA! HELP! MAMA!"

A hotshot call went out on the police network that a crazy man was chasing a small boy down the street with an ax. The call woke up every yawning, bored cop in town, and a dozen units responded, each officer hoping to get in some good police work and target practice by putting the ax man six feet under with a few rounds of double-aught buckshot. When the first six cars arrived on the scene, twelve excited, eager, bulging-eyed cops flew out the doors, shouting twelve conflicting orders at the busy woodchopper—most of them ending with ". . . throw down that ax and *FREEZE*, cocksucker!"

When the suspect didn't respond, a sergeant stepped forward, leveled his twelve-gauge shotgun and bawled a gender-bender, spit-spraying, incoherent order: "Drop it and get those hands on top of your head, prick! One more second and I'm gonna blow your nuts off!"

"Do it!" Gerald screamed from the treetop, "Do it! Do it! Go and shoot, goddamit!"

When the cops finally realized that the two-hundred-pound, jean-clad woodcutter was a female, four burly officers hopped on her and wrestled the squealing, biting woman to the ground. After a ten-minute battle, they pried the ax from her hands and clamped on the irons. It took over eight hours to determine who was telling the truth—the woodchopper or the boy. They finally arrested Gerald for rape.

Gerald claimed he didn't do it, of course, and in fairness, it should be noted that nowhere in the medical report of the doctor who examined the six-year-old child does it state that there was actual penetration of her vagina or rectum; furthermore, no evidence of semen was found on her body, including her mouth or hair.

Gerald lied, cried, and denied, and his statement to the police reads as follows:

Q: "What did you do to the girl?"

A: "I laid on top of her and went up and down like I seen the men do on my mom."

Q: "Did you take your thing out?"

A: "Yeah."

Q: "Did you stick it between her legs anywhere?"

A: "No."

Q: "Did you put it in her mouth?"

A: "No."

Q: "Where the hell was it then?"

A: "On her belly, I guess."

Q: "Did you come?"

A: "No, I never went anywhere until that crazy woman came after me with an ax."

Gerald's evaluation by a juvenile probation officer reads in part: ". . . his social traits are total failures, and he is an example of a hard-shelled young boy who evidences little or no motivation for improvement, or even a remotely remorseful insight into the crime he has committed. And in view of his numerous arrests for burglary, petty theft, shoplifting, and in particular, the felony knife assault upon a female burglary victim, this officer is regretfully forced to recommend that subject be confined at the Preston School of Industry until his majority . . ."

The judge acted upon that report by remanding Gerald to the Preston reform school until he was twenty one years old.

While Gerald was at Preston, he began putting on weight and developing his gorillalike physique. He finagled a job as gardener and lazed around the barracks all day, reading and listening to country music, pumping iron and planning major crimes with the other inmates. Gerald was far from a model prisoner. His record shows that he was involved in dozens of fights, and was thrown into solitary confinement for beating a six-foot-six seventeen-year-old aggressive homosexual almost to death with a piece of garden hose.

Gerald escaped five times, was caught twice within hours, and returned on his own three times. Despite his rebellious conduct, Gerald had served exactly twenty-three months when the staff psychiatrist decided he'd been rehabilitated and recommended he be released on parole to his mother. Lorraine signed the responsibility papers, and Gerald left Preston on a Greyhound bus.

When Gerald arrived in Sacramento, he was stunned to find that his dear mother had moved the night before and left no forwarding address. Gerald couldn't believe that his mother had deserted him. He sat down on the curb in front of her empty house and cried like a baby.

Lorraine had agreed to take her son in only because her grandmother, Mrs. Slone, insisted she do so, saying poor Gerald deserved another break. But Lorraine had just gotten rid of a very abusive alcoholic husband, George Bulgar, and didn't really want any part of Gerald Gallego, who'd been a thorn in her side since the day he was born.

It wasn't the abusive side of Bulgar that Lorraine wanted out of her life—it was the alcoholic one. Lorraine had probably taken more black eyes, split lips, and fractured ribs from boyfriends and husbands than any woman alive, and she considered that to be just another hazard of her lifestyle. But an alcoholic can't make a living, and Lorraine didn't want any part of that.

Gerald knew that if he didn't at least give the appearance of living with his mother, the probation department, lax as it was with its charges, would likely send him back to Preston. He didn't want them to catch him screwing up this early in the game. Fourteen-year-old Gerald stole a pickup truck and drove two hundred miles north to his mother's rented hideout shanty on Heraldsberg Street on the outskirts of the poverty-stricken former lumber town of Chico. He arrived there at midnight in a raging frenzy, burst through the door, and confronted Lorraine and her sister Ramona, who'd helped her move, scaring the hell out of both the women. Gerald demanded to know why his mother had ran out on the deal and put his freedom in jeopardy.

Ramona said later that Lorraine told her to leave, but when she refused, Lorraine took Gerald into the bedroom, saying she intended to calm him down, and Ramona said that after a few minutes, the shouting stopped and she heard them laughing. Gerald never told Lorraine that he had gotten her address from his great-grandmother, because the old family matriarch had promised Lorraine she'd never tell Gerald anything.

By the next morning, Gerald and his mother had apparently settled their differences, as they always did in one way or another, and after breakfast, Gerald started thinking up ways to make some money. Within a week, Gerald had teamed up with his sixteen-year-old half brother, David Hunt, and they went on a Wild West armed robbery spree of Chico, Sacramento, and Redding, knocking over about twenty motels. Two months later, they were captured while sleeping in their hot car near the small town of Willits and put in jail, on hold for a dozen law enforcement agencies. The crafty brothers escaped from the flimsy lockup that same night, but were taken off a freight train by railroad bulls in San Francisco the next morning.

This time, the judiciary system had a bellyful of Gerald Gallego. Over the objections of probation officers and social workers, Gerald was tried as an adult and given a five-to-life sentence at the Duell Youth Authority Correctional Facility near Santa Barbara. The California justice system was split between two warring factions—the judiciary branch, comprised of district attorneys and judges who claimed that they wanted to put criminals away for as long as possible, and the parole system, run by psychiatrists and social workers, who claimed to know what was best for everyone, and were determined to cure their criminals and put them back on the street as soon as possible. The parole system usually prevailed.

Things were looking pretty dark for Gerald Armond Gallego when he began serving that five-to-life sentence at Duell for armed robbery, jail break, and auto theft. But he was a firm adherent to the motto "Don't curse the darkness, light a lamp," so when the news arrived that his thirteen-year-old half brother, George Bulgar, Jr., had been hit by a car and killed, the ever-alert Gerald fired up a real beacon. Upon hearing the news, he opportunistically plunged into a deep depression and was placed in the prison psychiatric ward.

"I want to kill God for taking my brother away!" Gerald moaned to his shrink. "But I can't, so I'm going to kill *myself!*"

The frightened young doctor recommended that Gerald be transferred immediately to the comfortable minimum security psychiatric hospital at Vacaville, where he could have the loving care and attention he needed. The old, experienced warden vetoed the medical order, however, because he knew that Gerald was an escape artist and would be over the fence at Vacaville within twenty-four hours.

Gerald didn't get his transfer, but he did use George, Jr.'s death to convince the staff psychiatrists and parole board that he'd been "shocked back to reality" by the untimely demise of his beloved brother, and tearfully assured the board that he would "live the rest of my life as a decent citizen, trying to make up for all the wrong I've done."

Actually, Gerald barely knew his half brother, and hated him for stealing their mother's attention—what little of it there was. On one of the rare occasions when Lorraine had them together in the same house, Gerald had beaten his kid brother senseless with a cast-iron frying pan for stealing a slice of toast off his plate. Gerald put on his best crying-and-lying act, and the parole board released him before he'd even finished half of the minimum five years he was supposed to serve before being considered for parole.

Sixteen-year-old Gerald Armond Gallego had kicked the system in the ass again, and was out, a much wiser, harder, and determined young man. He hit the ground running, and didn't stop until he'd killed at least ten people.

Chapter 13

A Shave, A Haircut, And
The Big Swede

For a month after their third and fourth murders, Gerald and Charlene Gallego waited for any news of the murdered girls. When no word of the double murder appeared, they began to relax, guessing that the bodies hadn't been found, and after that length of time, the chances were good that they never would be.

Gerald and Charlene knew the desert, and that the big black rock rolled onto the grave wouldn't stop a pack of hungry coyotes from digging the bodies up and devouring them right down to the last thigh bone once they began to rot and smell.

After six weeks, Gerald was positive they'd gotten away with it again, and decided to celebrate by taking two weeks off and driving up to Oregon. He planned to sponge off a few of his relatives, fish a little in the Rogue River, then come back down through Idaho, visit some more kinfolks, hunt pheasants for a day or two, then take a leisurely drive back to Sacramento.

Gerald was an avid believer in vacations—job or no job, he

took one whenever he felt like it. Gerald fine-tuned the van for the long trip, then told Charlene to pack.

Charlene got up her nerve, covered her ribs, and told him that she thought she was about five weeks' pregnant. Charlene was very hesitant to tell him, because Gerald didn't like being around pregnant women, even in the early stages, and had always ducked out on all of his previous wives and mistresses the moment he became aware that a brat was looming up on the horizon. This time he was understanding, even jovial, and said jokingly that he'd never heard of a woman's tongue getting anyone knocked up. Charlene was really hurt that he would make fun of *her* sexual proclivities, considering his own. She got mad, hauled off and slapped Gerald so hard his eyes rattled. Then, like a pet dog who accidentally bites its beloved master, Charlene literally dropped to her knees, wrapped herself around his legs, apologized profusely, and begged him to forgive her.

Luckily for her, Gerald was feeling magnanimous. He told her to forget it, that he'd made a bad joke, and she should see a doctor the next morning to arrange for an abortion. Of course Charlene would pay for it, because Gerald kept his own paycheck and Charlene met their living expenses with hers.

"Don't tell your parents," Gerald warned, "they might want us to keep the damned thing, and if we didn't, we'd never hear the last of it."

Gerald even drove Charlene to the abortion clinic at Eighteenth and Broadway the next morning, waiting over three hours for her to be examined, have the ten-minute procedure, then rest for an hour before they'd let her go home. He was very sympathetic about her postabortion cramps, put her to bed, made sure that she took her tetracycline antibiotic capsules on time, and even gave her a quarter-grain codeine tablet when she complained that her dilated uterus really hurt as it started shrinking back to its normal size. Gerald had been intending to sell the codeine tabs, but he was still feeling good and let Charlene have a couple to ease the pain. Then Gerald cooked Charlene her favorite dinner: filet mignon, crisp fried potatoes, green salad, sliced tomatoes, and hot Parker House rolls. He served it to her in bed and sat beside her while she ate, even cutting the tender meat into bite-size portions.

Charlene was purring like a contented pussycat because of all the postabortion care and attention, and because Daddy Gerald was acting the way he had when they first met. She was really loving him again and planning to surprise him with one of her really special deep-throat blowjobs later on in the evening. But she changed from cat to tiger when Gerald patted her cheek, stood up, and said he had some business to take care of.

Charlene tried to choke back the tears as that good, warm feeling died instantly. She felt all her love for him slipping away again. Hanging on to Daddy Gerald emotionally was like trying to walk on water.

"What business?" Charlene said, sobbing. "Pussy business, I'll bet, or some barmaid who wants you to lay some pipe up her dirt road!"

When Charlene started talking convict slang, as she sometimes did in imitation of him, Gerald didn't like it. He didn't answer her, just slapped Charlene's face and walked out the door.

Charlene's accusation was in the ballpark. If the truth be known, while Gerald was waiting for Charlene at the abortion clinic, he'd made a date with the clinic bookkeeper, who was a five-nine, one-hundred-forty-pound, natural blond Swede with Ingrid Bergman looks named Hannelore. After an hour of mutual eye contact, Gerald had approached her cubbyhole office and started a conversation. The big beautiful Swede would later remark to an investigator that she knew Gerald had brought a patient in who was supposed to be his wife, that he'd given a phony name of John Smith, was low-class, a braggart and a liar, and obviously an unfaithful husband.

Knowing all *that,* why then, she was asked, had she agreed to see him?

Her answer was the same as ninety percent of Gerald's previous women—she said that it was because he was her living, walking, talking, fantasy sex object, and with those flashing, hypnotic, depthless black eyes, those wide shoulders, slim waist, and the cutest little ass she'd ever seen encased in tight corduroy pants, she simply couldn't resist.

The big Swede was third-generation American, and had inherited all the best characteristics of the Old Country. Her skin was like smooth silk, she had a wide mouth with full, sensual lips, and those one hundred forty pounds were distributed in a way that gave her body the look of a slimmed-down Venus de Milo. Her parents were college-educated professionals, owned property, had money in the bank, and harbored great expectations for their favorite daughter.

Hannelore knew exactly what she wanted from life. She did accounting for a doctor who owned several abortion clinics, was working toward her CPA license, and intended to go into business for herself. At twenty-eight, she had no doubts about her future—until she had the bad luck to run into Gerald Armond Gallego. By all odds, she should have missed him entirely. Most certainly the big Swede didn't even remotely resemble Gerald's usual female prototype—being too old, too big, too intelligent, too ambitious, too high-class, and far more interested in getting ahead in life by working rather than stealing. But in all those lonely years, the big beautiful Swede had never found a man who could even come close to satisfying her super high-level libido and dark sexual fantasies. Because she hadn't found that special man, and wouldn't settle for second best, she was emotionally vulnerable and love-starved.

After that first night in bed with Gerald Armond Gallego, who was a rabid, Tasmanian Devil sex machine with her, she knew she'd found the man who could satisfy her enormous sexual appetite and, she hoped, someone on whom she could lavish all her suppressed love and attention.

As for Gerald, he got a blackjack-hard erection just from *looking* at the big Swede. He told his mother later on that she was the most erotic, sexually satisfying woman he'd ever been to bed with. Gerald told Charlene about the beautiful Swede because he had to, and because she had $5,000 in the bank, a brand-new 1979 Buick, and a very hefty five-hundred-dollar-per-week paycheck. It was a con man's dream come true. Gerald forgot all about the trip to Oregon and went to work on Charlene, telling her that he intended to take every dime the Swede had, then they'd go to Texas, buy a bar–dance hall, make lots of money, and live happily ever after.

Charlene told him to shove his bar and happily ever after up his ass—that he wasn't about to do any outside fucking unless she could have her share.

Gerald tried to explain that the big Swede was not AC-DC, would never agree to a threeseome, and then he lied and said he couldn't get it up with the blond anyway, and other than a blowjob or two, and maybe a little anal sex now and then, nothing would happen. Charlene didn't see the difference, and said that blowjobs and anal sex *was* fucking as far as she knew, and unless *she* was there while it was going on, it wasn't about to happen. There are very few men who are still around after asking or ordering their woman to stand by while they have sex with another female. But Gerald did it all the time, and not one of his women ever really objected or took the issue past an hour of tears and threats. That's all Charlene did. She argued, cried, and screamed; she tried to brain Gerald again with that steel vacuum hose. Then she just gave up, told him to go ahead with it, but to call her every day so she'd know he was all right, and that she would wait for him no matter how long it took to swindle the Swede out of her money and property. She even promised not to tell her parents, to keep right on working at the packing plant, and to explain Gerald's absence by saying that he was in Texas looking at a bar he wanted to buy.

Charlene didn't see anything wrong with putting the horse before the cart—she knew that if Daddy Gerald *really* wanted to get a bar, he would get one, and nothing would stand in his way.

With Charlene pacified and agreeing to work as his outside man, Gerald moved himself and his baggage into Hannelore's neat-as-a-pin one-bedroom condo, which was located in an expensive area of American River Estates. For the next three months, Gerald woke up to a magnificent view of the river, satin sheets, expensive perfume hanging in the cool air, and breakfast in bed prepared and served by the big Swede, who was able to cook the way everyone imagines their favorite old grandma could.

Hannelore made delicious meals Gerald hadn't even heard of, much less eaten. She bought him more expensive clothes than a whore would have her new pimp. And the motherly Swede bathed him every night with her own loving hands in perfumed water, then gave him wonderfully relaxing massages that Gerald said felt better than orgasms. During those three months, Gerald's every want and desire was anticipated and taken care of by the big Swede. Later she said, "I was so much in love with him, I would have killed myself if he had told me to."

Just how much of that statement is fact and just how much self-serving camouflage can best be summed up by what Gerald said she demanded in return.

In exchange for all that loving domestic service, lavish personal attention and financial outlay, the big Swede demanded that Gerald perform twice in the early morning before she went to work, and again when she rushed home during her lunch hour for a nooner. And at night, there were *no* limits as to her sexual expectations from her extremely capable and cooperative sex object. She made Gerald a virtual prisoner of love, under orders not to leave the condo unless she was by his side; she was suspicious and called him almost every hour to make sure Gerald was where he was supposed to be—in the condo resting and thinking up new ways to fuck when she got home.

Gerald was secretly pleased by her sophomoric possessiveness because it fit right into his plan for separating the sexy Swede from her money. Gerald said that he felt like a mistress whose jealous sugar daddy laid down some stiff rules in order to protect his precious pussy from being used by anyone else.

Despite all the restrictions placed upon him by his passionate and ever-watchful lover, Gerald managed to call Charlene almost every day as he'd promised, assuring her that their scam was going well, that he had the Swede in his pocket, and was about ready to make his first move. According to Gerald, one of those calls went like this: "Are you fucking that bitch, Daddy?"

"Naw. All we do is sit around and talk. She's an *intellectual,* you know . . . and they'd rather talk than fuck."

"Yeah? What do you talk *about?*" Charlene asked, knowing Gerald's capacity for deep thinking.

"Lots of things. Books mostly, politics and . . ."

"Oh shit! I don't want to listen to any more of your lies, you dumb Okie prick!" And a sobbing, jealous, and frustrated Charlene slammed down the phone.

There was of course a grain of truth in what Gerald said. He was ready to make his first move on Hannelore's money and property. With a professional con artist's intuition, Gerald knew she would now give anything in order to hold on to her sex object.

That evening, Gerald sat Hannelore down for a talk. He tearfully confessed that his name wasn't really John Smith, but Armondo Galanto, that he was an Italian boy from LA who had worked for the mafia until he'd dropped fifteen thousand in markers at a crap table in Vegas. Not being able to pay it back, he'd made a run for it, and now the mob was closing in. But his dear old Godfather recently had a change of heart, Gerald said, and would now forgive and forget if he paid it back within a few days. If he couldn't do that—well, he'd be at the bottom of San Pedro Harbor wearing a cement overcoat. The terrified Swede had read *The Godfather,* and never doubted Gerald for an instant. She was furious—not at Gerald, but at the "mob," who wanted to drop her handsome sex object into forty fathoms of icy seawater.

"I just don't know what to do!" Gerald wailed, flanging himself down on the bed and allowing his robe to gape open, giving the scared Swede a good look at what she'd be missing if the mob got him. "I don't *want* to leave you, but I'll have to, unless . . ."

She threw her one hundred forty pounds of frightened, quivering flesh on top of her sex object, clamped her strong arms around his neck in a desperate, strangling, I'll-never-let-you-go full nelson, and said, "No one is going to hurt my sweet baby! How much do you need?"

Within thirty days, the Swede's bank account was empty, her Buick sold, and she'd taken out a five-thousand-dollar mortgage on the condo, which was all the bank would go for.

During the weekend of November 3, 1978, Gerald said that he and the Swede celebrated by making love twenty-four times—once every two hours. They were celebrating because on Monday, November 5, he would take fifteen grand in cash to his Godfather in LA, be pardoned, and then return to her loving arms so they could be together for always. Early Monday morning, Hannelore drove Gerald to the airport in her third-hand Ford, tearfully watched as he boarded a PSA flight to Los Angeles, then sadly went to work.

An hour later Gerald got off the plane at LAX, caught the next flight back to Sacramento, then took a taxi to the Swede's condo. He packed his expensive clothes in three new suitcases, all courtesy of the sexy Swede, took another taxi to downtown Sacramento, and called Charlene to tell her that her wandering boy would be home in a couple of hours.

"Oh thank God!" Charlene squealed, "I just love you to pieces, Daddy—and I've got a *big* surprise for you!"

"Uh-huh," a dead-tired Gerald replied. "Well, I ain't in no mood for surprises, baby. We got a lotta serious things to talk about. So don't get cute with no silly-assed surprises. Got it?"

"Okay, Daddy," Charlene said cheerfully. "Want me to pick you up?"

"If I'd wanted you to pick me up, I'd of said so." Gerald growled and dropped the phone.

During the taxi ride to 2067 Bluebird Lane, Gerald reviewed the possibilities of retribution from the Swede. All she had on him were two phony names, one phony address from the abortion clinic, and a whole lot of dead-end lies. And, Gerald thought, the likelihood of her running into me by accident is as remote as being struck by lightning. Still, he thought, maybe I'd better take that trip to Oregon. I could really use a good rest.

Gerald didn't hear anything from the big Swede until after he was arrested for the murders. When she read about him, saw his picture in the papers, and saw him on television, Hannelore wrote him a letter at the Sacramento County jail, saying how sorry she was to hear about his problem, and was there anything she could do for him? The police took her name and address off the envelope and put them on the list of people to be interviewed regarding Gerald's prior activities. Gerald kited a letter back to her, asking if she could get him out of the country should he manage to escape.

She never wrote back or contacted him again.

"After Gerald left me," she told an investigator sadly, "my life was as empty as my bank account. But I consoled myself with the fact that I had at least gotten something for my money. But I wasn't about to risk my freedom for him."

"I'll bet you just hate him!" The female investigator commiserated.

"Oh no!" The shocked Swede answered, "I love him. During the past eighteen months, I've been to bed with twenty men, trying to find something of what I'd had with Gerald. But all twenty of those guys put together didn't come close to what he made me feel."

The female investigator said that when she returned to her office and finished writing the report on Hannelore, she arranged a brief interview with Gerald because she just had to see for herself what twenty men rolled into one sexual athlete looked like. She was, she said later, very impressed with what she saw, and understood what the Swede was talking about. But she didn't think it would have been worth fifteen thousand dollars. At least not to her.

When Gerald walked through the door at his home on Blue-bird Lane, Charlene was waiting with her big surprise. She was poised stark naked in the middle of the living room, one foot on the floor, the other up on the coffee table, one hand on her bony hip, the other behind her head. She'd cut her hair very short, with bangs in front, then parted it on the left side, using a pink barrette to hold it in place. She'd put scarlet lipstick on the nipples of her bantam egg–sized breasts and shaved her entire pubic area as slick as a billiard ball.

"Hi, Daddy!" Charlene squealed happily. "Welcome home!"

Gerald dropped his suitcases and stared. It was the most uninhibited, erotic thing he'd ever seen in his life—something he'd always fantasized that his lover-daughter would freely and openly do for him.

"Mary Ellen!" Gerald moaned, reaching both arms out to Charlene. "My God, you look exactly the way you did when you were ten!"

An average thirty-five-year-old man with forty-eight hours of nonstop sex behind him would have been out of action for at least a week. But not the rabid Tasmanian Devil, Gerald Gallego. He threw Charlene on the couch and fell on her in a sexual frenzy that didn't abate for a whole week.

Charlene later told her cellmate that she lost count of the number of times they made love, but by the end of the week, she was worried that she might develop calluses on the walls of her vagina. She had, she told the informant, once known a retired whore who claimed that very thing happened to her after a summer of taking on some twenty tricks per night at a farm labor camp near Fresno. No, Charlene told her cellmate, she hadn't read *The Chinese Room*—the lipsticked nipples were something she'd seen in a porno movie. And yes, it *did* make her mad as hell when Gerald kept calling her Mary Ellen for a whole week.

Charlene said that the seven days and nights of wam-bam teenage screwing didn't make up for the big Swede having Daddy Gerald as her very own for three months, but the $15,000 would have gone a long way toward making her feel better. When she asked for her share, however, Daddy Gerald told her to shut up about it, that he had it put away and when they went to Texas and found that bar–dance hall, he'd produce it.

Unfortunately for Gerald, Charlene found out where he'd hidden the money at the wrong time—while she was in the Sacramento County jail waiting trial for murder. That accidental discovery gave her irrefutable proof of what Daddy Gerald had in mind all along as to their future, which threw her into such a jealous, hurting rage that Charlene decided to roll over on poor old Gerald and send him to the gas chamber.

Chapter 14

Willing Victims

Charlene's parents didn't believe a word of her story about Gerald going to Texas for three months. Of course they didn't say anything to Charlene about it, but when Gerald and Charlene showed up at their house a couple of weeks after Gerald came home, Charles Williams decided to have a man-to-man talk with his sneaky son-in-law. According to what Gerald told his mother later, he and Charles were standing in the Williams' back yard and the conversation went something like this:

"Now son, I'm not one to pry into your personal life," Charles told him.

"Uh-huh."

"But you've made my little baby very unhappy. Now son, I'm a man, and I understand that a fellow might go off after some strange stuff now and then. It's a natural thing to do."

How would *you* know? Gerald wondered. Your wife's had your balls in her purse for so long there's no way you could know what a *man* feels like . . .

"You've been away three months," Charles continued, "and you've lost your job, and my baby's still working every day, and . . ."

"Listen, Charlie," Gerald interrupted, punctuating his phrases by poking Mr. Williams in the chest with a stiff forefinger, "I don't care *what* you think. I'm telling you for the first and *last* time, stay the fuck out of my business. You want your baby back? Take her! That is if she'll let you. You wanna turn me in to Butte County? Go ahead—but your baby might not like it. And I'll tell her you turned me over. You want your baby arrested for hiding a fugitive? And maybe you and Mercedes too? I don't think so, Charlie. Fuck you *and* your chickenshit truck-driving job. I'm gonna work *where* and *if* I wanna from now on. You got it, Charlie?"

Charlie got it all right. He'd been taking a step backward with each poke, and was now clear across the yard, his back against the garage wall. Gerald poked his bony chest one last time, turned, and walked to the van and drove off without even saying bye-bye to Charlie's baby. Thirty minutes later a frantic and tearful Charlene burst through the door on Bluebird Lane, panting and out of breath because she'd run all the way home.

"You aren't leaving me, are you, Daddy?" she shrieked, leaping right up off the floor and throwing her arms about his neck, then clamping her skinny legs around his waist like an agile monkey.

"Naw," Gerald told her, staggering backward, "I just had to set your old man straight. You wanna stay with me, you can. But I'm not taking no more orders from your parents. Got it?"

"Oh, thank God!" Charlene said, sobbing. "I thought you were leaving . . . Daddy, you do whatever you want. I mean, you hardly ever went to work anyway, and I pay all the bills, and we have that fifteen thou—"

"Oh shut the fuck up," Gerald said gently, "I'm getting me a bartending job—right after we take a little trip to Oregon. *Then* I'll start looking for that place in Texas."

The trip to Wedderburn, Oregon, was a disaster. It rained every day and was so cold they rarely left Gerald's relatives' house. Charlene was miserable the entire time, and after one week, she convinced Gerald that they should go home.

Her middle-class, snobbish sensibilities were standing up like porcupine quills all the time, and she despised her dumb-assed in-laws and their musty, damp, cold, unkempt house that smelled of dirty socks, unwashed diapers, and a toilet that backed up every time someone took a crap. As there were nine adults and six babies living in the two-bedroom, thirty-year-old farmhouse, Gerald and Charlene had to sleep in the freezing van.

Dozens of chickens wandered in and out the open doors of the old house, and Charlene said she'd stepped in enough chicken shit to fertilize a ten-acre field. The family also had five large, wolflike mongrel dogs who were never fed. Each time Charlene went outside, they'd start barking and growling. She was positive that the dogs intended to make a meal of her skinny little body the first time they cornered her.

When they finally left, Charlene was an emotional basket case—not only because of Gerald's relatives, their house, chickens and dogs, but also because she missed her period and just *knew* she was pregnant again.

As Gerald drove the van through Oregon toward Sacramento that cold, gray morning, Charlene sat huddled in the front seat, staring out the windshield at the icy driving rain, wondering what the hell had happened to that brilliant girl student with an IQ of 160 who'd graduated high school at fifteen, to that almost-certain career as a classical violin virtuoso, to that lifestyle filled with sycophants and luxury that suited one with her artistic temperament, tastes and refinement. Here she was now, sitting beside a cold-blooded murderer whom she loved obsessively one moment and hated the next, aware that she was a user of almost every addictive chemical known to medical science, an alcoholic with an overpowering, aberrant, destructive sexual deviation more kinky than a roll of barbed wire, and which had, with Gerald's help, made her a murderess four times over. At that depressing moment of realization, the only future Charlene Williams Gallego could see through the rain-spattered windshield was a seat beside Gerald in the cylinder-shaped gas chamber at San Quentin prison.

Charlene sat on the floor in the living room, drinking straight gin, popping Quaaludes and staring glassy-eyed at Gerald, who was huddled on the couch watching Wile E. Coyote and Road Runner cartoons.

A thunderstorm with freezing rain rattled the windows at 2067 Bluebird Lane, a storm that typified the miserable March weather in Sacramento. Cold gray fog lay waist high on the street, and it was actually curling in under the front door like a scene in a 1930s horror movie. Gerald sat cross-legged on the couch, hunching forward, a blanket wrapped around his body and over his head like a hood, his Rasputin eyes gleaming in the shadows. Staring at him, Charlene thought he looked like a sad, meditating Buddha who hoped Nirvana was just around the corner. It was Gerald's day off and Charlene had stayed home too, just to be home with him.

When they returned from Oregon, Daddy Gerald found a job he liked: head bartender at Muskogee Joe's Place, a roadside bar –dance hall–poolroom sitting in a bare two-acre field between North Sacramento and Rio Linda. The male patrons at Muskogee Joe's were mostly working men who wore heavy leather, high-heeled, engineer's boots, K-Mart jeans and Western-cut shirts with the sleeves rolled up to their armpits in order to show off massive, bulging biceps. They drove pickups, loved to drink, use dope, fight, and dance the night away, then fuck their squealing, giggling women in their camper-covered truck beds after Muskogee Joe's closed at 2:00 A.M. In California, a place like Muskogee Joe's is known as an Okie Stomp Joint. It's a place where country music wails and thunders from a monstrous juke box with multicolored flashing lights, and fights break out every fifteen minutes, usually ending with the loser having the shit stomped out of him by his opponent—thus the sobriquet, okie stomp joint.

A bar such as Muskogee Joe's is a good place to pick up women, and a handsome burly laborer always had his choice of twenty or thirty females dressed in tight jeans and tank tops who sat at the long plywood bar, drinking up their welfare and child support money. The women patrons did their share of fighting too—not just hair-pulling, scratching and name-calling. They fought like their male counterparts, with roundhouse swings, kicks to the groin, ear- and sometimes tit-biting and eye-gouging. Occasionally a pistol or knife was pulled.

No one ever attempted to break up fights between men, and, unless weapons were drawn, women were also allowed to fight it out until one went down for the count. The reasoning was that a woman probably had a houseful of kids with no husband, and when a good bloody fight turned to guns and knives it wasn't worth making those kids orphans.

Muskogee Joe's rubbed Charlene's artistic sensibilities the wrong way, and she didn't go there very often. The women were overly hard, mannish and dangerous for her tastes, and the men a little *too* sweaty and macho. The place had a heavy, humid atmosphere of underlying physical violence, blatant sexual exhibitionism, expectant pleasure, and an aura of exhilarating, condoned illegality.

Like the skid row of his childhood, it was an environment in which Gerald flourished. He was a rat in a garbage dump. He could literally whip any man in the house and everyone knew it. He reigned supreme in his little kingdom behind the bar where he swaggered and preened like a male peacock, making small-time dope deals, stealing dimes and quarters out of the till, and graciously accepting five-dollar tips and free drinks from his female clientele, not to mention free pussy, which the females sometimes fought to be first in line to give.

Again, Gerald should have been a happy man. He was making $150 per week, stealing another hundred, and raking in about $200 more in tips from the panting, wet-crotched women and the shit-stomping Okie males who admired him because they knew he could whip *their* asses. But he wasn't happy, or even satisfied. As Charlene often said later, Gerald Gallego wouldn't have been happy with a million bucks and a perpetual hard-on. Gerald did like his job at Muskogee Joe's, but he'd recently developed another major sexual malfunction in tandem with his recurring limber-dick problem with Charlene. Now, when he could get an erection, he couldn't ejaculate!

I wonder what's the matter with him now, Charlene thought, as she sat there on the floor, gulping gin and staring at Daddy Gerald on the couch, hunched-over under the blanket, looking as lumpy as Quasimodo, morosely gazing at cartoons.

I'd hate to be a man, she thought drunkenly. Lucky for us women that we can do it anytime. All we really gotta do is be ready to fall on our backs whenever the man thinks he can do it, open our legs, wiggle a little, pretend we're having an orgasm by squealing and moaning some, then gasp "No one ever made me come like *you* do." And the dumb bastards actually believe it.

But when he can't get it up, all hell breaks loose 'cause there's no fucking at all and of course the prick always blames his woman.

If Daddy Gerald didn't get so mad, and cuss me and hit me, I wouldn't mind this no-come thing with him. I mean, at least he can do it long enough for me to have an orgasm or two. I wonder what the hell's really wrong with him? I mean, he has more trouble with that dick of his than any man I ever heard of. I hate to see him so worried. He said that if he couldn't ejaculate anymore, he didn't want to live. No matter *what* I do . . . I can give him a better fuck than I ever gave any man, then suck until my jaws crack, give him a hand-job until my arms get tired and he still can't do it . . . Maybe it's something psychological, maybe something to do with the abortion after we got back from Oregon . . . maybe he doesn't want me to get pregnant again because he can't stand being around women when they're knocked up.

At that moment, Charlene almost got her drug-pickled IQ of 160 working again, but there was too much LSD, coke, PCP, grass, and booze pumped through it, and now her narcotic-numbed thoughts would only weave and bob like flashing lights off the darkness, never coming clearly into focus. She poured another glass of gin, swallowed a Quaalude and dropped her head back against the wall with a dull thump. They'd gone to San Francisco for the last abortion because the big Swede was at the clinic in Sacramento. Daddy Gerald hadn't been so jovial about it this time, and he ordered her to start taking the Pill or get an IUD. But she disliked any kind of birth control method, even a diaphragm, so she hadn't gotten around to it yet, and probably wouldn't. Now Gerald got up, dropped the blanket, and without a word, motioned for her to get on the couch. It was the third time today that he had wordlessly directed Charlene to assume that position.

She got up wearily but obediently, staggered sideways, then caught her balance and weaved toward him, dropping her robe so as to give Daddy Gerald a good clear look at her shaved genitals, hoping that might help him this time. Gerald was hard almost instantly, but forty-five minutes later, he was sitting dejectedly on the floor, crying and sobbing, with Charlene still lying spread-legged on the couch, her vagina and pubic bone burning and aching from the long pounding they had taken from her man's frantic, rabbitlike attempt to reach a climax. Charlene had only come once because she'd been working so hard for Daddy Gerald she had lost her concentration and spent forty-five minutes using every trick she'd ever learned, tricks that she was fond of claiming had driven other men wild. But they didn't work on Daddy Gerald. He sat on the floor, head bent, staring uncomprehendingly at his still-erect member, tears running down his cheeks.

Charlene felt very sorry for him, and reached out to stroke his damp hair. Her gesture of sympathy made Gerald bawl even louder.

"I'm scared, baby," Gerald choked, "something's real wrong with me . . . my dick aches like a bad tooth and my nuts feel like they're gonna bust open . . . what am I gonna do, baby?"

"Don't you know, Daddy?" Charlene asked, her voice taking on a combative edge.

"Love slaves." Gerald stated in a whisper.

"That's right, Daddy," Charlene said emphatically, as her heart started that crazy pounding, sending the blood surging through her body like an electrical shock. Her vagina filled with sticky fluid; she later claimed that when Daddy Gerald whispered those two little magic words, she immediately had a tooth grinding orgasm right there on the couch while Gerald stared at her in astonishment.

On Thursday, April 24, 1980, ten months to the day after their last abduction murders, Gerald and Charlene were parked in the huge lot at the Tower Records in Sacramento. They'd spent the last hour strolling around, looking for potential victims among the crowd of teenagers swarming in or near the popular record store. There were lots of likely prospects, but also an unusual number of Metro police walking casually about, staring suspiciously at everyone. Gerald figured a robbery had taken place somewhere in the shopping area, and the cops thought the bandit was still around.

"This place ain't for us, baby," Gerald said, starting the van up again. "We'll go out to Sunrise Mall in Citrus Heights. That'll be brand-new territory for us. Wonder why the hell so many kids are out of school. Little bastards must be playing hooky," the old master hooky player mumbled, driving out of the parking lot.

Citrus Heights is a sprawling bedroom community some twenty miles north of Sacramento. Sunrise Mall is a monstrous uncovered shopping area that was laid out with the shopper in mind. There are benches to rest on under shady olive trees, usually facing a bubbling water fountain, and there are maps of the mall posted at every corner so that the average citizen can easily find his or her way back to the parking lot without resorting to the use of a compass.

Less than twenty years ago this was beautiful, open farming country, filled with pheasants, quail, doves, and jackrabbits. During the November-to-January hunting season, ranchers supplemented their income by charging city Nimrods twenty-five dollars for a day of good hunting on their property. Shotguns cracked from sunrise to sunset across a sixty-mile-square radius, making the entire area sound like a distant battlefield. Ranchers grew wheat, cattle, turkeys, and domestic rabbits. They were not wealthy as were their colleagues forty miles to the south, and when the opportunity arose to sell off their land to housing developers at enormous prices, they jumped at it. The pheasants, quail, doves and rabbits vanished when the middle-class housing went up, the shotguns were silenced, and Citrus Heights turned into an overcrowded suburb.

Gerald knew the area well, having spent a lot of time hunting, fishing, and prospecting for gold in or near the Sacramento River. When they'd first met, Gerald took Charlene on a week's gold-panning and fishing trip along the river, and she had found a three-quarter troy ounce gold nugget as large as her thumbnail. She wanted to keep it as a sentimental souvenir of what she later described as the happiest week of her life. But Gerald took it away form her and sold it for three hundred dollars to a modern-day gold assayer's shop in the little former gold rush stage-stop town of Folsom—which is less than five miles from the forbidding prison with the same name.

It really annoyed Gerald when Charlene discovered that nugget, because she was the one who *always* managed to pan a few specks of gold dust, catch the biggest fish, or find their way back to camp after Gerald became hopelessly lost. Charlene said that she got more cuffs and cusses by doing the right thing than when she screwed something up. Even though Charlene's IQ was badly impaired by alcohol and dope, she could still think circles around Gerald most of the time, especially when it came to logic and long-range planning. He knew it, and resented anything she said in the way of a correction. Charlene would have a major problem, for instance, if she told Gerald that he was going the wrong direction on the freeway, usually getting a hard elbow smash in her tender ribs.

As they approached Sunrise Mall, Gerald missed the entrance because Charlene was afraid to mention that it was coming up. They had to turn around—and Gerald shot her a few harsh words because she didn't mention it . . .

They parked at the far side of the mall lot, in a spot where their van was hidden on three sides by a high cinderblock wall.

"This is the place, baby," Gerald said, "let's go get us a coupla teenage pussies."

"Daddy . . ." Charlene said, mentally ducking, ". . . Daddy, do you think we might try for some black girls this time?"

"Shit!" Gerald said, snorting, "That's about what I'd expect from a nigger-loving cunt like you! Well, not with me, you don't. You want diseased black meat, get it by yourself!"

"Okay, okay," Charlene snapped back, "I just mentioned it, for Christ's sake!"

At 9:00 A.M., April 24, 1980, two pretty seventeen-year-old girls named Sharon and Tracy sneaked out of Sharon's mama's house with the intent of hitchhiking to Los Angeles and finding jobs in the movies—porn movies, that is.

A week before, they had met and made friends with a worn-out, herpes-infested porn bit player with a dope-fried brain who told them that young pretty girls with good bodies who were inclined to exhibitionism and who were totally comfortable with straight, lesbian, oral, and anal sex could make a fast fortune in pornographic films. The dope-addled ex-porn player went into great detail, explaining that porn is the most lucrative aspect of the film industry. She said that a first-run motion picture with famous stars might cost thirty mil and take ten months to produce, then gross eighty mil at the box office. In that same time span, forty porno flicks would be made at a total cost of one mil, then would gross a quarter-billion dollars worldwide.

Sharon and Tracy were impressed, thinking that all that money trickled down to the players. But their friend the former player explained that X-rated film companies are owned mostly by women, or at least fronted by women, and the big dough stays at the top. Like the wage scale everywhere, from Jack-in-the-Box to the corporate board room, pay is tilted in favor of males—in this case, she explained, for good reason. Young men with the proper equipment willing to work in porn films were very difficult to find, whereas thousands of eager girls appeared at casting offices every day looking for work. Those chosen to play were paid around two hundred dollars for five days' work on a film, while big-dicked boys made between five hundred and a thousand dollars, depending upon the size of their member, and how well it could be used on the sound stage in front of a film crew. As in private bedrooms around the world, if a guy couldn't get it up on the set, the gal was blamed for not being sexually proficient. The lucky ones were booted out without being paid (there were no SAG play-or-pay roles in the porn business!). The unlucky ones were sold to the pimps on Santa Monica Boulevard, who kept their girls supplied with cocaine, and gave them a fast, hard, painful lesson in the work ethic and discipline—something the girls had probably rejected from old Mom and Pop at home as being beneath their teenage dignity.

Sharon and Tracy weren't concerned with all those eventualities because that simply couldn't happen to a couple of smart, fine-looking and talented girls such as themselves. So with visions of a quick ascent to the heights of a Marilyn Chambers or a Linda Lovelace fluttering in their empty heads, but not carrying anywhere near the necessary pulchritude on their 32A-cup breasts and 34-inch hips, they headed down that yellow brick road toward Hollywood on a bright sunny April morning. First stop was the local Frederick's of Hollywood shop in Sunrise

Mall to buy each of them a pair of red crotchless panties and a black garter belt. Those items would consume most of their cash, but the girls felt that it was a good idea to have on hand all the necessary props for future screen tests.

After buying their crotchless panties and garter belts, Sharon and Tracy were standing in front of Frederick's, trying to decide if they should hitch to San Francisco and offer their services to the Mitchell Brothers in order to get a little porno experience, or go directly to LA and the big time. They saw a tiny, almost delicate, girl walking toward them, dressed in tight faded jeans, awkward-looking jogging shoes, and though it was chilly, a thin white T-shirt. Her hair was unstylishly short. Sharon and Tracy figured she was maybe fifteen, and that she was going to talk to them about some kind of religion.

Gerald and Charlene had been watching the girls for over ten minutes. They were sitting on a bench when he went into his bird dog point and said, "There they are, baby. Sic 'em." Charlene put a hand into her purse and gripped the little .25 auto as she stood up and walked slowly toward their targets.

She looked them over with an appraising stare. Both girls resembled Mary Ellen—slim almost to the point of pubescence, one with long light-brown hair, the other a pale blond. They wore ragged-at-the-knees jeans and men's gray sweatshirts. Charlene's brain camera clicked on now, and would record the next twenty-four hours for posterity—at least as *she* claimed to have seen and heard it.

"Hi," Charlene said, walking up to them and going directly into her pitch. "You girls doing anything for the next twenty-four hours?"

"Whaddaya wanna know for?" Sharon asked suspiciously. "You ain't no cop." But she did wonder if her mom had missed them already and called the law.

"Of course not," Charlene smiled, shaking her head, "my old man and me need a coupla cute girls to make a foursome for a pot-and-pill party we're throwing this afternoon. You interested?"

"What's your sign?" Tracy asked belligerantly.

"Huh? Oh, Aquarius," Charlene said, lying, "why?"

"Cause my horoscope today says to watch out for Capricorns. But I like Aquariuses—they're nice people."

"Good . . . listen, you guys wanna join in or not?"

"Who's gonna be there?" Sharon asked, looking around the mall, thinking that this bony-looking girl might be an undercover vice cop. It wouldn't be the first time she'd been snagged in this shopping mall trying to buy grass.

"Just me and my old man . . . we've got some real good Maui wow-ee, 'ludes and an ounce of shit right off the boat from Colombia . . ."

"Why you wanna share it?" Tracy interrupted.

"We don't," Charlene said testily, "but it's my old man's birthday and I wanna give him a real nice surprise. And I need you . . ."

"Oh wow!" Sharon exclaimed, and both girls broke into smiles, all suspicion and distrust vanishing from their faces. "I get it!"

"Me too!" Tracy cut in.

"What you want is *us* for the big surprise," Sharon continued, "a three-on-one pot-and-pill party! Oh wow!"

"Yeah, that's right," Charlene mumbled, somewhat taken aback by their perceptiveness, but happy she wouldn't have to explain things in detail because this scam was new, and she'd been making it up as she went along.

"Wait a sec," Sharon said, "where's this party gonna be? I mean, I don't want no motel room or nothing like that. Somebody might call the cops, and we got enough trouble."

"Oh no," Charlene assured her, "It's a nice cabin up in the mountains near Lake Tahoe. Uh, whaddaya mean, you got *enough* trouble?"

"Aw, it's just my mom, like, you know, we ran away again and she might turn us in and all."

"Oh," Charlene said, very relieved because you had to be super-careful nowaways. Some of these kids running the freeways and malls would actually kill you just for the hell of it. The last thing she wanted was to pick up a couple of red-hot on-the-lam female outlaws—Daddy Gerald wouldn't like that at all.

Charlene's 160 IQ came on full force for a few seconds as she assessed the potential victims. Both appeared to meet her estimate of typical lowlifes—dirty clothes, runaways, loved dope, probably had grown up on their own with no respect or love from or for whichever parent they lived with, on welfare, no purpose in life other than their own immediate gratification, started using dope and having sex before they even knew what it was, had lost count long ago as to the number of men and boys they'd fucked and/or sucked—in other words, all the things Charlene had always despised in other females. But again, she knew that they weren't all that different from herself—a fact that always depressed Charlene.

". . . and we'll get our share of all the shit?" Sharon was asking.

"Yeah, everything split four ways," Charlene answered, "whaddya say?"

"Well, we were gonna hitch to Hollywood . . . but I guess we *could* put it off till tomorrow. Okay with you, Tracy?"

"I guess . . . listen, you and the guy're clean, ain't you? I mean no clap or herpes or crabs or nothing like that?"

"I should say NOT!" Charlene snapped back indignantly. I'll remember that, you smart-mouthed little cunt, Charlene thought, trying to keep the anger she felt from showing in her eyes.

"What's your name, kid?" Sharon asked, fumbling in her huge plastic purse, pulling out a large red sucker, ripping off the paper and putting it in her mouth, making her left cheek stick out like a squirrel hiding a walnut in its jaw.

"Millie," Charlene answered shortly, "what's yours?"

"I'm Sharon," the pale blond-haired girl mumbled around her sucker," and she's Tracy. Where's your old man?"

"In our van, back of the lot. What's this about Hollywood?"

"Oh. We're gonna be in the movies." Sharon said.

"Really?" Charlene smirked to herself at the idea of these two being star material.

"Un huh. Porno flicks. We been told all about how to break in and everything. All we gotta do is go up to Hollywood and tell 'em we wanna do pictures."

"Really?" Charlene sneered. You two flacky little turds couldn't even get into animal sex pictures, she thought.

"Uh huh," Sharon rambled on, "we're gonna make us a lotta money and stuff, then buy a marijuana farm up in Mendocino . . . an' I'm gonna get me a new 'Vette."

"Sure. Sounds real interesting," Charlene said condescendingly. "Tell me all about it . . . while we walk to the van." She put a hand behind her back and showed one finger—a signal for Gerald to follow them. The three childlike girls sauntered off, Charlene in the middle, nodding and listening to both victims as they chattered inanely about their future in porn pictures.

"Oh wow! Nice van!" Tracy said as they approached the rear door. "I'm gonna get me a van right after my first movie."

Charlene unlocked the door, nodding for them to get in. Sharon and Tracy sat on the cot and Charlene took her usual place on the blue ice chest, wondering where the hell Daddy Gerald was, hoping he hadn't gotten lost or dropped his keys again. Then the back door flew open and Gerald stood there, like some apparition materializing in a flash of sunlight that flooded the dark van for a second.

"Oh wow!" Sharon gasped as Gerald slammed the door, "You scared me! Are you the birthday boy, hon?"

"What?" Gerald asked.

"He's the one," Charlene said quickly, remembering that she and Daddy Gerald hadn't rehearsed this particular scan. "It's his birthday, and the three of us are gonna give him a real party." That should bring the dumb prick right up to date, she thought.

"Oh wow!" Sharon said, her cute face lighting with a wide smile. "He's *really* nice! And big too. I like big guys—there's so much to hang on to."

Gerald grinned his appreciation, shot Charlene a see-how-lucky-you-are glance, then sat down cross-legged on the floor facing the victims.

"Where you girls from?" Gerald asked, offering them a cigarette.

"I'm from Reno," Sharon said, "an' Tracy's from right here—no thanks, hon, we don't smoke. It's bad for you."

"Whaddaya mean you don't smoke?" Charlene asked belligerently. "I thought you liked pot?"

"Well, we do . . . but grass don't hurt you. I mean, it ain't like smoking tobacco and all . . ."

"Oh shit, what's the difference?" Charlene said. "Smoke's smoke, for Christ's sake!" She was still pissed at Tracy for her crabs and clap remark, and Sharon's obvious liking for Daddy Gerald made her jealous. She had a feeling that this party wasn't going to be much fun.

"I'll just bet you girls are runaways," Gerald cut in, not fully understanding Charlene's hostility toward the victims this early in the game.

"Yeah," Sharon confirmed, "we're running away and're gonna be in the movies."

"That's really exciting," Gerald said with a wide smile. "Tell me all about it."

"Oh shit!" Charlene mumbled, rolling her eyes upward as Sharon told Gerald the same story she'd been listening to for the past twenty minutes.

When they finished, Gerald nodded solemnly, his face serious. "That's the most exciting thing I've ever heard. I never met a movie star before." Then he reached under his jacket and drew the big .357 Magnum.

"This is a kidnapping, girls. Just do as we say and you'll be okay. Scream or try to run, I'll kill you both."

Charlene and Gerald waited eagerly for the usual reaction.

"Oh wow!" Sharon giggled, "I never played kidnap before!"

"Me neither," Tracy squealed, wide-eyed, "but it's nice

. . . I mean, long as there ain't gonna be no whips and chains. I mean, you just gonna *play*-rape us, right?"

"Shit!" Gerald grumbled.

"Cunts!" Charlene hissed.

"Whatsa matter?" Sharon asked, a surprised look on her face.

"Tie 'em up," Gerald snapped at Charlene, "use that macramé rope under the seat. And tape their mouths shut."

"Tie us? Oh, now wait a fucking minute, hon . . ." Sharon didn't like this one bit.

"We gonna play kidnap, right?" Gerald said, "So we'll do it right. Got it?"

"Yeah, but I dunno 'bout this tying business." Sharon looked worried now, and Tracy was downright pale. "Oh, now listen, hon, I don't think . . ."

Charlene gave Sharon a hard cut across her face with the thick macramé rope, knocking her head back against the van wall. "Shut up and stick out your hands," Charlene told her.

Charlene wrapped the rope tightly around Sharon's wrists three times, then tied a double knot. She ripped off a piece of duct tape and clamped it roughly across the victim's mouth, then pressed it hard into place with the palm of her hand.

"Take it easy, baby," Gerald said, "You'll knock her teeth out."

"Yeah," Tracy chimed in, "I don't understand this . . . why're you so mad, Millie? I mean, we're willing to play-party, but no real rough stuff."

Charlene didn't answer, just grabbed Tracy's hands and tied them as she had Sharon's, then taped her mouth.

"Let's get the fuck out of here," Charlene told Gerald.

With Gerald driving, they took Interstate 80 north toward Reno. Charlene sat in the passenger seat, turned slightly so she could watch the victims, holding her little .25 pistol on them. The girls lay side-by-side on the cot, glaring indignantly at Charlene, obviously not understanding how a simple pot-and-pill, play-rape party required them to be treated like real victims. Charlene said later that they reminded her of someone who'd just been bitten by their own dog.

As they were passing through Baxter, Charlene turned to look for the little side road they'd used to take their first love slaves into the forest. When she saw it, Charlene felt her sphincter muscle contract involuntarily, and for the first time that day, the hot, bubbling volcanic lava began creeping slowly up from her toes until it reached her vagina, where it stopped, then settled in a warm, sticky, glowing pool. Suddenly, Charlene was feeling good. She had that lazy, euphoric feeling of anticipation she got when a man was between her legs and ready to put it in.

She glanced at the victims, and a sort of gender-bending déjà vu flashed through her mind—a fifteen-year-old boy virgin she'd spent two months with, teaching him everything she knew about sex. She had been very patient with his almost uncontrollable, hair-trigger eagerness, teaching him to make love the way she liked it, forcing him to learn control and to satisfy her first, making him understand that if mama wasn't happy, there wouldn't be a second time with her—or any other woman he didn't sexually satisfy. Then she would do all the things a teenage boy daydreams a woman will do some day. Charlene loved his reaction to her sexual expertise almost as much as her own orgasms, sometimes even more. When Charlene grew tired of him and was ready to move on to a new experience, she wasn't surprised that the boy was in love with her, and begged her not to let him go. As far as she knew, that boy was the only male other than her father who ever *truly* loved her for what she was. He was willing to accept her, warts and all, and didn't seem to realize that she had limitations.

She spent one last night with him, gently explaining things. "You aren't really in love with me," she whispered in his ear, "It's just that I'm your first woman, and you are in love with my pussy, not with me. In a couple of months, you'll find another girl, and when you use all the things I've taught you on her, she'll be the one begging you not to leave."

Charlene still treasured his final romantic words to her: "I'll never forget you, Charlene . . . no matter how many girls I have in my lifetime, none of them will ever *really* take your place in my heart."

It was one of the few private experiences that Charlene was proud of, and she just *had* to tell someone. That someone was her so-called best girlfriend, who spread the story to every girl in the locker room and then to the teachers so that finally even her mother got wind of it. To that very day, though, she liked to think that somewhere out there, a man was making love to a woman the way she had taught him, and whenever that woman felt good sexually, it was indirectly because of Charlene Adelle Williams.

They were now passing Donner Lake, a breathtakingly beautiful spot in a small valley, with snow still on the ground, the large lake looking like a giant sapphire jewel under the bright sunshine.

Some Californians claim that Donner Lake is haunted by ghosts of the hard-luck pioneer Donner party, which became snowbound at the lake in 1859. The survivors admitted that before a rescue party reached them some five months later, they stayed alive by cooking and eating those who had died. Some claimed, however, that when the strong got really hungry and nobody died, the weak and sick were killed, then boiled in a huge iron wash pot with wild onions and watercress. Three of the healthiest-looking members of the Donner party were tried for murder and cannibalism at Fort Sutter in Sacramento, but were acquitted by a military court. Those who have camped there overnight claim they've heard screams and moans in the darkness and seen misty shapes floating over the lake. Only a few out-of-state tourists have the nerve to even drive down to the lake in daylight and take a look.

They drove past the lake and arrived in Reno around noon. Gerald stopped at Sears, saying he had a purchase to make. He ordered Charlene to keep a close watch on the girls with both front windows rolled up. When he left, both victims started grunting and humming through their noses, and giving Charlene pleading, desperate looks with their eyes like dogs who want to come in out of the cold. Charlene made sure the .25 was off safety, then went back and removed the tape from Sharon's mouth.

"Whaddya want?"

"Oh, listen hon, I gotta pee. Real *bad!*"

"There's no place here . . . you gotta wait . . ."

"No way!" Sharon groaned. "I gotta go now!"

"No, you can't . . ."

"Oh, hon, I'm gonna piss right in my jeans . . . I just gotta!"

"Okay, okay," Charlene said, looking around for some kind of container. The only thing available was Gerald's empty quart Thermos bottle, and she started to hand it to Sharon, then realized she'd have to untie her. Gun or no gun, she couldn't risk that.

"No, you gotta wait until he gets back," Charlene said, annoyed that she suddenly needed to pee also.

At that moment Gerald got back into the van, tossed a paper bag on the dash, then turned to glare at Charlene. "What the fuck're you doing back there?"

"They gotta pee, Daddy, and—"

"Fuck 'em," Gerald said, starting the van and driving back onto Interstate 80, heading toward Winnemucca, Nevada.

"Oh Daddy, hon, please lemme pee!" Sharon moaned.

"Yeah, we better let 'em," Charlene said to Gerald, "otherwise she's gonna do it right on the cot." Then to Sharon, "Don't call him Daddy again—got it?"

Gerald saw a small rest area just down the road, turned into it and stopped, cursing Charlene and the girls. "All right now, how and where they gonna piss?"

Charlene untied the victim's hands and feet as Gerald watched, then handed Sharon the open Thermos.

"Are you fucking crazy?" Gerald shouted, "Not in my coffee bottle!"

"There's nothing else, Daddy," Charlene told him, her face turning red with the strain of holding back her own overwhelming need to urinate.

Both victims hurriedly dropped their jeans, and Gerald watched in disgust as Sharon more or less urinated in the narrow opening of his Thermos bottle while Tracy kept muttering, "Hurry, hurry, for God's sake!" As she did a little dance on her knees.

Charlene had to open the back door and empty the bottle twice before the girls were finished. Then she jerked down her jeans and squatted awkwardly over the bottle as Gerald threw both hands in the air, rolling his eyes upward and groaning, "Godalmighty! This is supposed to be a kidnapping? More like the Three Stooges is what it is!"

Charlene sensed the ludicrousness of the scene, and started laughing as she retied the victims. "Poor Daddy," she said with a chuckle, sitting down in the passenger seat, "saddled with three women . . . if we were men, we could just open the door and piss out on the ground."

"Yeah," Gerald agreed, pulling back onto the highway, "we're treating two kidnapped girls like they're our *kids*—a coupla three-year-olds, for Christ's sake . . . Throw that fucking bottle away!"

Charlene checked the rear for following traffic, then tossed the Thermos into the roadside sagebrush.

"Where're we taking them, Daddy?" Charlene leaned over and whispered in Gerald's ear.

"I was thinking about Limerick Canyon—you know, that kinda oasis place way up in the high desert?"

"Yeah, I remember we were there a long time ago. You think it's still the same . . . just as isolated?"

"What the fuck *ever* changes in this goddamned desert?" Gerald asked. "Of course it's the same."

"What's in the sack?" Charlene asked, nodding at the brown paper bag he'd put on the dash.

"A claw hammer."

"A hammer?"

"Yeah."

"Why?"

"*Why?* Cause there's no connection to the tire iron or the shovel we used the last couple times."

"Yeah," Charlene said softly, nodding her head. "Smart, Daddy. I wouldn't have thought of that."

But thanks to the TV shows, she *did* think of something else. And it scared hell out of her. They grabbed those two kids in California and now they were in Nevada, which made it a federal case. And the FBI weren't like ordinary cops . . . they caught people. Charlene mentioned it to Gerald and he didn't speak for a minute.

"Yeah, but even the FBIs can't do anything if there's no bodies or witnesses or nothing . . . they've never found the ones over at Humboldt Sink . . . so we just gotta make sure nobody finds these two. Just a coupla more teenage runaway cunts who disappear and're never heard of again. Nobody misses 'em. Happens thousands of times every day," Gerald laughed softly and added, "We oughta know, baby . . . we're the magicians who *make* 'em disappear!"

They stopped at Lovelock at a typical rundown desert gas station on the barren highway to have the tank filled. Charlene covered the victims with a blanket and sat near them, gun in hand. The teenage attendant had a copy of *Hustler* sticking out of his back pocket, and the only thing that interested him was getting in out of the cold and back to checking out the yawning beaver in his magazine. He didn't even glance at Gerald or the van.

Less than halfway between Lovelock and Winnemucca is a desolate junkyard village called Oreana, with a rusty, bullet-punctured sign reading LIMERICK CANYON posted near a dusty graveled road that leads off into the high desert toward Mt. Tobin. This area of Nevada is part of Pershing County, one of the largest counties in the state, with a population of about 3500. Most of them are tough, dawn-to-dark hardworking, bare-subsistence farmers and ranchers whose ancestors arrived in covered wagons and decided they could live here in one of the most desolate places on earth. They were mostly Mormons out of Utah looking for an uninhabited spot where they could practice their religion without interference from the hypocritical, antipolygamist government in Washington, DC. It was make it or die, and most were tough enough to live on boiled rattlesnake and jackrabbits until they got their farms and ranches going.

The Western frontier spirit is as strong in Pershing County today as it was when the wagon trains arrived, and if the citizens had their way, rustlers, sheep thieves, and petty criminals would still be having their necks stretched in front of the Lovelock courthouse on Saturday afternoons. Gerald and Charlene Gallego couldn't have chosen a worse place than Pershing County to commit the crime of murder. During Gerald's trial there some years later, a British news reporter asked a local citizen if he actually believed that an execution was a deterrent to murder.

"Mister," the jean-and-boot-clad rancher replied, "you ever heard of a man killing anybody *after* he was hanged?"

Gerald took that gravel road toward Limerick Canyon at about five in the afternoon. In April, the high desert darkens early and is bitterly cold after sundown. It was twilight when they parked at one of the empty, trash-littered campsites in Limerick Canyon. Charlene was lightheaded and dizzy from the 9,000-foot altitude and staggered when she got out of the van to stretch after a three-hundred-mile drive. Charlene's parents claimed their daughter had had asthma since birth. By now, Charlene believed it herself, and actually experienced symptoms of the affliction. Gerald shook his head in disgust as he watched Charlene gasp for breath in the thin air, knowing her asthma was as imaginary as her elitist family background. Gerald was a little dizzy himself when he got out and walked over to a rusty camp stove sitting beside a termite-infested wooden picnic table, both state-owned items deeply buried in thick concrete to prevent them from being carried off by thieving campers.

"Why don't you make a fire?" Charlene called to him.

"Don't be stupid. Every starving desert rat within fifty miles would see the smoke and come in, hoping for a free meal . . . untie the girls and bring them over here—maybe all three of you gotta piss again?" Gerald added sarcastically. And they surely did. After their three-hundred mile ride lying on the narrow cot bound and gagged, both victim's legs folded and they fell to their knees when they stepped out of the van. But they scrambled up, got their balance, hurriedly dropped their jeans, squatted, and urinated like two water hoses.

"Oh, wow!" Sharon said to Charlene, "What a relief! Where's the cabin, hon?"

"Cabin? Oh! We couldn't get it. We're gonna camp here tonight and have our party in the van."

"Oh, now wait a minute, hon," Sharon said, looking fearfully around at the empty, hostile, darkening desert, "I don't know about that . . . this place is real scary an' all . . . I mean, it's so cold . . . no bathroom or nothing, and . . ."

"I don't like it either," Tracy said, cutting in. "You said a nice cabin. I ain't gonna get naked and fuck in no freezing van . . ."

Charlene lashed out with her purse, which was weighted with the pistol, twenty extra rounds of loose ammunition, and all the other necessities carried in a woman's handbag. The flat side struck Tracy square in the face, and she hit the ground on her rear, blood spurting from her nose.

"Hey, baby!" Gerald said sharply, walking over. "Why all the rough stuff?"

"I don't like that smart-mouthed cunt!" Charlene shouted in a shrill voice.

"Okay, you don't *have* to like her. They're just love slaves, baby. No point in getting mean about it."

"Yeah?" Charlene screamed again, "You know what she asked me back at the mall? 'Do we have clap or crabs?' "

"Okay," Gerald said gently, putting his arm around Charlene, "maybe we oughta ask them the same thing . . ."

"Oh no, Daddy hon," Sharon broke in, "we ain't got nothing like that!"

"I told you not to call him Daddy!" Charlene squealed, trying to lunge at Sharon, but Gerald held her firmly by both arms.

"All right, knock off the bullshit," Gerald ordered sharply. "Get back in that van—all three of you. From now on, I'll do all the hitting around here—now get in that fucking van!" Gerald shoved Charlene toward the rear door, then took each victim by an arm and more or less dragged them over to the vehicle.

"Get in there and sit on the cot—and you baby, on the ice chest. Watch them while I look around . . . and no more arguments, got it? We're here to fuck, not fight!"

Gerald closed the door, then went to a toolbox bolted under the van, unlocked it, and removed his trusty surplus infantry folding shovel, then walked a few yards down a slight incline to the dry sandy creek bed. Thick clumps of short willow trees grew along the bank for a mile or so in both directions, and Gerald figured that when the snow melted in the mountains that spring, a raging flood of water would come roaring down this little creek bed, adding at least a three-foot layer of new sand and debris. Gerald walked to the middle of the dry creek and looked carefully at both sides. There was a sharp bend in the bank, like a crooked arm, and Gerald decided that was the perfect spot to bury the girls, because sand, gravel, and sagebrush would catch there . . . and hopefully, by June, the bodies would be covered under ten feet of debris. He stuck the shovel in the sand to mark it.

Gerald was standing there urinating when he heard the van engine start. His legs were already pumping hard by the time he turned around, driven by the sudden knowledge that Charlene was taking off—leaving him here in the middle of nowhere, fifty miles from the nearest town, where temperatures would drop to zero that night, and if he fell asleep, he'd freeze, or worse, be eaten alive by coyotes. The thin air made him pant as he ran up the slight hill. He saw the van, vapor pouring from its tailpipe, and drew his .357 Magnum. He knew that if he could put all six rounds through the side of the van, he was bound to hit someone, hopefully Charlene, and stop her from leaving.

Gerald would say later that he'd never been so frightened in his life. It wasn't freezing that scared him—it was being eaten alive by coyotes. Just as he started to aim his pistol, the back van door opened and he heard Charlene's voice: "Hurry up, Daddy. Get in out of the cold."

Gerald walked cautiously up to the door, fully expecting her to shoot at him through the dark-filmed window. When Charlene threw open the door, he came within a heartbeat of firing point blank at her head.

"Hurry up," Charlene said breathlessly, "I started the engine and turned on the heater . . ."

"What for?" Gerald asked foolishly, kneeling beside her and glancing at the victims sitting stiffly on the cot.

"To warm up the van, silly. What else?"

"Uh huh," Gerald mumbled, trembling slightly from what he still believed was an attempt by Charlene to leave him to die in the desert.

"Oh wow!" Sharon suddenly giggled, pointing at Gerald's crotch, "You got a nice-sized pecker there, hon!"

Gerald looked down and was surprised to see his member hanging out of his unzipped pants. He'd been so frightened when the van started, he had even forgotten to put his dick back in.

"That's *nothing,*" Charlene said proudly, "it's all shriveled up from the cold. Wait till you see it in action."

"I'm ready when you are, hon," Sharon said cheerfully.

"How about *you?*" Charlene asked, nodding at Tracy.

"Yeah, I guess. Can we have some coke first? I mean, you promised, and I really need something to get my engine running for this fuck-party . . . I mean, no bed or nothing, colder'n all get out, and this tying business . . . if I'd known all this, I wouldn't have come along . . . how about some coke at least, Millie?"

Charlene hesitated. She had a quarter-gram of weak, stepped-on stuff taped to the arch of her left foot, but Gerald didn't know, and she sure didn't want him to beat the shit out of her in front of the love slaves—which was what he'd promised to do if he ever caught her carrying narcotics when she was out with him.

But Gerald smiled and nodded. "Go on, give 'em a good toot. It'll make things easer when we finish."

The victims missed his meaning because they were totally engrossed in watching Charlene remove her clunky-looking shoe and untape the small plastic bag from the bottom of her left foot. Gerald held out a stiff thumb and Charlene sprinkled a small mound of cocaine on his nail. He stuck it under Tracy's nose and she sniffed it clean, then greedily licked his nail. Sharon cleared her nose by blowing it into a hand, then wiped it on her pant leg. That made Charlene gag and her stomach queasy, but she didn't say anything as she sprinkled coke on Gerald's thumbnail. Sharon closed her left nostril with a finger, then sniffed in so hard Gerald's thumb was sucked up against her nose.

"Oh wow!" Sharon said, "That's good *stuff!*"

Charlene knew that it wasn't good stuff, that it was street coke cut to twenty percent. I wish I had some pure shit, Charlene thought angrily, I'd give you such a hotshot your heart would stop like a bullet hit it . . .

"Let's give 'em another round," Gerald said, holding out his stiff thumb. Within seconds, the victims eyes were sparkling, they became overly animated, giggling as they took off their clothes. Even the chronic fault-finder Tracy was doing a sort of burlesque strip-tease with her gray sweatshirt.

"I know what," Sharon squealed, "give me those shopping bags! We'll show you how we're gonna do our first screen test!"

Gerald tossed over the Frederick's of Hollywood shopping bags, and the girls took out their red crotchless panties and black garter belts. He turned on an overhead light, watching with a smile as Sharon and Tracy slipped into their movie props.

Tracy flopped down on the floor, bent her knees, opened her legs wide, then wildly rotated her bony hips, giggling at the top of her voice, looking at Charlene as she flicked her tongue in and out like a snake. At that moment, Charlene felt her animosity toward Tracy temporarily disappear and she let herself get into their little camping trip for the first time that day. She began taking off her clothes, and after a moment's hesitation, Gerald followed her lead.

"Hey, birthday boy, let's get it on!" Sharon yelled, then reached down and grabbed Gerald by his still cold-shriveled dick.

"Which one you want first?" Gerald asked Charlene.

"I'm gonna take that smart-mouthed Tracy," she answered.

"You want me to fuck her while she's eating you?"

"Yeah. But do it to Sharon first. I wanna watch."

At around 2:30 A.M. Charlene was standing outside the van, listening to Gerald doing it one last time with Sharon.

Her breath steamed in a gray cloud around her head as she stared up at the twinkling stars. A pale three-quarter moon leered down, looking, as it always did in the desert night, low enough to touch. The pale moonlight reflecting off the cobalt-blue sky made the entire desert look as if it was bathed in a dim bluish gray glow. Charlene wondered if the desert ever really became black-dark at night. Looking off across the sagebrush and hills was like looking through a sniper scope that turned everything bluish gray rather than green.

A coyote screamed off in the sagebrush and Charlene shivered violently. The cold was almost unbearable, but she didn't want to get back in the van. Both girls were totally unfamiliar with feminine hygiene, and the strong fishy smell permeating the van made her stomach turn.

She heard Sharon's high-pitched phony whore voice urging Gerald on: "Oh, yeah . . . yeah . . . fuck me, hon . . . oh, hon . . ."

Charlene walked over to the picnic table, which had been decimated by termites, and sat down, taking deep breaths of pure, icy air. We might as well have hired two Tijuana whores, she thought, there'd been no fear, no begging, no absolute terror, just two typical, modern-day teenage girls who knew every sexual trick in the book, and enjoyed showing off their talents. Daddy Gerald had been so disappointed he'd barely managed to keep a halfway hard-on, and if the three of them hadn't given him a group blowjob every few minutes, he couldn't have done anything. According to Charlene, Gerald finally managed to ejaculate, but only after an episode of nipple-biting and screaming. Gerald was having sex with Tracy, holding her down, while Charlene chewed on her nipple like it was a stick of Juicy Fruit. It hadn't been *really* real, of course, but if they used their imagination, it was enough to trigger Gerald's climax—and Charlene said it was a relief to know that her love-slave idea had saved Daddy Gerald once more by arousing his hopelessly screwed-up sexual psyche.

Charlene saw Gerald getting out of the van, and called softly, "Over here, Daddy . . . you tie them?"

"Yeah," Gerald said walking over and sitting beside her on the picnic table, "but I don't think we really need to tie 'em . . . I mean, you couldn't run them off with a shotgun." Gerald lit a cigarette and inhaled deeply. "You know what that Sharon said to me just now? Said, 'we really like you guys, and we'll get together every time we're in town.' "

"Yeah. Well . . . it's almost three, Daddy. Maybe we better get it over with."

"I guess," Gerald stood up, knocked the fire off his cigarette and dropped the butt in his shirt pocket. "Nice moon. The only thing I like about this fucking desert is the sky at night . . . why anyone would want to *live* here, I'll never understand. Okay, let's go get 'em."

"Daddy, we don't *really* have to . . . they wouldn't tell anyone," Charlene said, touching his arm.

"I know . . . I thought about it. But suppose the cops pick them up as runaways? They tell 'em they were with us. We get hit with contributing to the delinquency of a minor . . . and maybe even forcible rape . . . can you imagine anyone having to *rape* those two?"

Charlene shook her head, not saying anything, waiting for Daddy Gerald to decide the future of Sharon and Tracy. Like everything else in their relationship, it was his decision whether the love slaves lived or died tonight.

". . . And once the cops start checking," Gerald was saying more-or-less to himself, "they might tie us in to those other girls. No, we gotta do it."

"Whatever you think is best," Charlene said.

Gerald opened the back door and leaned in. "Okay, girls, we're gonna spend the night here. I found a nice spot down by the creek where we can build a big fire, roast some marshmallows, and have a little more coke. That suit you girls?"

"Okay, hon," Sharon chirruped cheerfully. "Whatever you say . . . but you ain't gonna keep us tied, are you?"

"Nope. No need for games now. You come with me, Sharon, I need you to help gather some firewood."

"Sure thing, hon." Sharon turend on the cot and stuck out her ankles for Gerald to untie. "No more tit-biting, okay?"

"Okay. Wait a sec," Gerald said, then walked to the front door, reached in, and picked up the paper sack with the claw hammer.

"What's that, hon?" Sharon asked, putting her arm around Gerald's waist, hugging him tightly.

"Just something to light the fire with . . . baby, you stay with Tracy."

"Oh wow!" Sharon gasped, shivering and folding her arms across her chest. "It's really cold out here!"

Gerald removed his gray nylon jacket and placed it around her shoulders. "Better?" he asked, his voice soft and kind. It was the voice he used to talk to dogs and kids, Charlene always told him.

"Oh, yeah, hon. Thanks a million."

When Gerald walked down the hill, Charlene sat on the blue ice chest, watching Tracy. She'd left the back door open because of the fishy smell.

"Didn't you two ever take a douche?" Charlene asked, wiggling her nose at the odor.

"Huh? Oh. Naw. We read in the *National Inquirer* that it's bad for you. We don't do it 'less we start itching real bad down there."

"That's disgusting."

"Whatever," Tracy said, yawning.

Charlene heard Sharon's high-pitched voice floating up on the cold, thin air: "Oh, now hon, wait a fucking minute . . ."

Charlene imagined Gerald swinging the hammer, and Sharon going down, her shrill, irritating voice silenced at last.

Tracy felt something, too, and stirred nervously, then held out her hands. "Untie me, Millie. I don't like this shit . . ."

Then Gerald was standing at the back door, breath steaming around his head, hair disheveled, dark spots covering his face like black freckles—dark spots that Charlene knew were spattered blood.

"Come on, Tracy," Gerald said gently, "Sharon wants you to help with the firewood . . . come on, now."

"I'm not going nowhere till my hands and feet are untied!" Tracy announced belligerently.

Gerald leaned in the van, grabbed Tracy's ankles, dragged her forward, lifted her out, and effortlessly threw her body over his shoulder, turned and walked down the slope, paying no attention as Tracy writhed and twisted like a snake on his back, then screamed so loud she was answered by a lonesome coyote a few hundred yards away in the sagebrush. Charlene got out and stood in the eerie bluish gray desert night, trying to spot

Gerald down at the creek. She couldn't because he was behind a clump of sickly willow trees. But she could hear Tracy screaming and the lonesome coyote answering hopefully.

"EEE-EEE!" Tracy would scream.

"ooooOOOO!" The coyote would answer.

Charlene suddenly had to urinate again; she quickly dropped her jeans and squatted.

"EEEE-EE . . ." Tracy's scream was cut off in mid-screech.

"ooooOOOO!" The lonesome coyote answered.

Charlene's bare rear end was stinging with cold. She stood, pulled up her jeans, closed the zipper, and listened.

"ooooOOOO!" The lonesome coyote howled inquiringly.

Charlene knew it was all over for Sharon and Tracy. Her nervous bladder filled again and she squatted hurriedly, wondering where so much liquid had came from.

"Hey, Charlene," Gerald's voice floated over to her on the icy wind, so faint she wasn't sure of the direction.

"Hey, Charlene," he called again.

Charlene opened her mouth to answer, then her jaws froze in place. Why was he calling her Charlene? In all their years together he'd always called her baby or cunt—never Charlene. Why now? A cold, bloodchilling spasm of fear and paranoid suspicion rippled down her spine like icy fingers, making her knees rubbery.

"Hey, Charlene, you there? Come on down here . . . I wanna show you something," Gerald's faint voice sounded as if he was trying to suppress a laugh.

Charlene ran to the driver's side and looked in the van window. The keys were gone. I knew it, she thought, her head spinning dizzily with fear. He's gonna kill me too. Took the keys so I can't get away. He's got a grave for me down there . . .

Gerald had slowly snuck up behind her and was poised like a shadow. He placed his cupped, freezing-cold hand on the back of her neck.

"EEE-OW!" Charlene let out a scream that would leave her hoarse for days.

"ooooOOOO!" The lonesome coyote immediately answered.

"JESUS FUCKING CHRIST ALMIGHTY!" Gerald shouted, leaping backward and drawing his gun. "You scared the shit outta me! What's wrong with you, you stupid cunt?"

Charlene was charged with so much static terror, she could have jump-started a B-1 bomber. But now she was so happy to hear that familiar name, she threw herself into his arms and sobbed hysterically. "Oh Daddy, oh Daddy . . . I was so frightened . . ."

"What of, for Christ's sake? I was right down there . . . you know I wouldn't let anything hurt you . . . baby, I got blood all over me. You better stand back. I'm gonna have to change my clothes."

Charlene finally got her voice box unparalyzed and whispered, "It's all finished then?"

"Yeah. I wanted to show you where the grave is and how it's hidden. Why didn't you answer?"

"I don't know, Daddy," Charlene half-lied, "I got scared . . . I mean, every time she screamed, the coyote . . . it was like it was *answering!* Oh, those fucking coyotes . . ."

"Yeah, they scare me, too. There's so damn many of them out there. I read someplace that five coyotes can kill and eat a deer in less than ten minutes, bones, hide and all."

"Uh huh," Charlene mumbled, thinking she'd been wrong again about Daddy Gerald. He had no intention of killing her—at least not *tonight.*

"Come on, baby, take a look at the grave."

They walked arm-in-arm down to the creek, and Gerald pointed at two heavy, splintered tree trunks on top of which a large boulder rested.

"They're under all that?" Charlene asked, her arms gripping Gerald's waist as her cheek rested against his chest, ignoring the bloodstains on his shirt.

"Yep. I dug the grave way back under the logs and rocks, five feet deep. Nobody'll find 'em, baby. Except maybe some coyotes . . . and they don't matter."

"Oh Daddy, I gotta pee," Charlene said, gasping, dropping her jeans and squatting so fast Gerald's arm that had been resting on her shoulders was crooked around thin air. They went back up the hill and sat on the ramshackle picnic table, smoking and looking up at the gleaming stars and three-quarter, pale yellow moon.

"I'm real sad," Gerald told her, his shoulders drooping.

"I know . . . me too. It wasn't worth the effort. At least, I don't think so."

"I wonder if it'll ever be like that first time again? That was . . . I mean, it was *perfect*. The two up in Reno weren't bad, but only after they realized we were gonna . . . you know."

"Yeah . . . I'm sorry about these two, Daddy. But there's no way I could tell they were so . . . *promiscuous!*"

"Don't be silly, baby," Gerald told her. "It's not *your* fault if every teenage cunt in the country is selling pussy or swapping it for dope almost by the time they're out of diapers. When I was a boy, you couldn't hardly get pussy at all 'less you were engaged or something. That goddamned Free Love Movement back in the sixties just flat ruined everything!"

After *that* profound statement, Gerald stood up, yawned and stretched. "Well, we better go, baby. I think we ought stay in Winnemucca till morning, then go home by way of Lake Tahoe. Tell you what! Let's stay tomorrow night at a good hotel in Tahoe, have a nice dinner, and play the slot machines? What say?"

"Oh, that's sweet of you, Daddy! I'd love to!"

Gerald and Charlene spent the rest of that night sleeping in the van at a roadside campground just outside Winnemucca, Nevada. Gerald had changed his bloody clothes, shoes, and socks, then placed them in the Frederick's of Hollywood shopping bag, along with two pairs of red crotchless panties and two black garter belts. Charlene put the bag in a locked toolbox for safekeeping, and somewhere between Limerick Canyon and Winnemucca, she threw the blood-covered hammer out a window into the shifting desert sand and sagebrush.

The combined contents of the victim's purses came to twenty-one dollars, a box of Tampax, two black lipsticks, a half-roll of toilet paper, eight Polaroid color photos of the victims in various nude poses (probably intended to be their movie resumés) an almost toothless comb, and two red suckers—not much to show for seventeen years of life each. The Polaroids were burned, the ashes buried, and all other evidence would be dropped in the American River or thrown into a dumpster in back of the Safeway market in North Sacramento. On the drive to Lake Tahoe, Gerald pulled into a willow thicket beside a mountain stream and watched while Charlene washed, wiped, and cleaned every inch of the Dodge van, inside and out.

Around 2:00 P.M., April 25, 1980, Gerald and Charlene Gallego arrived at Stateline, Nevada, on the east shore of Lake Tahoe, just a few feet across the California border. The little town is a cluster of first-class gambling casinos conveniently located at the California line so that people from around Sacramento can take a scenic Sunday afternoon drive over the Sierra Mountains, lose a couple hundred dollars, then be back home in time for the eleven o'clock news. Gerald and Charlene took a fifty-dollar-per-night room at the Silver Dollar Hotel and Casino, where they soaked for an hour in a hot bath, then fell into bed exhausted.

They woke at seven that evening, dressed in clean jeans and shirts, then went to eat. According to Charlene, Gerald had sautéed chicken livers and mushrooms, while she had her usual, filet mignon. After dinner, they split a bottle of California wine between them.

Gerald played the slots and lost sixty dollars. Charlene lost ten dollars, then hit a two-hundred-dollar jackpot. That pissed

Gerald off so much he wouldn't speak to Charlene until she gave him the money. They went to bed around one in the morning.

Charlene remembered that they had "normal" sex before going to sleep, that Gerald got on top and ejaculated without trouble in about three minutes. She had a very strong orgasm, and when they were finished, she just "knew" that she was pregnant again.

As Charlene drifted off to sleep, she was a little worried about being pregnant, but pleased that her love-slave idea was still working for Daddy Gerald.

Some three weeks later, Charlene's premonition of pregnancy proved correct. She fearfully told Daddy Gerald, but he was surprisingly very pleased that another little Gerald Armond Gallego was about to take his place in the world. He remarked that they must have been destined to have a child because she kept getting knocked up all the time. And he solemnly decreed that this one would be a keeper.

Charlene didn't want a baby at that time in her life, but didn't dare argue with Daddy Gerald's mystically inspired decision. Now she was scared shitless because she had a strange, gnawing fear that something might be wrong with that fetus, considering the conditions under which it was conceived, and she knew that if she delivered a defective baby for the egotistical Gerald Armond Gallego, there was no telling what he would do to her.

Chapter **15**

Experiment At Gold Beach

Within a few days of their last abduction murders, Gerald slipped into a genuine deep, dark depression that left him lying on the couch in an almost catatonic state, wearing only his red silk bikini shorts, once again staring glassy-eyed at Road Runner cartoons while Charlene sat on the floor beside him, once again drinking gin and popping pills.

Somehow, from some source, the two lovebirds had been overtaken by an extremely powerful case of guilty conscience.

Gerald Armond Gallego had never before felt the slightest quiver of guilt about *anything* he'd ever done in his life. When it comes to criminal psychiatry, cops and shrinks are farther apart than Israel and the PLO, but there is one area they do agree upon: that a sociopath has no social conscience and is totally incapable of feeling guilt about anything he does simply because he believes that it is his right to do it if it makes *him* feel good. Gerald fit very few pigeonholes, but he fit this one as snugly as he did his teeny-weeny red silk bikini underwear, which Charlene bought for him because she said she just loved to see them on his cute little behind.

On top of the guilt, they were feeling really sorry for themselves because Sharon and Tracy had turned out to be such lousy love slaves.

"We went to all that trouble for almost nothin'," Gerald whined, his eyes filming over with tears of self-pity, "I mean we could of been caught with them little freeway runners . . . and they were so dirty and all! And we could have got a disease from them! That was a real cruel thing they got us into."

"You're so right, Daddy," Charlene mumbled around a mouthful of gin and Quaaludes. "Those two were immoral and they were promiscuous. They should have been locked up to protect innocent people! God! I still shiver when I think of what those two little whores could have done to us and our baby!"

"Yeah. The no-good little cunts," Gerald mumbled, grunting and heaving himself up off the couch. He went to the front window and stood staring out at the van parked in the driveway.

"You going to work tonight?" Charlene asked.

"Yeah . . . uh, I don't know . . . I'm so tore up over all this, I mean what rotten luck! Hey, did you leave the van door open?"

"Of course not. Why?"

"*Well, it's open now.* Maybe it's the cops . . ."

Gerald ran out the front door dressed in his bikini shorts, followed so closely by Charlene, wearing only pantyhose and bra, she was stepping on his bare heels. They stood there on the sidewalk, disheveled, blurry eyed, squinting in the bright sunlight, fearfully checking up and down the street. There wasn't a parked car as far as they could see, and certainly no sign of cops.

"Maybe the door just came open," Charlene said, reaching for an explanation through the haze of Quaaludes and gin.

"Uh-huh," Gerald whispered, bending over and sneaking toward the van like a lion stalking an elephant. He stopped and stared at the open door as if he'd never seen it before.

"What is it?" Charlene whispered hoarsely.

"Don't know . . . something. I can *feel* it but I can't *see* it," Gerald hissed. "Feels like a cold wind coming outta the van."

Charlene was now bending over too, just like Gerald, staring wide-eyed at the open door, thinking she could hear that cold wind.

"Mornin' folks!" A gruff male voice boomed out behind them, causing Gerald to snap erect fast enough for his spine to pop like a cracked knuckle and Charlene to squeal as if she'd been goosed. They whirled to face the voice and saw the postman staring at them with a half-puzzled, half-fearful look in his eyes.

"Sorry, folks, didn't mean to scare you," he said, throwing an envious glance at Gerald's red silk bikini shorts, then fastening his furtive eyes on Charlene's pantyhose, which bagged at the knees, sagged in the crotch, and had a gaping four-inch-wide run down the left leg from hip to ankle.

"Are you all just getting up or going to bed?" the postman asked.

"Holy fucking Jesus!" Gerald suddenly screamed, leaping eighteen inches in the air and slapping wildly at his feet, belatedly realizing he'd been standing barefoot on the sun-baked sidewalk for ten minutes without feeling the pain.

The postman did a fast sidestep off the curb into the gutter, smiled weakly as he edged past Gerald, then boogied on down the street, glancing back over his shoulder every other step.

It was the first time he had seen the people who lived at 2067 Bluebird Lane and he intended to make damn sure he didn't run into them again. He was interviewed by the FBI five months later; when he was asked if he knew where the couple might have moved to, the postman said he had no idea, adding that if there'd been a spaceship around lately, those two raggedy-ass weirdos had probably left in it.

"Close the van door," Gerald ordered Charlene from where

he stood on the lawn, rubbing the soles of his scorched feet on the cool grass.

"Oh, no, wait a minute—" Charlene stopped abruptly and clamped both hands over her mouth, realizing she'd sounded exactly like Sharon. Gerald noticed it, and paled.

"Close that fucking van door or I'm gonna knock you on your bony ass," he said.

Charlene slouched toward the van nervously, reached out and pushed the door closed with her index finger. She then whirled and ran to Daddy Gerald, stood behind him, and peeped under his arm at the van.

"They're in there," Gerald said, wheezing, "them two little freeway runners have come back to haunt us."

"Oh Lord!" Charlene wailed. "I knew it! I just knew it! Oh, Daddy, I' so scared!"

"Why now?" Gerald lamented from his prone position on the couch, those depthless black eyes brimming with tears as he reached both arms imploringly toward the ceiling.

"Why now what?" Charlene asked, slipping off her saggy pantyhose and sliding on a robe.

"Why do I feel bad about those girls now? I never felt bad about the others." Suddenly Gerald sat bolt upright and stared at Charlene. "Do you suppose I didn't kill 'em? I mean, could they have dug out . . . naw, I smashed their skulls . . ."

"Are you sure, Daddy?" Charlene whispered. She had been highly superstitious all of her life, and it didn't take a whole lot of Gerald's ghost talk to get her in the mood for some real first-class "Twilight Zone" fantasizing.

"You better go back up there and take a look," Gerald said.

"Not me!" Charlene squeaked, ready and willing to commit mutiny if Daddy Gerald insisted.

Gerald flopped back down on the couch. He realized the impossibility of enforcing his order, knew that she'd just drive off and hide for several hours, come back and say the graves were undisturbed. The only way he could be sure was to go himself—and Gerald had absolutely no intention of returning to Limerick Canyon. He firmly believed at that moment that Sharon and Tracy had reached their bony hands out of the grave to destroy him and Charlene and Gerald Jr., who was on the way. He was convinced that their spirits had taken up permanent residence in the Dodge van and would devote the rest of eternity to getting even with them for taking their lives.

And if Gerald believed the spirits were there, Charlene was *positive* of it. Very few murder victims have the opportunity of handing their killers a kind of retribution from the grave, but poor little Sharon and Tracy did—and they were far from finished with them yet.

The next morning Charlene had an acute, gut-wrenching attack of morning sickness that caused her to vomit profusely every five minutes, gave her a migrainelike headache, made her dizzy, and after an hour, left her lying on the bathroom floor curled into a fetal position, suffering total exhaustion, her face a waxy greenish white.

"Oh, Daddy," she gasped weakly as Gerald knelt beside her on the floor, "it's worse than being seasick . . . my stomach gets tied in knots . . . oh, Lord, do you think it might hurt our baby?"

"You through puking?" Gerald asked, and when Charlene nodded, he picked her up and carried her into the bedroom. "It's them freeway runners that's making you so sick," Gerald said morosely, sitting beside her on the bed and rubbing a cold washcloth over her pale, sweaty face.

"I'd better see a doctor," Charlene said. "Maybe he can do something."

Gerald didn't really believe that a medical doctor could do anything, but he took Charlene to her mother's Ob-Gyn specialist that afternoon.

The genial doctor laughed and told Charlene not to worry, that gravidarum was quite common in the first trimester of pregnancy, that her uterus and digestive parts were totally separate and that nothing short of surgical invasion was likely to harm a fetus at this early stage of a pregnancy. He gave her a scrip for some antinausea pills, told her to take large doses of vitamin B, eat some crackers, and drink a Coke as soon as she woke up in the morning. It didn't help one bit. The next morning at seven, Charlene was on her knees in front of the toilet again, heaving, groaning, and turning greener than the Incredible Hulk.

Over the next couple of weeks, Gerald went to work at Muskogee Joe's once or twice but his heart just wasn't in it anymore. He didn't enjoy being pawed and fawned over by the regular female customers. Those five-dollar tips barely made him smile, and he turned down any and all offers of a quickie in the beer-storage room.

He made Charlene drive him to work in her Olds at six, then pick him up at two, after he'd closed the bar. Gerald candidly admitted to her that he was frightened to death of being in the van alone because he could feel that cold wind on the back of his neck. He told her how the brakes had suddenly failed a couple of days earlier, causing him to swerve around another car and narrowly miss smashing into a telephone pole. Gerald tried to rid the van of Sharon and Tracy by running a garden hose from the exhaust pipe into the closed van. He let the engine idle for an hour, then absentmindedly opened the door, breathing his own lungs full of carbon monoxide, which caused him to turn blue and cough all night. His next idea was to pour boiling water inside the van, but Charlene said that was stupid because if carbon monoxide wouldn't work, hot water was useless and would probably ruin the interior to boot. Then he burned about a pound of lilac incense inside the closed van, which only succeeded in making it smell like a San Francisco bathhouse.

Charlene recalled that Gerald went around in a sort of frantic daze, mumbling to himself, making and discarding plan after plan to dehaunt the van. He would sit in the dark living room half the night, staring out the window at the van parked in the driveway, mumbling, and, Charlene claimed, praying for God to give him a sign as to what he should do about the spirits of Sharon and Tracy. But there was no writing on the wall, no thunderclaps or messages in the sky forthcoming.

Around the end of May 1980, though, Gerald, with his usual resilience, seemed to snap back to reality. It wasn't that he'd stopped believing the van was haunted—just that there was something he had to do that required his undivided attention, a plan that no one except himself and one other person could know about. Like all of Gerald's long-range plans, this one included a female, and it would backfire on him with the devastating force of a lightning bolt. The plan was the worst mistake Gerald Armond Gallego would ever make because it was the one that landed him on death row.

Early one morning, Gerald drove away in Charlene's Olds without saying a word, and disappeared for forty-eight hours. Charlene wasn't overly concerned, figuring that he was just getting away from her daily early-morning ordeal on her knees in front of the toilet, groaning and vomiting. Gerald told her that he couldn't enjoy his breakfast anymore, that listening to her heaving in the bathroom for an hour made him so sick he might as well be pregnant himself. For the first time, Charlene was happy that Daddy Gerald's usual sexual problem seemed to be cropping up again. She was so ill in the morning, and so worried about being sick the next morning, she had lost interest in just about everything. She even quit her job, borrowed a few hundred from Mom and Dad in order to keep Daddy Gerald from being worried about living expenses, then just gave herself up to those terrible bouts of morning sickness. She became hollow-eyed and sunken-cheeked; she was losing weight she couldn't spare. She was positive in her own mind that the evil spirits of Sharon and Tracy were now inside her own body, taking their deadly, ghoulish revenge upon her and little Gerald. She had had a terrifying dream in which the baby was born with Gerald's body and Tracy's head, then another where a Frankensteinlike doctor held up a bloody object and told her that the baby was an idiot, then laughed hysterically until she woke up with a scream that scared the hell out of Gerald.

All this made her angry and resentful; after all, she hadn't killed the girls—Daddy Gerald had done the deed, and he didn't even have a headache! She became even more resentful when Gerald returned from his mysterious two-day trip, looking and acting like a new man. The minute Gerald walked through the door, he hopped on Charlene's weary, aching bones. When it was over forty-five minutes later, she had to admit that he was at his very best that day. She fleetingly wondered why, but as Gerald had the most unpredictable male libido she'd ever encountered, she knew that it was useless to speculate about it. She was, however, a bit peeved that he'd whispered "Mary Ellen" several times in her ear during that otherwise pleasurable forty-five minutes.

The next morning after she'd recovered from the usual ordeal, Gerald made the announcement that they were going to get married again. Charlene didn't understand that at all, and because of her illness and irritability, she said so.

"Don't you see, baby?" Gerald said in that rare, gentle, talking-to-dogs-and-kids tone, "to beat them freeway runners, we gotta get on the good side of God!"

This statement confused Charlene even further, and she wondered for a moment if Gerald might have gotten himself born again while he was gone those two days.

"You see," Gerald continued earnestly, "you know I got this devil in me, from my parents, and I've been doing bad things all my life because of that. When Sharon and Tracy came back, that devil in me helped 'em do all those things they're doing to me . . ."

"But they aren't doing anything to *you!*" Charlene interrupted Gerald's rambling explanation. "I'm the one who's sick . . ."

"But don't you see, you're mine, and the baby's mine, and they are using my devil to get at *you!*"

Charlene rolled her bloodshot eyes upward and mentally threw in the towel. She was too sick to argue, and what the hell, if he wanted to get married again, how could it hurt? Gerald never got around to explaining just how getting married again would put them on the right side of God, or get rid of the evil spirits. At the time, the whole thing made about as much sense to Charlene as an Ingmar Bergman movie. But she would remember it very clearly some months later.

On Sunday, June 1, 1980, Charles and Mercedes Williams drove Gerald and Charlene to Reno, where they were married under Gerald's now well-established alias of Steven Robert Feil. Charlene was about eight weeks' pregnant, looked like a Nazi concentration camp survivor, and other than to say, "I do," didn't open her mouth during the entire proceeding.

On the drive back to Sacramento, the Williamses seemed tense, nervous, and unfriendly. Obviously they did not understand Gerald's reasons for marrying their daughter again; though they couldn't quite put their finger on it, they were inwardly suspicious about the whole thing. Charlene was so weak and exhausted, she didn't give a damn about anything, and just wanted to get home, where she could lie down and be miserable in private.

Gerald was the only one in the wedding party in a cheerful, talkative mood. He hadn't spoken to his father-in-law since the chest-poking incident, but he now engaged Charles in a long question-and-answer session about life insurance.

When they arrived at 2067 Bluebird Lane that evening, Gerald was unusually jovial, even ignoring the haunted van sitting in the driveway. He immediately informed Charlene that they were taking a honeymoon to Oregon, and ordered her to pack all their camping gear because they'd be staying at an isolated campground near Gold Beach. Charlene didn't want to go, but was just too weary to argue. At least, she thought, they wouldn't be staying with his relatives, with all their dogs and chickens. She spent half the night packing and loading the van while

Gerald snored on the couch. Each time she passed him while carrying a load of camping gear, Charlene would mutter "lazy Okie prick" under her breath.

There were up at five o'clock and she sat groggily in the passenger seat as Gerald backed the van out and headed north toward Oregon. By seven, she was on her knees in the back of the van, gagging and throwing up into an empty coffee can, wishing she were dead, or better yet, that Gerald Armond Gallego was.

She stretched out on the cot, her head throbbing with every jolt of the van, miserably nauseous, dizzy, hating herself, Daddy Gerald, Gerald Jr., and most of all, those two despicable freeway runners who were to blame for it all. Charlene finally fell into a deep sleep and didn't wake up until twelve hours later, when Gerald stopped for gas in Ashland, Oregon, a small town about ten miles past the California border. They ate dinner in a pseudo–log cabin tourist-trap highway cafe, and Charlene begged Gerald to check into a motel so she could have a hot bath and get some more sleep. Gerald was worn out after the twelve-hour, nonstop drive, and he readily agreed.

Early the next morning Charlene had an unusually severe attack of gravidarum, and tearfully pleaded with Gerald to take her home. He refused, saying he'd came to Oregon for some fun, and intended to have it. It was after ten o'clock before Charlene was able to travel.

Gerald crossed the Rogue River at Wolf Creek about four o'clock and decided to make an early camp so he could get in some fishing that afternoon and again at dawn the next morning. Rather than sleep in the haunted van, they'd brought a small tent, and Gerald supervised Charlene while she put it up.

At daybreak, Gerald was standing hip-deep in the Rogue River fly-fishing when a female game warden walked up behind him. She asked for his fishing license, which of course Gerald didn't have, then for his ID. While she was running the name Steven Robert Feil through the state police computer via her hand-held rover radio looking for any outstanding warrants, Gerald Armond Gallego was staring at her with those wide, black eyes. The game warden was barely five feet tall, slim almost to the point of being skinny, had long blond hair cascading down from under her Smokey the Bear hat. She didn't look a day over seventeen. She gave Gerald a ticket for fishing without a license, told him to have a nice day, walked back to her jeep parked in a clump of trees, and drove off, most likely to enjoy a long life with a happy family, children, and grandchildren. Gerald stood there on the river bank with the sun coming up behind him, cursing and mumbling to himself, kneading and tugging at an enormous erection with both hands while his gleaming eyes burned a hole in the game warden's back as she walked out of sight.

The fact that her badge represented the power of the people of Oregon, that she carried a pistol, a lead-loaded sap, a canister of Mace, and probably had a hideout gun strapped to her leg didn't mean a thing to Gerald Armond Gallego. He could have easily dropped the blond minicop with one surprise punch to her forehead or belly. The only thing that saved her life on that lovely June morning was the rover radio she carried. Gerald knew that if she whispered "officer needs help" into that radio and gave her location, one-third of the Oregon State Police would be on top of them within ten minutes—and most of them over six feet tall and at least 180 pounds, ready for battle, willing and able to stomp, maim, and/or kill the old street fighter, Gerald Armond Gallego.

When Gerald got back to the tent, he just hauled off and slapped the shit out of Charlene without saying a word, then went over to the camp stove and started making breakfast, still mumbling and growling under his breath. Like most women who are habitually on the receiving end of a man's fist, Charlene knew instinctively that this wasn't the moment to fight back or even demand an explanation. If she did so, Gerald would only end up giving her a real beating. Furthermore, Charlene was expecting her usual bout of morning sickness at any moment, so she just rubbed her stinging cheek and glared at Daddy Gerald, hunched over the camp stove making pancakes, bacon, and coffee. She didn't learn until the next day that Gerald had hit her because of his rabid, seething frustration at not being able to grab the mini–game warden—a female representative of all the power of the social system he hated, an ideal candidate for kidnapping, humiliation, sexual assault, and that final indignity—an ignoble, violent death at his own hands.

For the next three days, the honeymooning couple alternated between camping near Gold Beach and staying at cheap motels along the state highway. On June 7, 1980, at around three in the afternoon, they were driving on a remote two-lane road that ran through an endless pine forest that Gerald claimed would eventually take them to the Pistol River, where he wanted to fish—illegally of course—for steelhead salmon. When Gerald first saw the hitchhiker from a mile down the road, his only thought was that he'd have a little fun and swerve the van, forcing whoever it was to jump back and fall into the muddy ditch.

As he came closer, Gerald saw that the hitchhiker was a female with coal-black hair hanging to her waist, wearing an ankle-length Mother Hubbard–style black dress like the San Francisco hippies used to wear back in the 60s. He noticed that the dress was sticking out so far in front the girl seemed to be leaning backward to keep from falling forward on her face. Suddenly all the pent-up frustration he'd felt at missing the little blond game warden exploded in a frenzy in Gerald's brain. He was seeing red, and Charlene was startled out of her misery when he let loose a deep, menacing growl that reminded her of a frustrated tiger she'd seen at the San Diego Zoo when she was ten years old. Gerald slammed on the brakes and sat gripping the wheel so hard his knuckles turned white, staring vacantly ahead as if he was waiting for someone to cross the road in front of the van.

"What's the matter?" Charlene asked.

"I'm . . . I'm goin' back and get her."

"What? That pregnant little hippie? You can't be serious . . . what *for?* She's got a belly like . . . like, well, she should have a wheelbarrow to carry it in!"

"I don't care," Gerald said doggedly, "I *want* her."

"But what for?" Charlene asked. She was totally confused because the girl, who looked Mexican, was so far removed from Gerald's usual fantasy, and most importantly, was at least six months' pregnant. It just didn't make sense.

"Don't you see, baby," Gerald said, turning his wide head on that thick neck to stare at her with those hypnotic eyes, "she's a gift from God! Sent to us so I can use her to get over my phobia about being around pregnant women."

Charlene stared back at Gerald, still trying to comprehend. She knew the "phobia" bit was right out of one of Gerald's prison psychiatric group therapy sessions. But surely he didn't expect her to believe he could have sex with a pregnant woman—not after all those weepy, whiny stories he'd been telling her ever since she'd know him? Or were they just lies to excuse his abandoning his pregnant wives and girlfriends . . . how many was it? At least six she remembered hearing about.

"But you said . . ." Charlene stopped, recognizing that sudden flash of light in Gerald's eyes, the spark that caused his eyes to glow and turn a mud-brown color, like he was a werewolf about to attack. Charlene hadn't seen it often. This time it scared her so badly she started hiccuping—a spastic, uncontrollable nervous reaction.

"But Daddy—hic—if you can't—hic—do anything—hic—with her, why take such a—hic—chance?"

"Because she was provided by providence," Gerald said softly, "and if I'm gonna be able to stay with you while you're knocked up, I gotta get rid of this phobia the devil put into me . . ."

"Will you stop with the jailhouse psycho shit?" Charlene screamed, regardless of that werewolf glow in his eyes. "I don't—hic—even know what that phobia bull means—hic—and I don't think you do either!—hic!"

"Don't fuck with me, cunt," Gerald snarled menacingly. "You'll get your share like always."

Charlene thought it over but couldn't get very excited as Gerald made a U-turn on the narrow two-lane road and drove back to where the dark-haired girl still had her thumb hopefully stuck out even though there wasn't a car in sight.

"Hey, girl," Gerald called out cheerfully, pulling up beside her on the wrong side of the road, "where you heading?"

"Home," the five-foot-tall hitchhiker answered, looking death in the eyes as she glanced up and smiled coquettishly at Gerald. "Want to drive me there?"

"Sure baby," Gerald said, really pissing Charlene because he'd used her pet name on another woman, "where you live? And what's your name?"

"I'm Helen, and me and my old man got a house trailer back in the woods, near the Old Bridge. You know where it's at?" The victim was smiling as she climbed clumsily into the van and sat down on the blue ice chest. Gerald said he didn't, and the pretty little victim told them the whole story about the Old Bridge trailer camp, a story that even held Charlene's interest. It was a place, Helen said, that the state welfare people had leased, then installed sewer, phone, and electric lines, and parked several small used house trailers in the woods. They moved a couple dozen welfare mothers and their numerous children in, and sent out a nice welfare check each month, which kept their charges out of sight and out of mind.

She told Gerald and Charlene about the men who latch onto welfare women for those checks, how they move into the tiny trailers, take over the welfare money, sell the food stamps for sixty cents on the dollar, beat the shit out of the kids and their mothers whenever they feel the urge, and how they're eager to get the women pregnant as soon as possible because every kid is worth another three hundred bucks per month in welfare as soon as the baby is registered with the state.

Charlene was horrified. "If a man treated me like that, I'd throw his ass into the street," she said truculently to the victim.

"Oh, I don't know," Helen answered softly, "it's better than not having a man . . . I mean, it's not so lonely and all, and really, if you're on welfare, what other kind of guy can you get?"

Charlene's indignation reluctantly faded as she remembered that Daddy Gerald treated her exactly the same way as the welfare-moochers did their women—beat her up when he was in the mood, took her money, kept his own and did whatever the hell he felt like doing, with or without her consent. She even admitted for a moment that the females she and Daddy Gerald preyed upon were no worse than she was, even though she despised them for being lowlifes with no ambition beyond the moment, because they were dirty, stupid, and uneducated, and most of all, because they weren't like she wanted to be.

Helen explained that she lived with an out-of-work lumber-jack who often locked her in the trailer for two or three days while he was out peddling dope or chasing other pussy, that she had a three-year-old son by him, but she didn't know exactly who the father of the new one was (no, that didn't bother the lumberjack one bit because he was more interested in the extra three hundred than in who the kid's dad might have been).

"Are you Hispanic?" Charlene asked.

"Hell no!" Helen said indignantly. "I'm Mexican—and god-damned proud of it! 'Hispanic' is a name the gringos decided to call us. Us Mexicans don't even know what that means!"

Charlene was somewhat impressed with Helen's pride in her heritage. Upper-middle-class white liberal or not, Charlene had never had much use for Mexicans; she would have liked to explore with Helen what it was like being one—just as she had discussed what it was like being black with Tyrone.

Gerald slowed the van and nodded off to the right. Charlene looked and saw a large meadow covered with ten-foot-high weeds with a small clump of dense woods about a half-mile in.

"There's a dirt road going over to those trees," Gerald said out of the side of his mouth.

"How do *you* know?" Charlene asked nervously.

"Because I saw it, that's why! While you've been bullshitting,

I've been watching . . . hey, Helen, we're gonna drive over to those woods and pick up some camping stuff we left there last night. Won't take a minute."

"Okay. I'm in no hurry," Helen answered amiably, bracing herself on the ice chest as Gerald turned off the highway onto the dirt road.

As the big van bounced and rocked along the nearly invisible trail, Charlene kept looking back at the highway because she'd seen a blue pickup stop for a moment, and knew that the driver was watching them. She was very relieved to see the truck drive on. This is really dumb, she thought, we're way out here in broad daylight, in a strange place, driving a van that stands out like a cockroach on a white dinner plate, about to rape and kill a hitchhiker almost in her own backyard . . . Jesus, we must be nuts . . . or are we just getting careless because we haven't come close to getting caught yet?

Charlene shivered violently as a picture of the gas chamber flashed across her eyes, so vivid it shut out everything in her line of vision for a full second. As her head bobbed up and down in rhythm with the bouncing van, Charlene recalled the old movie about Barbara Graham (*I Want to Live* with Susan Hayward playing the lead). Graham was another lowlife petty thief, hugger-mugger, con artist–whore who finally made the fatal mistake of taking one step up the ladder from two-bit thievery to real crime by helping two hardcase ex-cons beat an elderly widow to death while trying to make her tell where she'd hidden her money and jewels. The movie had been very sympathetic to Barbara, making her appear to be a victim of police entrapment rather than her own greed, and the scene where she was strapped into the chair, her final minutes of spastic jerking, groaning, and gasping for breath as the cyanide gas filled her lungs was the most terrifying thing Charlene could imagine— and now, that part of the movie was rolling in her mind's eye so that when Gerald stopped the van in the clump of woods, Charlene was soaking wet with perspiration and so frightened her teeth were chattering.

"What's wrong?" Gerald demanded.

"Oh, Daddy, I'm so scared!" Charlene wailed, throwing her head back, opening her mouth, and cutting loose with an ear-splitting howl.

"Uh-huh," Gerald said under his breath, then gave her a backhand across the mouth that not only shut off her howl abruptly, but also split her lip and knocked her head against the window.

"What's up?" Helen inquired from where she sat on the ice chest.

Gerald didn't answer. He got out, walked to the rear, unlocked the door, leaped in, squatted down, drew his .357 Magnum, shoved it in Helen's face and snarled, "On the floor on your face, cunt. This is a kidnapping!"

"Oh God—oh God—oh God!" The victim screamed so suddenly and loudly that Gerald dropped his pistol and was fumbling for it, trying to finish his command and keep an eye on Helen in case she tried to jump him.

"I said," Gerald began again, "get on the floor . . ."

"Ugh . . . Ugh . . . Ugh . . ." Helen gurgled, then her eyes rolled upward and she pitched headfirst off the ice chest right into Gerald's lap, the top of her head banging into his unprotected pubic bone with such force that he fell backward and tumbled right out the open door, hitting the ground on the back of his neck, his feet still inside the van. Because she was still deep in her own nightmare, Charlene wasn't exactly sure just what had happened in the back of the van. She did see something that looked like Helen butting Gerald in the belly, and she saw him fall backward out of the door. Charlene gave a primordial scream, then dove headfirst over the seat, landed on top of the unconscious victim, grabbed her hair, and started pounding her head on the floor. Gerald had managed to get to his knees; he fell over, groaning and rubbing his aching pubic bone with one hand, waving the Magnum in the other.

When he could stand, Gerald stuck his head and shoulders inside the van and saw Charlene banging the victim's head against the floor. Charlene's hair flew wildly around her face and her blue eyes were fixed in a vacant stare.

"What the hell are you doing?" Gerald yelled, climbing in and shoving an enraged Charlene away from the limp victim. "She's no good to us dead."

"Rip her clothes off and do it to her now!" Charlene screeched. "She's just another lowlife welfare cunt who doesn't deserve to live—do it, goddamn you! If you don't I will!"

Gerald would say later that for the first time, Charlene really scared him. He'd seen her angry of course, hysterically so, but this rage went beyond a normal anger. This was what the prison shrinks like to call "severe transitory maniacal frenzy," a temporary psychosis that they claimed was the reason many convicts were in prison. Simply put, certain individuals couldn't control their sudden bouts of violent rage, thus causing them to commit heinous crimes against society. When Gerald first heard this explained to him by a fatherly prison shrink, he'd put his head on the naive doctor's knee and wept buckets of crocodile tears because he said he'd finally seen the light, now he knew why he kept doing all those bad things the unforgiving DA had sent him to prison for. There, again, the kindly shrink had said, patting Gerald's head, now that I've shown you what's wrong, all you have to do is learn to control that anger, and you'll never rob, assault, steal, or want to kill anyone ever again. Gerald always managed to have that wonderful mystical revelation just before his parole hearing, and it had never failed to set him free.

Charlene was sitting on the blue ice chest, her body shaking and heaving with dry sobs, but her eyes were clear of that maniacal, vacant stare, and her anger seemed to have faded away. The victim was conscious and hogtied facedown on the cot, grunting and groaning as she lay on her bulging belly.

"You don't have to do this, Mister," Helen was saying, her beautiful black eyes bright with tears. "I'll give you a good fuck or suck, or both . . . or whatever you want. But for God's sake, don't hurt me or my baby!"

Gerald watched her closely, a faint smile beginning to show on his lips as the girl's obvious terror mounted. Maybe, he thought, this was going to turn out to be worthwhile after all.

Even Charlene had stopped her dry sobs to watch and listen as the victim begged for her life.

I got a three-year-old kid at home," Helen went on, "and I'm about to become a mother again . . ."

"Well, hurrah for you!" Gerald cut in. "All that means is that you've fucked at least twice . . . why do you cunts always pretend being a mother is something special? All you got to do is fuck to get a kid . . . even a halfwit like her," Gerald nodded at Charlene, "can get knocked up."

"Oh, Mister, what do you want me to do? I'll do it—anything you say . . . please don't hurt us . . ."

Now Charlene got up and knelt on the floor beside Gerald in front of the victim. Maybe Daddy Gerald was right in picking this one, she thought. Maybe, just maybe, she'll be as good as the first two love slaves had been . . . if she'll just get more scared it might be . . .

"We're gonna rape you," Charlene said, "and you're gonna have sex with both of us, and . . ."

"Okay, okay," the victim agreed eagerly, nodding her head rapidly up and down, cutting off Charlene's threat in midstride, "whatever you say . . ."

"And then I'm gonna cut that bastard outta your belly and feed it to you!" Charlene screamed, putting her face almost nose-to-nose with Helen's.

"Ugh . . . Ugh . . . Ugh . . . !" Helen said, gurgling, then fainted again.

"Shit!" Gerald muttered.

"Untie her and get her clothes off," Charlene ordered, committing a serious breach of protocol that would have ordinarily gotten her a smack in the mouth or an elbow in the ribs from Gerald, who was hypersensitive about being told what to do by any female, especially Charlene. Gerald untied the yellow macramé rope, then he and Charlene undressed the victim and rolled her faceup on the floor. She was tiny but well built, and Charlene knelt on her knees, inspecting the girl's body. She was particularly curious about the awkward-looking mound of belly that stuck up like a turtle's back, and Charlene bent over to stare at a narrow, brownish line that ran from just above the victim's navel to her pubic hair, looking as if it had been drawn with a pencil.

"What's that?" Charlene asked suspiciously, tracing the dark line with her finger.

"Just the skin on her belly starting to stretch," Gerald said. "You'll get it too."

"Yeah? You sure, Daddy? I mean, it's not a disease of some kind?"

"Nah. I remember seeing it on my mom. When you get big, your belly skin's gotta stretch . . ."

"Mine too?" Charlene interrupted fearfully.

"Of course," Gerald said, rolling his eyes upward in disgust at her stupidity, "you're no different than any other woman—no matter what you think . . ."

"Okay, okay," Charlene interrupted again, "I just asked! You see any sores or stuff on her down there?"

"No, but you better check it out real close."

Charlene spread the victim's legs and opened her labia lips with a fingertip. "I don't see anything . . ."

"No pus or anything like a discharge?"

"No . . . you look too, just to be sure."

Gerald inspected the victim's privates with great care. When satisfied, he nodded and said, "Okay. Let's get on with it."

"Are you gonna kill her?" Charlene asked, taking off her clothes and folding them neatly on the blue ice chest.

"Yeah. We got to, don't we?"

"I suppose so . . . but you can't do it here. I saw someone in a truck watching us from the road as we drove across the field. If they find the body here, that driver might remember the van."

"Was that why you got so scared?"

"Partly . . . she's waking up."

The victim opened her eyes to see a naked Charlene, felt her fingers running through her pubic hair, and saw a smiling Gerald Armond Gallego stripping down to his bare skin.

At around 4:00 P.M., Gerald and Charlene left the clump of trees and drove back to the highway, their victim now dressed and hogtied again, lying facedown on the cot, moaning and begging them to turn her over on her back in order to take the weight off that protruding stomach, complaining that she couldn't breathe, and that her baby might be injured.

Gerald and Charlene ignored her pleas as they talked about their own little Gerald Armond Gallego, Jr., who would arrive in about seven months, and how sweet and pretty he'd be, and how they'd play with him, and buy all kinds of toys, and dress him in the finest clothes, and Gerald said he would get his son a pair of snakeskin cowboy boots just as soon as the kid could walk.

Oh, they said almost in unison, it was going to be so much fun to raise another Gerald Armond Gallego.

Gold Beach is a desolate, wild, surf-pounded stretch of coastline, a beautiful area that begs passing tourists to stop their cars, get out, and walk along the cold, windy sand, to smell the damp, clean breeze, and perhaps to contemplate what America must have looked like before the white man came in and turned most of it into an asphalt jungle.

The kidnapper-rapists and their victim arrived at an isolated, rocky area of Gold Beach at about six o'clock. Helen was now complaining that she had to urinate, and begging them to let her go home, that she wouldn't tell anyone about her ordeal, that her young son was locked in the house trailer alone, that he liked to play with matches and she was afraid he'd set the place on fire if she didn't get back.

"You mean you left your kid locked up alone?" Charlene barked indignantly at the victim, then reached back and slapped her. "What kind of mother are you? You outta be put in jail!"

"Okay, okay," Gerald said placatingly to Helen, "I'll take you down to the beach behind one of those big rocks and you can take a pee. When it's dark, we'll let you go if you promise not to tell on us."

"I won't, Mister! I swear to God I won't!" Helen said, gasping, clinging to his promise like a drowning man to a life raft.

"Okay, I believe you," Gerald said. "Baby, get back there and untie her ankles so she can walk . . . but leave her hands tied."

He got out and went to the rear door, opened it, and helped Helen out, holding her up until she could carry her own weight.

As they walked toward the beach, Charlene called after them, "Don't you need something?"

"Naw," Gerald answered, "I got everything I need right here," and held up his right hand.

When Gerald and Helen were hidden from the road by a huge boulder, Gerald jerked her jacket down over her arms, picked up a rock and smashed it into the back of her head. Helen fell to her knees, whimpering, "Oh, you lied, oh, you lied . . ."

Gerald put his powerful hands around her neck and squeezed until she went totally limp. As he dragged her across the sand, her heels uncovered a half-buried hubcap. He dropped the body, picked up the hubcap, and used it to quickly dig a shallow, narrow grave. He dropped the victim in, choked her until he heard the bones in her neck crack, then covered the body with damp sand.

Charlene stood by the van watching Gerald walk slowly toward her. He was throwing the shiny hubcap into the air then catching it, like a frisbee, a wide smile on his face.

"All finished, Daddy?" Charlene asked.

"Yep. No trouble at all."

"Why was she yelling?"

"Oh, just that I'd lied about letting her go home."

"That's a dumb Mexican for you!"

"You know something, baby," Gerald said as he started the van and lit a cigarette, "we could kill fifty girls every day—and there's no way they'd ever catch us."

"You think so, Daddy?" Charlene asked, shivering at the delicious thought of them having that many love slaves under their control, then frowning when she thought of the logistics involved in hiding that many bodies.

"I know it. Long as we stick to freeway runners, dopers and lowlifes, no one in the whole fucking world gives a damn. Like you say, everybody'll be *glad* they've disappeared and won't cause any more trouble."

"Well, there's a whole lot of that kind around."

"Yep. All we gotta do is make sure we don't grab no important ones. Even the law don't give a shit about the lowlifes."

As usual, Charlene was way ahead of Daddy Gerald. She'd realized from the very first there would be very little concern for their flaky victims as far as both the public and law enforcement were concerned. The public didn't care as long as it didn't happen to them, and law enforcement was far too busy keeping their heads above the slimy torrent of crime that swept over them night and day to worry about kidnap-rape-murder victims whose own families didn't have the slightest idea of where they were in the first place. Of far more importance to Charlene right now, even though Daddy Gerald hadn't mentioned it, was that she was weak in the knees with the pleasant, warm knowledge that he *could* have sex with a pregnant woman. He'd even made love to her after they'd finished with Helen. Charlene knew that Daddy Gerald wouldn't leave her now, that they were locked together until the day they died.

On June 22, 1980, twelve days after she had disappeared, Helen's badly decomposed, crab-eaten, unrecognizable body was discovered at Gold Beach. A couple of West German tourists had stopped to let their dog run and play in the sand. When it started barking, the man and wife went down to take a look. The dog was digging in the damp sand, and tugging at what looked like a pale, bony foot. Helen's body was taken to a morgue, where an autopsy showed that her lungs were filled with sand—proof-positive that she'd been buried alive. Otherwise, the body was too far gone to determine the exact nature of the indignities to which she had been subjected. Her fetus was estimated to be six months, three weeks old, and would have likely been viable outside its mother's womb. The victim was ID'd by partial fingerprints. Her live-in, out-of-work lumberjack boyfriend was immediately arrested. But his alibi stood up and he was released the next day, even though a police statement to a local crime reporter indicated that he was still the prime suspect.

There would be no irate, grieving family members to cry in front of TV cameras for the eleven o'clock news. The little hitchhiker's lifestyle, her years of dependency upon welfare, the fact that she probably hadn't worked for wages a single day in all her twenty-one years, would label her as of no real value to society, and her case would soon be forgotten in some dusty unsolved homicide file.

When the great state of Oregon was finally notified by California authorities that Helen's killers were in custody, the state's response was, in essence, you guys in California go ahead and prosecute them. We do not have the time, money, or inclination to get involved in a complicated extradition and trial—from which we probably couldn't get a conviction anyway. And besides, Oregon doesn't have a death penalty . . .

Chapter 16

The Birthday Present

Gerald and Charlene were back in Sacramento long before Helen's body was discovered. In fact, they didn't know she had been found until over a year later. Charlene was in horrible shape when they arrived home from Oregon. She collapsed into bed and lay there shivering and shaking.

"I'm gonna die, Daddy," she said with a gasp as Gerald stood in the doorway looking at her skin-and-bones body, pale waxy face, and trembling hands. Charlene thought she heard him say, "Not yet you ain't, baby," but when she managed to open a bloodshot eye, he was gone.

Gerald had once pretended to flirt briefly with voodoo and devil worship. Through a black ex-con he'd served time with, Gerald was introduced to a small cult of voodoo phonies in Del Paso Heights who claimed to be in direct contact with the Devil. Gerald, ever on the alert for anything that might prove profitable in turning a dishonest buck, joined them as an observer for a few days.

194

Gerald wasn't remotely interested in the devil business itself, but he hoped to make a good, solid, coke-buying connection through the cult. He enjoyed watching a half-dozen black girls dance a devilish hip-swinging, bosom-flopping mambo, even though the incessant bongos and devil chanting got on his nerves after a few minutes. He especially liked the fact that when the girls were finished dancing, they went to bed with any male or female who cared to take them on. When the cult leader started dragging cats and dogs in to be chopped up as live sacrifices, Gerald got mad. The very first time it happened while he was there, Gerald grabbed the sacrificial knife away from the head devil, beat and stomped him to a bloody pulp, then told him that if he ever heard of another animal being killed there, he'd come back and break every bone in the voodoo man's body—starting with his toes and working up to his neck. Gerald turned all the animals loose and vowed never to go back.

But today he had to.

Gerald drove the van over to Del Paso Heights and entered the small stucco house that was surrounded by a ten-foot-high chain-link fence. The place smelled worse than a battlefield covered with rotting corpses. Gerald found the same voodoo man he'd beaten up two years before.

Fifty dollars found their way from Gerald's pocket to the witchdoctor's hand, and they walked out to the van. After thirty minutes of goofy, limber-legged leaping, arm waving, rattling of dry bones, mumbo-jumbo, and shrieks that made Gerald's hair stand up, the voodoo witchdoctor declared that it had been a tough case, but that the van was now clean, Whatever evil spirits might have been camping out inside he'd sent them back to the other side, where they'd stay for eternity. As Gerald drove away he had the uneasy feeling that he'd been screwed out of his fifty dollars by the witchdoctor. But he had to try everything. He knew he couldn't let the spirits destroy Charlene now because if she died, it would ruin his last chance for lifelong happiness.

When Gerald arrived home an hour later, he was shocked right down to his toes when he saw Charlene sitting at the kitchen table, up to her elbows in empty Kentucky Fried Chicken boxes, her face still gaunt but slowly taking on a healthy glow.

"Hi, Daddy!" Charlene said, squealing a greeting between bites. "I'm feeling lots better! In fact, I got so hungry about an hour ago, I went out and got all this." She waved her hand at the pile of junk, food detritus left over from the feast she was just winding up. "Want some?" she asked, holding up a gnawed, extra-crispy chicken leg.

"You're not sick any more," Gerald stated in a flat voice, ignoring her question and looking a little pale in the face.

"Unh-uh. It went away just like that." Charlene snapped her greasy fingers. "I was asleep, then something woke me up. I mean, I think I felt the bed shake, like maybe a little earthquake. I was feeling marvelous and so hungry! There wasn't anything to eat in the house, so I went down to Kentucky—"

"Okay, okay," Gerald mumbled, "eat it, for Christ's sake, and shut the fuck up."

Gerald went into the living room and sat down on the couch, staring at the blank TV screen. It worked, he thought, it couldn't have been anything else . . . that skinny, wrinkled, dried-up little nigger did a Lazarus on Charlene by jumping around and rattling some bones and . . . goddamn! That means he really *does* have the power . . . maybe he ain't no phony witchdoctor after all. Maybe he is a disciple and does own the devil franchise in this area just like he claims. If that's true, then all this bullshit I've been giving people about a devil inside me could be true also. I may not have the power to cure but I do have the power to kill—to kill and get away with it. I see it all now . . . Gerald figured the devil in him was just testing to see what he'd do. Would he take Charlene to a hospital, or would he go to another devil and ask him to help her? It was all clear now; he figured he could keep on killing until he was on social security and the law couldn't touch him. He was under the protection of the devil that he inherited from his dear old Dad and Grandpa Pullin.

Over the next two weeks Charlene blossomed out like a spring rose in the early morning sun. She rapidly gained weight, her strength came back, and, she claimed, she could actually feel little Gerald Jr. moving around for the first time. Within three weeks Charlene had that extra-special, self-satisfied glow that all happily pregnant women are supposed to have; she looked like the typical, first-time-mother-to-be pictured in one of the top women's magazines.

When Gerald told Charlene how he went to the black witch-doctor in Del Paso Heights, she was so ecstatic that he had cared enough about her to go out of his way to get help, she hopped on his bones. When he couldn't perform, she happily gave him one of what she liked to call her extra-special, super-slurpy blowjobs.

During those three weeks, Gerald was overawed, subdued, and a little frightened at having his devil theory more or less verified by Charlene's miraculous recovery, not to mention the fact that there was no longer any cold wind blowing out of the van—and no policemen knocking on his door with questions about seven dead bodies. All that marital bliss couldn't last, though, and by the end of June, Gerald and Charlene were like two caged jungle beasts in their small house. They tiptoed around each other, glaring and muttering insults under their breath. Charlene had her full youthful strength back, and with that newfound vigor, her old feeling of superiority over Gerald came back with such force she had trouble controlling it. She received several painful elbow smashes to her ribs for, as Gerald put it, talking when she should have been listening. The tiptoeing and mumbled insults started when they woke up, but by afternoon it escalated into shouts that could be heard up and down Bluebird Lane.

"Whore!"

"Oh yeah? Well, at least all the other Johns could get it up, you monkey-dicked, peanut-balled, dumb Okie prick!"

"Oh yeah? With that Grand Canyon pussy of yours, you wouldn't recognize a big dick unless you had it in your ear!"

"Oh yeah? Shorty!"

"Juicy Lucy Pussy!"

"Old limberdick!"

"Lizzy!"

"Tiny balls!"

"Dyke!"

And so it went. By nightfall both were so physically and emotionally exhausted, they would finally collapse into each other's
arms on the bed, crying, apologizing, and trying to reestablish
that fragile thread of warped love that had so far managed to
bring them safely through every crisis. By July 10, Gerald and
Charlene were throwing day-long screaming fits, and actually
beating on each other to such a degree their neighbors called
the police on two separate occasions. Two tired, cynical, fif-
teen-year veteran cops answered disturbance calls at 2067 Bluebird Lane, one clocked in at 3:00 A.M., Saturday, July 12, and
the other at 4:00 A.M., Monday, July 14. Both reports read, in
essence, "Parties claim loud voices, screams, etc. were coming
from TV . . . claimed they had fallen asleep after drinking two
beers and didn't realize TV was so loud . . . neither party
appears to be under the influence, and wife states she was
not assaulted . . . husband said he was sorry for trouble and
it wouldn't happen again . . . verbal warning issued to both
parties . . ."

Those two visits from the cops really scared Charlene because
she knew that if they continued attracting police attention with
their perpetual fights, they could end up in jail on charges of
disturbing the peace. Their house and cars could be searched,
and who knew what overlooked clues the cops might find? Charlene was like most civilians in that she believed cops solved
homicides with clues. She didn't realize that your average big-
city homicide officer has more unsolved cases in his file than he
can crack in two lifetimes, that clues helped solve crimes for the
convenience of one-hour TV scripts, and that those TV clues
would be totally inadmissible in a real court unless they had
been obtained under a search warrant, which required that the

clues be enumerated prior to issuance of that search warrant. The scale of justice is in fact tilted in favor of the criminal, and every DA prays for a 180-degree turn someday that would enable him to go back to the good old days of solving crimes with clues rather than hard evidence. But in the meantime, it's ". . . forget the clues and gimme a good, believable informant anytime, because without that informant or a confession in a stranger-killing-stranger homicide, my chances of even accidentally cracking that case is about as likely as my ex-wife letting me have the house back . . ."

At approximately 10:00 A.M. on July 15, Charlene made breakfast for Gerald as a sort of peace offering. Gerald took one bite of scorched scrambled eggs and threw the whole plate on the floor, then backhanded Charlene so hard she fell against the sink, knocking the breath out of her. Gerald turned around and saw her bent over, gasping, arms folded across her stomach, face white with pain—then Gerald did an extraordinary thing. He burst into tears, picked Charlene up, carried her to the bed, and lay down beside her, holding his surprised wife in his arms while he begged forgiveness.

"I'm no good for you, baby," Gerald wailed. "I'm mean, and I treat you like shit, and I beat you even when you don't deserve it. When you go to the gas chamber, it'll be my fault cause I got you into all this!"

"No you didn't, Daddy," Charlene whispered soothingly between gasps for breath. "I wanted it as much as you did. It was my idea, remember? I wouldn't trade the past two years with you for anything in the whole world . . . it's been the happiest, most exciting time of my life."

"But I'm a no-good husband!" Gerald tearfully protested. "You should be living in a nice house like your folks have, and me coming home from work in the evening and sitting down to a good dinner . . ."

"No! That isn't you and it certainly isn't me. We're different, Daddy. I'm no typical housewife and you're not the All-

American husband. I have no idea why you're so sexually screwed up, or even why *I* am. There's something wrong with our genes. That's the way we are, that's the way we always will be—and there's nothing we can do about it.''

"Maybe we could go to a shrink," Gerald said, rolling over and wiping his eyes on the sheet.

"Daddy, it's okay to pretend to believe that shrink bullshit if it'll get you outta prison, but you should know better than anyone that it's all nonsense. You should know that your personality isn't going to change just because a shrink tells you you did something because of what happened during your childhood . . . come on, Daddy, did that shrink crap ever stop you from doing anything you really wanted to do?"

"I guess not," Gerald admitted. "But maybe if we pretend we believe it . . . Oh, I dunno—how could we ever tell a shrink what we've done?"

"That's right, Daddy. There's no turning back . . . it's just you and me right down to the very end."

Gerald sat on the edge of the bed, head in his hands, staring at the wall with those depthless, unblinking, black eyes. "Are you sorry we done it, baby?"

"Not for a minute. If my life's gonna be a short one, at least I'll have had something no other woman's ever had—a guy like you for a husband and our love slaves."

That night Gerald and Charlene went out looking for two more victims. They drove to a teenage dance hall in Roseville and sat in the parking area for over an hour. There were lots of girls, but not a single pair ever showed up. They were all in large groups, or accompanied by boys. Gerald and Charlene knew that it was simply too dangerous to make an attempt to grab more than two. They returned home at 2:00 A.M., tried to make love and failed, then fell into a restless, moaning, sweaty sleep.

For the next week, the lovebirds of Bluebird Lane, in a desperate frenzy of sexual frustration, prowled the freeways, shopping malls, teenage hangouts, and even drove up and down dark residential streets looking for their next victims. As they cruised past lighted houses and peered in curtainless windows at the people inside, Gerald wondered whether they should do a creepy-crawly Charles Manson attack and sneak into one of the houses where they spied at least a couple of females with no man in sight. But they decided it was too risky and reluctantly gave up the idea. They worked a twenty-mile area around Sacramento both day and night, but every time they'd see a likely pair of victims, some small occurrence would cause them to back off. A cop car would suddenly cruise by, or the potential victims would be followed too closely by other people, or Gerald would simply not like the "feel" of the situation.

They did manage to stop and talk to a pair of pretty teenagers, but the girls flatly refused to get into the van despite Charlene's offer of dope, sex, and finally money. Like two starving jungle predators who instinctively realize that they must depend upon each other, Gerald and Charlene declared a silent truce between themselves while they concentrated on finding their prey. As always in times of trial and tribulation, they drew closer to each other, neither blaming the other for their failed efforts to entrap a couple of willing teenage girls. Their frustration at not finding anyone to kidnap, rape, and murder became unbearable. Gerald would jump violently at the slightest sound, and Charlene started having headaches that came on with lightning speed, caused horrible pains in her forehead and neck for a few seconds, then vanished as quickly and inexplicably as they had started.

Gerald's birthday, July 17, was coming up in a couple of days; Charlene knew that nothing would be more appreciated by him than a pair of young, clean, pretty, and easily terrorized teenagers—and she was determined to get Daddy Gerald what he wanted. Charlene went out hunting on her own, dressed in her best teenage costume, carrying her little .25 pistol. She prowled every record store, fast-food outlet, public swimming pool in the area, and even spent an hour in the parking lot of a state unemployment office. But she failed to make a single contact. That evening, Charlene made several clandestine phone calls to Gerald's daughter in Butte County, but hung up when Lorraine or her husband, Ed, answered. When Charlene finally managed to reach Mary Ellen, the girl was unfriendly, in fact downright hostile, refusing even to discuss making another birthday visit to her father. Charlene was very surprised at the girl's attitude, and would remember it clearly some months later.

On the night of July 16, Gerald and Charlene tried unsuccessfully for several hours to make love. When they realized it simply was not going to work, Gerald turned over with his back to her and whispered, "I'm sorry, baby."

Charlene answered, "Don't be silly, Daddy. It's not your fault. One way or the other, we'll get someone to help us tomorrow . . . after all, it's your birthday."

Gerald and Charlene spent most of Thursday, July 17, which was sizzling hot, driving around town looking for prospective victims. In the late afternoon they stopped for a few minutes at Charlene's parents' house to drop off a cake she had bought for Gerald's birthday. Then they drove across the American River to West Sacramento, where Gerald insisted they do some fishing. After two hours without even a nibble, he gave up and sat forlornly in the shade of some willow trees, drinking gin and staring at the water. He urged Charlene to drink with him, but she refused, saying that it might harm Gerald, Jr. Charlene had even given up coke and pot because she'd heard they could be addictive to a fetus, and she wanted the future little Gerald Armond Gallego, Jr., to be a perfect specimen, with *her* brains and *Gerald's* looks and body. It was well after eight o'clock when Gerald snapped out of his catatonic state and offered to take his mind off their miserable failure at finding a couple of teenage victims.

"Let's stop at the Boat Inn and play some pool," Gerald said, slowing the van to make a U-turn in the middle of the busy street, oblivious to the blaring horns, the indignant gestures and shouts from other drivers.

"If you want to," Charlene said, "but I'd rather keep looking. I mean, it's real late, it's Thursday, everybody's gonna go home early . . ."

"Forget it," Gerald said impatiently, "we're not gonna find anything anyway. I wanna relax."

Charlene knew the decision had been made, and she didn't bother to comment as they pulled into the six-car parking lot in back of the Boat Inn, a small working-class bar and pool parlor that she and Gerald had visited a couple of times before. There were six or seven people in the smokey room. It smelled of beer and there was a guy behind the bar who Gerald didn't know but who instantly recognized him. The normally congenial bartender didn't let on, because Gerald was one of the few people he didn't like, a man he knew to be extremely dangerous and hot tempered. Gerald immediately went to a pool table and began playing against a small elderly man who reminded Charlene of Gerald's stepfather, Ed Davies. Charlene watched Gerald play for a few minutes, then turned to check her hair in the mirror behind the bar. She was startled to see a very pretty woman standing there. The woman looked to be in her late twenties, with shoulder-length blond hair, blue eyes, petite but with a pleasingly curvaceous body. Looks like Mary Ellen, Charlene thought.

"Where'd you come from?" Charlene asked the woman bartender.

"Oh, I've been here all the time," she said, smiling and showing a nice set of white teeth. "I'm on duty till closing time. The guy you saw was just helping me set up some stock from the back room. He's really the morning bartender."

"Gimme 'nother gin," Charlene ordered, forgetting about making Gerald Jr. an alcoholic as she stared hard at the woman's hips when she bent over to pick up something from the floor.

"What's your name?" Charlene asked as the woman set a glass of gin in front of her.

"Betty . . . and usually called Betsy," the bartender answered, smiling again. "What's yours?"

"Mildred . . . and mostly called Millie—and I hate both names."

Betty laughed and turned away to serve a beer to the little old man. Charlene covertly watched the female bartender for about twenty minutes, then went over to join Gerald at the pool table.

"Do you like her, Daddy?" Charlene whispered, nodding her head at the diminutive blond behind the bar.

Gerald glanced up briefly, uninterested, then leaned over to make his shot. When he was done, he suddenly snapped erect, then froze into that bird-dog point, those depthless black eyes locked onto the blond bartender like a radar beam. He stared until Betty felt his eyes on her. She turned to look directly at him, smiled uncertainly for a second, then frowned and turned back.

"Yeah, I like her, baby. I like her a whole lot," Gerald muttered. "I was psyching her out real good just now . . . she'll do anything, baby . . . but how we gonna get her?"

"Leave that to me," Charlene whispered, "just do exactly as I say."

Gerald and Charlene left the Boat Inn at 1:45 A.M., fifteen minutes before closing time. They were sitting in the van, which was now parked across the street in the dark shadow of a large tree, when the last customer, the little old man, left the bar, got into his pickup, and drove away. There was now one car, a blue Pinto, left in the parking lot. They waited another five minutes, then Charlene nodded and said, "Let's go. Move it!"

Gerald whipped the van across the street and parked alongside the blue Pinto. Charlene got out and half-ran, half-walked across the lot to the door of the bar. She knocked several times until Betty shouted, "Who is it?"

"Me, Millie. I left my jacket in there, Betty. Could you please get it for me? It's in the booth behind the pool table."

"Okay. Just a minute."

She heard Betty unlocking the heavy door, then saw her standing in the darkness holding out Charlene's light-green nylon jacket.

"Oh, I really appreciate this, Betty," Charlene said. "I was afraid to leave it until tomorrow. It might be stolen and . . . is someone picking you up? I mean, we'd be happy to give you a ride home."

"Thanks anyway, but that's my Pinto over there . . . uh, excuse me, Millie, I gotta go to the bathroom, then get right home. My babysitter worries when I'm late."

"Sure. Listen, we'll wait for you to get in your car. It's so dark out here."

"Okay, but you don't have to. I'm not afraid."

Charlene walked slowly back to the van, then nodded. Gerald got out on the passenger side and stood at the rear of the blue Pinto.

"I'll wait until she's in the car, then take her," he said, holding the .357 Magnum behind his right hip.

"Okay. Just do it the way I told you. I'll keep watch—and whatever you do, don't let her scream."

The intended victim was now slamming, now triple-locking the heavy door. She walked rapidly to her car, nodding at Charlene as she said, "Thanks for waiting. So nice of you."

"Oh, no problem, Betty," Gerald said, stepping around the Pinto. Betty looked startled, as if she'd forgotten that Charlene's companion was this man with the scary eyes who had undressed her with that stare of his.

"Here," Gerald said, "let me unlock your car."

Betty handed him the keys, watched as she opened the door, looked inside, then laughed and said, "Okay. All clear. No crazies hiding in there!"

"Thanks," Betty said, getting in and rolling the window halfway down. Gerald quickly shoved the pistol barrel against her forehead and grabbed a fistful of her hair with his other hand.

"This is a kidnapping, cunt. Get out and walk to the rear of that van. If you make a sound, I'll blow your fucking brains all over this parking lot."

Gerald pulled Betty out of the car by her hair, jerked her head back, pressed his pistol barrel into her ear, and marched her to the van, where Charlene was holding the rear door open.

"Get in," Gerald ordered, then crawled in behind her. "Lay on the cot. Baby, hand me the tape."

Gerald quickly clamped a strip of tape over the victim's mouth, then nodded to Charlene. "Let's get going."

Charlene started the van, then screeched, "Oh shit!" She leaped out, ran to the Pinto and used her nylon jacket to wipe Gerald's fingerprints off the door and half-opened window.

"That dumb Okie prick's gonna get us caught yet," Charlene mumbled as she ran back to the van.

At 5:00 A.M. Betty was lying on the bedroom floor of the house on Bluebird Lane. She was fully conscious but had lost count of the number of sexual indignities that had been inflicted upon her during the last three hours. Her kidnappers had used an illustrated paperback book on S&M as an instruction manual. They whipped her with a piece of rope, the female sodomized her with an eight-inch black rubber dildo, then they hung her up by her wrists from a nail in the wall and whipped her again. She was forced to perform cunnilingus and fellatio on her kidnappers, separately and together; her nipples had been chewed and pinched. She was sodomized three times by the man while she performed cunnilingus on the woman, then forced to fellate him until he climaxed in her mouth. Betty was now looking up at her two tormentors from her prone position on the floor. There was no fear in her eyes or voice as she whispered, "Why don't you kill me?"

"You want to die?" the woman asked.

"No. But I can't live after what you've done to me."

"Bullshit!" the man said with a snort of disgust. "You cunts are all alike . . . listen, bitch, you never done nothing tonight that you ain't done before, 'cepting maybe get your ass beat with a rope."

"If I did those things," the victim told him in a matter-of-fact voice, "it was because I wanted to, and it was with someone I liked . . ."

"So why do you wanna die now?"

"Because I can't face my kids or my boyfriend or anyone else after what you two did. I'm so ashamed. Just kill me, *please.*"

"We might do that. How would you like to die?" the man asked, smiling and dropping to his knees beside her.

"Shoot me," Betty whispered.

"Okay, bitch," the female said sharply, "that's enough playacting. It'll be daylight soon, Daddy. You'd better get it done."

As the male hands closed around the victim's throat, the woman suddenly screamed, "No! Not here! Not in our bedroom!"

The man looked up, startled. "Huh? Why not?"

"The spirits, Daddy, the evil spirits, remember?"

"Oh yeah. Good thinking, baby. I'll take her to the van."

Charlene sat in a rocking chair by the window after Gerald got into the van with Betty. Five minutes later she jumped up, went to the door and opened it. She heard a furious argument coming from the van, but couldn't make out all of the words. She hurried outside and knocked on the front window. "For God's sake," she whispered hoarsely, "I can hear you from the house! Get it over with before someone comes by."

As Charlene walked back inside, she felt a hot rush of anger and jealously because she knew that Daddy Gerald was having sex with the victim one last time, alone and without sharing with her. She sat back down in the rocking chair and watched the van for about fifteen minutes. Gerald finally got out and walked toward the house. She met him at the door and whispered softly, "Is it finished? Did you kill her?"

"Yeah."

"How?"

"Choked her."

"I want to see," Charlene said, brushing past Gerald and running toward the van. She opened the rear door, climbed in, and switched on the overhead light. Betty lay faceup on the cot, naked, her eyes wide open and staring, as blank as the glass eyes

of a toy animal. Her throat was swollen into a grotesque greenish blue knot, and her body was covered with welts, scratches,
and red bumps. It reminded Charlene of pictures she'd seen of
people in the last stages of leprosy.

"Satisfied?" Gerald asked sarcastically as he got behind the
wheel and started the van.

"Yeah. Was it hard?"

"Naw. Only took five minutes. But she did flop around
some."

"Uh-huh. What now?"

"We'll take her out to the river, throw her in. With any luck,
she'll float down to the bay by tomorrow and the sharks'll have
a real tasty treat."

"Good thinking, Daddy. Let's go . . . and happy birthday. Did
you like your present?"

The victim's body never reached San Francisco Bay. In fact,
it didn't leave the spot where it landed when Gerald, misled by
the darkness, heaved her corpse into what he thought was deep
water. It landed on a sandbar, then settled slowly into the muck
as the tide went out, and that was where it would be found on
October 2, 1980, some three months later.

When the blond bartender's babysitter filed a missing-person
report in the afternoon of July 17, it was definitely not a priority
call. Missing-person reports are the most time-consuming, bo-
thersome, and the least productive of all police work. The police will not even take information until the person has been
missing for twenty-four hours, simply because that missing husband, wife, teenager, or senile old grandpa will more than likely
call or show up within that time span. With people reported
missing at the rate of one million per year, it is logistically
impossible for the police to do anything but a superficial check
into fewer than one percent of those cases. The only exceptions
are missing children under ten years of age. That kind of report
will usually generate a full-scale search and investigation not

only because of the media coverage, but also because most cops have sympathy for young kids.

Three days after Betty's disappearance, a harried missing-persons cop showed up at the Boat Inn to interview whoever he could find, hoping it wouldn't take too much effort and time.

As luck would have it, the bartender who knew Gerald happened to be on duty, and when the cop asked for names of people who were in the bar that night, Steven Robert Feil was the first name he took down, along with that of Feil's female companion, a little blond called Millie. Those names, along with a few others, were dropped into a file and forgotten until approximately two and a half months later, when, on Thursday, October 2, 1980, a fisherman found what was left of the blond bartender. Fish, crabs, worms, and birds had done nearly as much damage as the sharks would have. There was a skeleton frame, some teeth, and a piece of turquoise jewelry left, all of which were used to ID the little blond bartender.

Chapter **17**

The Distaff Side

According to the gospel of social workers and shrinks, Charlene Williams should have grown up to be a normal American woman. She seemed to have had the background—loving parents and a stable upbringing—that most psychiatrists claim will guarantee a normal adult. Of course in the psych business what does it mean to be normal? Charlene certainly would have faced the mandatory number of identity crises, attempts to assert herself in a chauvinistic society, and most certainly, all kinds of sexual problems.

This author once spent three hours, like Alice in Wonderland, looking through a glass darkly, listening to a half-dozen off-duty shrinks' argue among themselves as to just what caused Charlene to go wrong. One female psychologist claimed that Charlene was downtrodden and had been dominated by males all of her life—first by her father, then by her boyfriends, husbands, more boyfriends, and finally, by that grand master of all male chauvinist pricks, Gerald Armond Gallego. Two male psychiatrists claimed that the only thing wrong with Charlene was

210

that, like Agamemnon's daughter, she suffered from a good old-fashioned Electra complex, which, simply put, means that Charlene had a suppressed sexual attraction for her father.

One male psychiatrist said that Charlene was loaded with more personalities than Bridey Murphy, that she had been a witch back in the Middle Ages and was acting out that personality when she committed the kidnap-rape murders with Gerald. This shrink claimed that Gerald was none other than the reincarnated guru of the Inquisition, the monk Tomas de Torquemada himself, that it was a lead-pipe cinch that when those two bloodthirsty personalities met in space and time, there would be bodies scattered all over the place. Another shrink claimed that the only problem Charlene had was a hooded clitoris, and hooded clits caused more problems for women than all the chauvinist pricks, split personalities, and Electra complexes in the world. If she had only had an operation to remove that damned hood, she'd be right as rain for the rest of her life.

Just how male chauvinist pricks, Electra complexes, split personalities and a possible hooded clitoris caused Charlene to team up with Gerald for the ten vicious murders may never be fully explained . . .

Her own statement says much more, and there isn't an experienced cop in America who would doubt one word of that statement: *"We had this sexual fantasy, see, so we just carried it out . . . I mean, like it was easy and fun and we really enjoyed it, so why shouldn't we do it?"*

Charlene Adelle Williams was born on October 10, 1956, in Stockton, California, a small inland seaport fifty miles south of Sacramento. California penal authorities show her to be five feet in height, with blond hair and blue eyes, weighing about one hundred pounds. Prior to November 18, 1980, she hadn't been arrested or accused of any crime.

Her father started as a butcher with a supermarket chain and worked his way up to a top executive position. Charlene gradua-

ted from Rio Americano High School in Sacramento, where she
was classified as having an IQ of 160, placing her in the top one
percent of the population as far as brains go. Charlene was later
described by some of her classmates, including a girl who said
that she had been Charlene's best—and as far as she knew,
only—friend, as standoffish, shy, and mousey. Others called her
a snooty, phoney little smart-mouthed bitch who acted as if she
were better than everyone else. They said that she'd fuck anything with a dick, that she had a black boyfriend she often
bragged about but whom no one ever saw.

Everyone said that Charles and Mercedes Williams pampered
their only child until it was sickening, giving her whatever she
demanded, and allowing her to do anything she wanted. One
day Charlene decided she was going to be a "businesswoman,"
so her parents invested $15,000 in a junk-gift shop for her in
Folsom. Charlene whimsically named it "The Dingaling Shop."
It lasted about as long as her attention span.

One of Charlene's husbands said that she was a whiny, sneaky
daddy's or mama's girl and her parents interfered in their marriage so much that it didn't stand a chance from the start. This
particular husband was damned glad to get rid of her, because,
in addition to the parental interference, Charlene was a fake, an
habitual liar who couldn't keep her hands off other men and
talked incessantly about "weird sex." Her favorite sexual fantasy was a ménage à trois with two women and a man. On top
of that, she wouldn't wear makeup or fix her hair, she dressed
like a hippie, and said that if her natural beauty wasn't enough,
to hell with everyone. Charlene claimed to have an asthma
problem, he said, which she used as a weapon when she didn't
get her way. She'd throw a phony asthma attack until her parents appeared and gave her whatever she wanted at the moment. Her ex said "Charlene was a sex-nut before she met that
Gallego guy, always talking about being raped by another
woman, and even wanted me to hire a whore to go to bed with
us. I'd have done it, but I was so strung out on heroin all the

time I couldn't get my head straight long enough to follow through."

Just prior to meeting Gerald, Charlene had had a powerful, sexually satisfying affair with a married man. She discovered that she loved to have sex with him if he told her he'd just made love to his wife. She would sometimes sneak over to his house late at night and meet him in the garage where they'd make wild, passionate love on a cot in the corner. The fact that the man's wife was sleeping in her bedroom just a few feet away always drove Charlene into an extra-special fantasy-fed sexual frenzy. On at least one occasion, after they'd finished in the garage, Charlene insisted that he go back to his bedroom, raise the windowshade an inch or two, turn on the light, wake his wife, and make love to her while Charlene peeped through the crack. The affair abruptly ended when Charlene scared the hell out of the guy by suggesting that she join him with his wife in bed. Her husband said that after receiving a mysterious phone call late at night, Charlene attempted suicide by drinking Pine-Sol disinfectant. He figured that call was from her married lover, telling Charlene bye-bye forever.

The chances of Gerald Gallego and Charlene Williams ever meeting were about as likely as Menachem Begin throwing an afternoon tea party for Yasser Arafat. If Charlene hadn't willingly and deliberately stooped to Gerald's level, the odds of her ever laying eyes on him were totally nil.

On September 10, 1977, one month to the day short of her twenty-first birthday, the tiny, twice-married, twice-divorced, sparkling blond, blue-eyed, cute, upper-middle-class girl with the All-American looks drove over to South Sacramento to buy some coke from a dealer she knew who operated out of the Black Stallion Card Room, a licensed, legal poker parlor. Charlene made her buy, went into the restroom to snort up, and came out five minutes later flying at 20,000 feet. She ran smack into Gerald Armond Gallego with such force they both bounced off the walls in the narrow hallway. Charlene took one look at the roughly handsome, all-around career criminal, and felt her crotch getting wet.

Gerald looked at this expensively dressed young lady, obviously out of his class, and immediately smelled money—an amenity he was fresh out of because he'd just lost his last dollar in a poker game with a bad-assed, mean-talking black man who was bigger and uglier than Idi Amin. So instead of yelling "Why don't you watch where you're going, bitch?" Gerald immediately assumed his most charming con-man personality, took Charlene gallantly by the arm, led her out to the parking lot, got a good look at her new car, then invited her to have a late dinner with him. Of course she ended up paying.

Other than supposedly losing his wallet, Charlene would recall that Gerald was a perfect gentleman, lighting her cigarettes, opening car doors, and doing all the little things that a guy does for a gal on a polite date. Charlene liked it; she especially liked the fact that Gerald asked for her phone number, then shook hands instead of grabbing her crotch, and didn't even kiss her when they drove home at midnight. The next day, Charlene received twelve long-stemmed red roses with a note that read, "To a very sweet girl. Love, Gerald Gallego."

A week later, Gerald and Charlene rented the place on Bluebird Lane and moved in together. Whatever deadly attraction there was between them was now solidly locked into place. Exactly one year to the day after their meeting in the Black Stallion Card Room, they started their murderous spree.

During her almost thirty months with Gerald, Charlene would marry him not once but twice, and never, in all that time, did she attempt to leave Gerald for good. Never for a moment did she consider turning him over to the police, which she could have done at almost any time.

After her confession, Charlene never claimed to be insane, nor did she deny that she and Gerald were anything other than what they were accused of being—a pair of murderers who kidnapped and raped to satisfy their sexual fantasies, then killed to cover their identities. That fact, all think-tank speculation aside, is the bottom line as far as Charlene Adelle Williams standing by Gerald Armond Gallego is concerned.

A few criminologists and a large number of psychiatrists have claimed that individuals who can't bring themselves to commit certain crimes on their own will do so if they can find a partner whose personality fills the gaps necessary for them to commit that crime. It's a transference of personalities, to use the correct psychological terminology. If this theory is true, Gerald and Charlene would be a case in point because their secret sexual fantasies meshed perfectly. And while it is highly doubtful that either would have committed a fantasy-motivated kidnap-rape murder on their own, together they formed the optimal serial killer team.

Chapter 18

I Wanna Be A Daddy So Bad!

There are records of Gerald marrying at least seven times. But under California law, it is highly doubtful that any of those marriages were legal. In each case, Gerald had either lied about his age, name, or previous marital status, and any one of those false statements, among others, renders a marriage in California legally null and void if challenged. Most certainly, all but one of Gerald's marital adventures were bigamous because his divorces from previous spouses were not yet final. Gerald didn't worry about technicalities, though. He knew that no one is ever prosecuted in California for bigamy unless there is another compounding charge, such as marriage bunco—in essence, marrying in order to obtain money under false pretenses, an embarrassing accusation and almost impossible to prove even if a plaintiff could be convinced to bring charges and testify in open court that they were dumb enough to be taken in by a false-hearted lover who wanted their money.

Gerald never went out of his way to look for women with money. He didn't have to because every woman who knew him

216

willingly contributed in whatever way she could to Gerald's financial advancement.

With the exception of Charlene and the Big Swede, his wives and girlfriends came from Gerald's own social stratum. Like most criminals, Gerald hated to work because he simply didn't see the sense in it. What the hell, it interfered with stealing, robbing, travelling around when the mood struck him, and all the other activities he loved to pursue.

Those who knew him best always wondered why Gerald didn't become a pimp. His mother stated matter-of-factly, "All of Gerald's women would do anything for him, and he could have been the wealthiest pimp in the country if he'd worked at it. Christ, Gerald was born for that kind of life!"

Lorraine claimed that Gerald's first wife had been an amateur whore when he first met her, and would have gone on the street full-time if he'd agreed to it. Gerald grew up around whores and he surely knew the value of a good, docile, working girl to her pimp. But Gerald's mother had worked for a Sacramento pimp named Chubby, and perhaps that was the real reason he wouldn't touch the whore business or allow any of his women even to suggest it.

The way Lorraine told it, Gerald's first adventure into matrimony came when he was sixteen, and the woman, Ellen Weed, was twenty-five. Ms. Weed lived in Bakersfield and worked as a waitress at a truck stop on Freeway 405, the crowded, dusty direct route from San Diego to the Oregon border.

According to Lorraine, when the couple met, Gerald was on parole for a series of armed robberies. His parole officer had found Gerald a job as a door-to-door book salesman; within minutes of his knocking on Ellen Weed's door, they were in bed together. In keeping with Gerald's propensity for almost immediate impregnation, Weed was knocked up very soon after their first encounter. When she was about nine months' pregnant, Gerald decided to marry her. Why is anyone's guess. The fact that he was on parole and needed permission from his parole officer to do just about anything, or that he was sixteen, five years short of legal age at the time, didn't concern Gerald one bit.

"I was madly in love with that son of a bitch," Ellen Weed told Lorraine. "When we got married, our daughter was a week old, and I had three other kids. We were living in a crappy little two-room apartment and Gerald was making fifteen dollars a day. He never sold no books, so he didn't get any commission.

"Like I said, I was madly in love with him . . . he'd told me he was twenty, and when I found out he was only sixteen, I like to shit! I mean, they could have arrested me for contributing to the delinquency of a minor. Can you imagine *anybody* contributing to the delinquency of Gerald Gallego?

"But it was worth the risk to me. I mean, Gerald may have been sixteen, but he knew more about screwing than any man I ever went to bed with. I'm not all that pretty, and Gerald seemed to like me, I guess. See, most people think a hooker gets all the fucking she can handle. Well, that ain't so. I mean, tricks are business and you get it over quick.

"But when you come home, a girl likes her main man to know how to make her happy. And Gerald could do it. We used to make love for hours and hours, and he wouldn't stop until I had all I wanted. When things got bad between us, I think that was the only reason I stayed with him.

"Our marriage only lasted eight months. I mean, he started beating the shit out of me right off. Accused me of sleeping with guys while he was out selling books. I'm not denying *that* part cause one of us had to bring in some money. I could turn two, three tricks in an hour or so, and make twenty, thirty bucks. I mean, I wasn't overdoing it or nothing, like walking the streets at night.

"I'd just go down to the Norway Bar and Grill, which was a block from home, get me a trick or two and take them in the back room there for a fast one. But I never brought nobody home like Gerald told that social worker I was doing.

"Then one night, just before Christmas, I think it was, me and Gerald got into a real big fight because the apartment hadn't been cleaned in days—maybe weeks, I don't know. Truthfully speaking, I'm not much of a housekeeper, and a little dirt and stuff don't bother me none. I remember there were shitty diapers all over the place, even in the kitchen sink, and Gerald said they made him so sick to his stomach, he couldn't eat.

"I said something like 'poor baby,' and if he wanted it cleaned up, he could do it himself. That's when it happened. He grabbed me by the hair and threw me clear across the room. Now, I knew better than to fuck with Gerald when he was mad, but I got to admit I'm a pretty good fighter for a woman, and don't mind a little domestic brawl now and then. Fact is, when I was younger, I'd start a battle with a new guy just to see if he was a real man, and how much shit he'd take from a woman.

"Anyway, I grabbed a big glass ashtray and hit Gerald right in the eye. He pulled his switchblade knife and slashed at my throat. I jumped back just in time, but he put a two-inch gash on the side of my neck. And that was *it!* Good sex or not, I wasn't about to get killed for a pecker, even his!

"So I ran down to the Norway Bar and called my dad and three brothers. They came over and ran Gerald off, but they had to point a shotgun at him to do it. I mean, Gerald Gallego was no coward!

"But Gerald paid me back . . . boy, did he ever! The bastard took our daughter away from me! I'll never understand how a man with Gerald's background and criminal record could legally take a child from its natural mother, but he done it. I mean, here he is, on parole and all, and he goes to the child welfare people and they gave him a free lawyer! The next thing I know, a man and a woman from there bust in one night, throw a court order in my lap and walk out with her. They were real smart-mouthed and insulting. The woman said the apartment was the filthiest place she'd ever seen, and that any self-respecting hog wouldn't live there.

"I never laid eyes on that kid again. Gerald hid her at one of his goddamned relative's, I think his mother, and I was afraid to look for her. I tried to get social welfare to give *me* a free lawyer, but they wouldn't do it. I never had any money, so I just gave up."

The child would be the one known later in court records as Mary Ellen, Gerald's lover-daughter. How Gerald ever managed to obtain full and permanent custody of her boggles the legal mind.

The social worker who was directly responsible for removing Mary Ellen from the custody of her natural mother, without so much as visitation rights, wrote the following report to the judge who would decide whether Gerald, a sixteen-year-old ex-convict and career criminal without a job or a home, would be awarded custody of the ten-month-old baby:

". . . Gallego seems genuinely concerned about his daughter, and when discussing her, he becomes fearful of losing custody and breaks into tears. He says that he wants to be a daddy so bad it's painful when he looks at his little girl. Mr. Gallego, in direct contrast to the natural mother, is polite, neat and clean, well-dressed, and entirely cooperative with this investigator. It is my professional opinion that Mr. Gallego needs the responsibility of this child, and that she will help in rehabilitating him, and will contribute greatly in shaping Mr. Gallego's future life . . ." And indeed Mary Ellen did—in a roundabout way.

The day he was awarded full and permanent custody of Mary Ellen, Gerald shipped her off to his mother and didn't see her again until she was six years old—at which time Gerald decided that she was just ripe to have sex with him.

Chapter 19

In The Wrong Place At The Wrong Time

Gerald and Charlene didn't really get to enjoy the euphoric aftermath of their ninth killing. They were still discussing it and trying to decide how good Betty had been as a love slave when the news reached them that the bodies of Sharon and Tracy had been found and ID'd.

On the morning of Tuesday, July 1, 1980, a family had been picnicking in Limerick Canyon, Nevada. At around ten o'clock A.M. they heard their dog barking down the hill in the dry creekbed. Fearing that the beloved family pet might be challenging a rattlesnake, they rushed down to call it off. The sand was still flying as the busy dog vigorously dug under a large log. While the now amused family watched, their pet dragged a human arm out of the sand, turned, and triumphantly brought the grisly trophy over to his people, dropped it at their feet, then looked up happily, waiting for the expected pat on his head and a "good boy!"

A few days later Sharon's skeleton was ID'd in the morgue from dental records. The cops finally put the girls together as friends, then identified the bones of Tracy. None of their personal effects were recovered.

When word of the discovery reached Gerald and Charlene, they decided to take another trip to Oregon. Even though there was no indication in the newspaper report that any evidence linked them or anyone else to the bodies, Gerald figured it couldn't hurt to make themselves unavailable for a while. He ordered Charlene to pack the van again and they hit the road. They wandered through Oregon, Washington, and Montana, then down to Idaho, camping and fishing along the way while keeping an eye open for possible targets. But they didn't see any, not even a female hitchhiker. Charlene called her parents collect every other day, just to let them know where she was and to check surreptitiously whether anyone was asking about them. When it appeared to be safe, after a relaxing month on the road, they went home.

When they pulled into the driveway, they saw a man sitting on the front porch, dozing and smoking a cigarette. He introduced himself as a missing-persons cop. He wanted to know if they remembered being in the Boat Inn on the night of July 17. Gerald asked the cop why he wanted to know, and he said it seemed that the woman bartender had disappeared that night and hadn't been seen since.

"Yeah, we were there," Gerald told the cop, "drinking and playing pool. But I don't remember much 'cause we got real drunk and . . ."

"How about you?" The cop interrupted impatiently and directed his attention to Charlene.

"I'ma . . . I'ma—hic—I don't 'member anything either," Charlene gasped.

"You talk to the woman?"

"Hic—I might have . . . I mean, we ordered lotsa drinks . . ."

"She say anything about meeting someone after work?"

"Unh-uh. Not to me—hic—she didn't."

"Me either," Gerald said. "I don't remember talking to her at all. Did I, babe?"

"Unh-uh."

"Then you can't recall anything because you were both under the influence?"

"Yeah, I guess," Gerald said, and Charlene nodded vigorously.

"Did you see or hear anything suspicious, I mean like someone else talking about the woman?"

"Naw," Gerald answered, "but I wasn't really in shape to hear much . . . and like I said, I never paid no attention to her at all."

"Okay." The cop shrugged his shoulders and put away his notebook. These two were his last interview before deep-sixing the case. "Sorry to have bothered you. Here's my card on the off-chance you think of something later. It'll probably turn out that she took off with some guy and just forgot to check in."

"You and them fucking hiccups," Gerald growled at Charlene from where he lay on the couch, alternately watching Road Runner cartoons and glaring at her sitting on the floor in a corner sipping gin. "That cop was either stupid as hell, or he was shining us on. I mean, a fucking *fool* would've known you was lying."

"I couldn't help it, Daddy," Charlene whined. "You know I get 'em when I'm scared. Anyway, I don't think he's got a thing . . ."

"Yeah? Well, I'm not so sure. Course I'm not smart like you, but I think we oughta hit the road for a while."

Charlene slumped and rolled her eyes in disgust. She was sick and tired of living out of the van, camping and sleeping with millions of chiggers, spiders, and other bugs that always gnawed and sucked on her but wouldn't touch Gerald if they were starving to death. (Charlene figured it was because they couldn't stand his rotten blood.) And she had had more than enough of squatting down to relieve herself in scratchy grass, then jumping up half-finished because a stick looked like a snake and scared the hell out of her.

"I'm not going," Charlene said belligerently. "You wanna go, go on! I'll stay with Daddy and Mama until you come back."

"Oh yeah?" Gerald was instantly suspicious—of what he wasn't sure, but it was totally out of character for Charlene to challenge such decisions.

"Yeah! Listen, Daddy, that cop said he was closing the case . . . I mean if he had anything, wouldn't he have pressed it, or read us our rights or something?"

"Maybe," Gerald conceded reluctantly, "but I'm still not sure. I got a feeling . . . well, okay, we stay."

"Thanks, Daddy," Charlene said, relieved. It wasn't only the bugs and squatting in the woods that made her want to stay home. She was pushing six months' pregnant; because she was so tiny and Gerald Jr. was growing like a baby elephant, Charlene was beginning to feel very awkward. She found it a real struggle just getting in and out of the van. She imagined that she was like most women she'd talked to who were this far along: they just wanted to make their nest and stay in it until the baby arrived.

"Well, if you weren't knocked up, I'd go. And you'd come along—or else. But out of consideration for you . . .

"Listen, baby, I think we'd better get rid of the van. I don't like it no more."

"I been thinking that ever since we . . . you know, did that girl in Oregon. I know someone saw us up there. And we've used it eight times around here."

"If you felt that way, why didn't you say so?" Gerald demanded.

"What for?" Charlene snapped. "You wouldn't have paid any attention to me!"

"You better watch that mouth of yours, cunt," Gerald shouted, sitting up and glaring at her, "you keep smart-talking me, and you're gonna need some new front teeth!"

"I'm sorry, Daddy," Charlene murmured, properly contrite. "You wanna blowjob?"

"No, goddamit! Is that all you ever think about? Get me the

phone. I'm gonna put a For Sale ad in the *Pennysaver* and get rid of that fucking hard-luck van."

Charlene sat as quietly and unobtrusively as possible while Gerald made his phone call. She knew that he was very agitated, even fearful. The blowjob offer had been made only to calm him down if that was what he needed. Lately, she hadn't been interested in any kind of sex with Daddy Gerald, though she was always careful to make herself appear to be ready and available. It had come to the point where she couldn't have an orgasm with Gerald unless a love slave was involved. Charlene was far from pleased at this unexpected turn of events, because she'd always enjoyed making love to Gerald, even when she'd had to work like a sled dog to help him get an erection. Like all the other bizarre circumstances that had shaped her life over the years, she accepted the fact that without the stimulation, danger, and excitement of the love slaves, her days and nights of normal sex with Daddy Gerald seemed to be over.

The van was sold almost immediately to a couple in Orangevale. They offered a reasonable price, and Gerald and Charlene were happy to be rid of the vehicle that had served them so well as a traveling house of horrors. But Charlene quickly got very pissed off when Gerald took the money and disappeared for a couple of days. Upon his return, Gerald had pecker tracks all over the front of his pants. Nevertheless, Charlene let him throw her big-bellied body in the sack and make love to her for several hours. She even faked a few squealing orgasms while Gerald whispered "Mary Ellen" in her ear again, just like he did the last time when he'd vanished with the Big Swede's money. The obvious pecker track around his fly made Charlene real mad, but she didn't challenge Gerald's explanation that he'd spilled a bowl of oatmeal in his lap when he'd stopped for breakfast.

"Yeah?" she had commented cautiously. "You could have fooled me . . . it looks like you were fucking with your pants on and got pussy juice and come all over the front."

Gerald snorted and shook his head, but didn't deny it.

By the end of September they were at each other's throats again. Charlene got bigger and more uncomfortable, and Gerald became even more morose and short-tempered. They had numerous battles, made up, then fought again. They went out almost every evening that month prowling for victims, but every prospect was either rejected by Gerald, or something else came up that forced them to abort their planned attack.

On the night of October 1, during a pitched verbal squabble with Gerald, Charlene fainted. When she came to, she went into a gurgling, slobbering, crazy-eyed hysteria. A shaken Gerald finally calmed her down to some semblance of normalcy, but she went to a fit of hiccuping that lasted for hours.

"Oh! God! Daddy!" she would scream every few minutes. "I got to have it! I just gotta have it!"

Gerald didn't ask what "it" was because he knew. He wanted it as much as she did. He was well aware that both of them were on the ragged edge of a frenetic sexual hysteria, and that sooner or later it would cause them to make that final, fatal mistake.

On the evening of Saturday, November 1, 1980, Gerald and Charlene went out on what was to be their last hunt for love slaves. It was a bone-chilling cold night with patches of fog hanging over the city of Sacramento like ghostly gray shrouds.

"Daddy, we've just got to get at least one," Charlene said to a nodding, grim-faced Gerald as she huddled next to him in the Olds. "I mean, I'm seven months' along and in a couple of weeks I can't hunt any more, much less enjoy it if we catch one . . . we gotta do it one more time, just to tide us over until the baby is born."

They prowled all the usual teenage hangouts, then residential streets, and finally even skid row without even a nibble. They were both so nervous, frustrated, and angry Gerald swore he'd grab the first female in sight, no matter how high the risk.

"Let's go back to Arden Park and try Restaurant Row," Gerald suggested after another hour.

"Okay, but it's awfully close to home," Charlene said. Arden Park is an exclusive area near North Sacramento, where Charlene's parents happened to live.

At approximately 1:00 A.M., after six hours of frenzied hunting, the silver-gray Olds, with lights out, cruised slowly and silently through the huge, dimly lit, foggy parking lot near the Carousel Restaurant. There were dozens of cars still parked around the well-known eatery, and Gerald stopped to read a cloth banner hanging over the door: "WELCOME TO SIGMA PHI EPSILON FRATERNITY FOUNDERS' DAY PARTY."

Charlene suddenly wished that she'd gone to college. If she had, she'd belong to an exclusive sorority like Sigma Phi, and she'd be in a place like the Carousel, dressed in a beautiful gown, dancing with a handsome, wealthy, frat brother . . .

"There's two!" Gerald's harsh whisper brought Charlene back to reality with a heart-pounding rush.

"One's a guy," Charlene whispered back.

"Yeah . . . And I don't like that cunt. Her tits are too big."

They sat there in the darkness, watching a tall young man walking arm-in-arm with a blond girl dressed in an ankle-length formal gown. The man bent his head and kissed the smiling girl, then patted her ample rear.

"Let 'em go," Gerald said, watching as the couple got into a car and drove away.

Five minutes later, they saw another couple walking slowly across the parking lot, then passing under a light. The girl was small with long blond hair and a slim body; she looked like a teenager even in the silk-ruffled blue evening dress. The man was of medium height, dressed in a dark tuxedo, and kept his arm around the girl's waist. Gerald waited until they stopped at a small Honda Civic parked in one of the darkest spots on the lot. When the man unlocked the door and reached inside, Gerald shot the Olds forward to within a foot of his targets. The young couple were so interested in each other, they didn't even notice the Olds until Charlene leaped out and shoved her .25

pistol under the man's nose. Gerald slid over to the passenger side, leaned out the open window, pointed his .357 Magnum at the girl, and whispered, "Get your asses in this car. You're being kidnapped. Come on, get in!"

Charlene, dressed in a thigh-length, loose-fitting ski jacket over dark slacks, snatched the keys from the boy's hand and threw them under the Honda.

"Look," the young man said in a normal voice, "take me and leave Mary here . . . she won't say a word . . ."

"Shut the fuck up," Charlene snapped. "Get in the backseat, goddamit. NOW, or I'll blow her fucking brains out!"

The couple got in and had barely sat down when a very tall, powerfully built young man walked up to the car.

"What's going on?" He asked, sitting down on the front seat beside Gerald.

"Stay out of this," the man in the back told him in a tense voice. "Go home and get away from here. I don't need you."

"Who are you?" Gerald asked, totally taken aback by the intrusion.

"I'm a frat brother of Craig's."

"Yeah? Well, take a hike, asshole," Gerald growled.

Then Charlene ran around to the door and grabbed the frat brother's elbow. "Get out of my car, motherfucker," she hissed like an angry tiger. "Come on, get out, you cocksucker!"

The frat brother got out and Charlene slid behind the wheel. "Hold it a minute," the big man said, catching Charlene by her arm. "Hold it . . . I want to talk . . ."

Then the five-foot-tall Charlene, seven months' pregnant, leaped out of the car, turned, and hit him with a right cross to the chin, knocking the six-foot-six, two-hundred-fifty-pound college football player to the pavement. (He had quite a few beers in him already and Charlene must have landed a lucky punch!)

Charlene then slid under the wheel again, backed the Olds up, then shot it forward, burning rubber. The frat brother, still dizzy from the unexpected punch, looked at the license plate number, ROV-240, and memorized it as the car disappeared into the fog. The frat brother was probably the luckiest man in the world that night—he had faced Gerald Gallego on a rampaging hunting expedition and lived to tell about it.

With their two captives in the back seat, Gerald and Charlene drove across the American River bridge into Sacramento, down Sixteenth Street to Capitol Avenue, then turned left. At Broadway, Capitol becomes Folsom Boulevard, which is the start of US Highway 50.

They headed some thirty miles east down this four-lane freeway toward Carson City, Nevada to a large recreation area called Bass Lake. The lake doesn't have any bass, but people come out to rent row boats, picnic, and enjoy the country atmosphere of the Sierra mountain foothills.

Charlene was driving and Gerald sat turned in the front seat, covering the prisoners with the .25 he'd taken from Charlene.

"What're your names?" Gerald asked politely, looking at the man.

"I'm Craig Miller and she's Mary Beth Sowers. What're you going to do with us?"

"I'm thinking of robbing you and leaving you barefoot out here in the boondocks to give us time to get away," Gerald said in his most friendly voice, "we were gonna kidnap you, but dingaling here thought you were somebody else. Looks like we got the wrong couple."

"I have a few dollars in my pocket, but we're sure not worth kidnapping," Miller said, so relieved that his voice cracked like a nervous teenager.

"We sure aren't," Mary agreed with a nervous giggle, "I have about ten—"

"Just shut the fuck up," Gerald ordered, "I'll find out how much money you got. Turn here!"

Charlene took a left off the freeway onto a paved road with a sign pointing toward Bass Lake. She drove through the deserted campground, passing darkened picnic tables, barbecue stoves, and rusty trash cans. She turned onto a dirt road, continued driving for ten minutes, then stopped in the middle of a small grassy cow pasture. The early morning fog hung low to the ground here, and it was cold and damp.

"Take your shoes off—both of you," Gerald told the captives. "All right, YOU", he indicated Miller with the barrel of the .25 pistol. "Get out and stand in front of the car. Watch her," Gerald told Charlene, who took the .357 Magnum from her purse and covered the girl. Miller was standing by the right front headlight, and Gerald stood with the right front door open, his left foot inside the car, his right on the ground.

"You wanna fuck this guy?" Gerald asked Charlene.

"No. Get it over with."

KERWHACK! KERWHACK! KERWHACK! The shots echoed around the fog-shrouded cow pasture as Gerald fired three nearly simultaneous rounds from the little .25 semiautomatic. Craig Miller fell, hitting the dirt road on his face.

"Oh God!" Mary moaned from the back seat, covering her face with her hands.

A coroner's photograph of the body would indicate that Miller took those three bullets, fired from a distance of about twelve feet, in a four-inch group around the heart, probably killing him within thirty to sixty seconds.

Gerald got into the backseat and put his arms around Mary Beth Sowers. "You're gonna be my little Mary Ellen tonight!" He said happily.

"We'd better do it here," Charlene told him. "It's getting late."

"No. Not after those shots. Let's go home."

At around 2:30 A.M., Charlene parked in front of 2067 Blue-bird Lane. Despite repeated assurances from both her captors, the victim must have realized that they intended to kill her. She knew their car, their faces, and now where they lived. Placing a palm over her mouth, Gerald helped Mary out of the Olds while Charlene ran ahead and unlocked the front door. She came back and helped Gerald half-carry, half-drag their captive into the bedroom. Charlene rushed around turning on all the lights, then checked the closed window shades and drapes—perhaps recalling her Peeping Tom days.

"Jesus, get her clothes off," Charlene whispered. "I can't wait any longer."

The sexual assault upon the Gallego's victim was frenzied, predatory, and vicious. She was sodomized while Gerald kept his hand over her mouth to silence the screams. She was forced to endure the usual fellatio and cunnilingus and nipple-biting. After an hour, Charlene gave it up because her big belly got in the way of her sexual acrobatics. She was totally exhausted, temporally satiated, and sleepy. She told Gerald to enjoy himself as long as he wanted, then pulled a rocking chair up to the open bedroom door, took out her violin and played a beautiful rendition of Brahms' *Lullaby* as she alternately dozed and watched Daddy Gerald vigorously molesting the victim while repeating, ". . . Mary Ellen, my sweet Mary Ellen . . ."

At approximately 4:00 A.M., Charlene and Gerald left 2067 Bluebird Lane in the Olds with Mary Sowers in the back seat. Charlene followed Gerald's directions and drove north toward US 80. Some fifteen miles from Sacramento, they turned into Greenback Lane, followed it to Sierra Boulevard, then turned left. Twenty miles later Charlene took another left onto a deserted road full of potholes with the pretentious name of Woodsdale Court. They were less than two miles from a one-street town called Loomis. This had been gold country in the old days, and the entire area was still filled with dredge holes, ditches, and other deep scars left by prospectors. Here Charlene parked and turned to Gerald, who sat with his arm protectively around an almost catatonic Mary Sowers.

"This the place you meant?" she asked.

"Yeah. You feel like doing it to her again?"

"Are you fucking crazy?" Charlene screamed. "It's almost daylight! Take care of the little rich-bitch and let's get out of here before some farmer sees us!"

"Why don't *you* do it this time?"

"No! Come on, Daddy, let's go."

Gerald carried Mary Beth Sowers, dressed in her blue evening gown, to a shallow ditch. By this time, she was too dazed to put up a struggle. Gerald dropped to his knees, lowered her into the hole, then shot her three times in the head. The autopsy would later reveal that she had suffered the same type of injuries as Gerald and Charlene's previous sex-slave victims—ripped anus, chewed nipples, and of course the head wounds.

If the FBI statistics on serial killers are correct—and they probably are—ninety-eight percent of such killer's victims are ". . . anonymous nonentities who insist upon going in harm's way and have no connection with their killers . . ." In the case of Craig Miller and Mary Beth Sowers, they indeed had no connection with their killers, but they were certainly far from nonentities going in harm's way. According to Deputy Probation officer Mary Frey, who would handle the background investigation of the Gallegos and their victims for the Contra Costa County Superior Court, ". . . if anyone happened to be in the wrong place at the wrong time, it was Craig Miller and Mary Beth Sowers . . ."

Miller was twenty-two, a senior honor student at California State University at Sacramento. He was vice-president of his Sigma Phi Epsilon fraternity, 1979 Man of the Year, a member of the American Marketing Association, and had been offered a full partnership in a prestigious advertising company some seven months before he was to graduate from college. He was a young man who knew where he was going and how to get there. He had family, friends, ambition, and the brains to exploit these assets. In addition, he was engaged to a pretty, twenty-one-year-old blond, Mary Beth Sowers, who had been runner-up for Miss Shasta County.

Mary Beth was the daughter of Harold and Cecily Sowers, and her father was a prominent nuclear physicist from Redwood City, California. She was a senior finance major and honor student at CSUS, a member of Alpha Chi Omega sorority, and like Miller, had been offered a management job with a financial firm seven months before graduation. She was an intelligent, strong-willed individual, always active, always looking for advancement. They were considered by everyone who knew them to be the All-American couple, two young adults who were certain to succeed.

Gerald and Charlene Gallego had finally made the fatal mistake that most sociopaths invariably make either through arrogance or choice—that is, either for the thrill of raising the risk factor or, as some might say, through pure stupidity. They had chosen two victims who were not freeway runners, dopers, welfare recipients, or nonentities. And those two victims would bring the wrath of society as well as a very hostile press down upon their heads with all the power of a biblical lightning bolt.

Chapter 20

The Escape

Gerald and Charlene were lying side-by-side in the bedroom at 2067 Bluebird Lane, shivering and shaking and holding hands as the cold sweat of pure terror seeped from their pores, all the while whimpering like two orphans lost in the forest. It had taken several hours for the euphoria to subside and reality to descend on their heads like a black fog.

"Oh Lord!" Charlene wailed in Gerald's ear, "that big guy got our license number! Oh, Daddy, I'm so scared!"

"Me too, baby," Gerald blubbered and snuffled, "it just ain't fair . . . I mean, why'd he have to come up and stick his nose in our business? We didn't bother him!"

"I know it, Daddy. Oh, I wish you'd have shot him!"

"I wanted to, but I couldn't do it in that parking lot."

"Oh, what're we gonna do?" Charlene screeched in Gerald's ear, gripping his hand so hard he squealed in pain.

"I don't know . . . I'm too scared to think . . . Jesus, leggo my hand!" Gerald sat up and blew his nose on the sheet. "Listen,

baby, first thing is you better get the Olds cleaned up, then this
bedroom. That'll give me time to think."

Happy to have a task to occupy herself, Charlene leaped up
and went to work, vigorously cleaning the entire house like a
Dutch maid. She even scrubbed the walls in case Mary Beth
Sowers touched them. When she'd washed and vacuumed the
Olds, they drove to the Sacramento River, where Gerald threw
the .25 pistol he'd used to kill Miller and Sowers into the muddy
brown water. They returned home and put all their dirty
clothes, including the things they'd worn the night before, into
a laundry bag, then headed for Charlene's parents' house to use
their washer and dryer, because, Gerald said, they shouldn't be
seen washing clothes at a laundromat. Charlene didn't think
that it mattered what they did, because when those two society-
types failed to pop up somewhere, the big guy was bound to go
to the police and tell them his story, and back it up with the
license number of her Olds. And then, as Daddy Gerald was
fond of saying, they'd truly be lip-deep in shit.

Charlene parked a block from her parents' house and they
walked down the street, Gerald carrying the stuffed laundry sack
over his shoulder like some sneaky wino bagman. They were too
upset to notice a stripped-down four-door sedan sitting in front
of the house as they went down the driveway to the back entrance. Mercedes opened the door before they knocked, and
when Charlene saw her mother's face, she knew that she and
Daddy Gerald were already over their heads in shit, that their
days and nights of rape and murder were finished.

"The cops are here," Mercedes whispered. "Get out—go
hide and call me later." She shut the door before Charlene
could ask any questions.

Gerald and Charlene hustled back to the car and drove to a
gas station, where he ordered her to go back to the house and
find out exactly what the cops wanted.

"It could be about that old warrant out for me in Butte
County," Gerald said, then added hopefully, "I'll bet that's it."

"I dunno, Daddy, I got a bad feeling about this . . ."

"Never mind that. Just watch yourself. If there's two cops, they'll play good-guy/bad-guy with you, so don't tell them nothing. Just say we went to the movies, then got drunk and you don't remember a thing. Got it?"

"Yeah," Charlene said. "Call me at the house in thirty minutes. I should know what they want by then."

As Charlene drove to her parents' home, she knew in her own mind that it was very unlikely the cops would be out on a Sunday morning lookout for Gerald on a two-year-old warrant from Butte County. She made up her mind at that moment that if she was arrested, she would protect Daddy Gerald no matter what, even if they kept her in jail for a thousand years.

While Gerald and Charlene were disposing of the gun and scrubbing the walls of their apartment and the inside of the Olds, the fraternity brothers and sorority sisters were having a very hard time convincing the police to pay attention to their story that their two friends, Craig and Mary Beth, had been kidnapped.

"Can't take a missing-person report until the subject has been gone twenty-four hours," they were informed by the desk cop.

"But they've been kidnapped!"

"Yeah? How do you know? Maybe they just drove off with someone to buy a six-pack." The cop didn't really give a fuck one way or the other, and he couldn't stop himself from yawning in their earnest little collegiate faces.

Eventually the word filtered down the chain of command that the missing couple were the son and daughter of some prominent community members and something had better be done that would look good on the eleven o'clock TV news. Even with that edict, it was noon before the police decided to listen, and put the license number into their computer for a DMV check. The computer kicked out the information that plate number

ROV-240 was a 1977 Oldsmobile Cutlass, registered to a Charles and/or Mercedes Williams at 4233 Berrendo Drive, Arden Park, California. A fast check on the Williams' drivers' licenses indicated that they were a middle-aged couple whose photos and descriptions didn't remotely match those of the young man and woman driving the Olds in the Carousel parking lot. The eager frat brother confirmed they were not the same people. Now, the police *were* interested in a possible stolen car used in a kidnapping, so they sent two detectives out to contact the owners of the Olds. The detectives arrived at 4233 Berrendo Drive at around 2:00 P.M., Sunday, November 2, 1980.

Mr. and Mrs. Williams said that the car actually belonged to their daughter, Mrs. Charlene Feil, who lived with her husband, Steven Robert Feil, at 2067 Bluebird Lane in North Sacramento. They said they had no idea where the car or their daughter had been the night before, or where she was now. At that very moment, like a scene from an Agatha Christie novel, the silver 1977 Oldsmobile in question pulled up in front of the house, and a young blond woman got out and walked slowly up to the door. If Godzilla had come in their front door, the Williams couldn't have been more surprised. The cops, with one glance, made Charlene as the female who had smacked the frat brother and was driving the Olds that carried Miller and Sowers away from the Carousel parking lot. Only one thing surprised the hell out of them—this female was in the latter stages of pregnancy, and there'd been no mention of that in the report.

"This is our daughter, Charlene Feil," Mercedes mumbled to the detectives.

In response to the question about her whereabouts the previous night, Charlene answered that she had been so drunk she couldn't remember where she, her husband, or the Olds had been. "Far as I know, we went to the movies and out drinking, but I can't remember where. And anyway, we weren't driving the Olds. We took my husband's Triumph."

Charlene sat on the couch, lying and denying to the cops until the phone rang. "That's my grandma," Charlene said, jumping up and hurrying for the kitchen phone. "I told her to call me here."

"It's me, baby." Gerald's voice was tense and hoarse.

"It isn't about Mary Ellen," Charlene whispered, "but I don't think they've got much."

"They read you your rights before they started talking to you?"

"No."

"Okay, then they ain't gonna arrest you right now. Soon as they leave, pick me up at the Red Sails. I'll be in the booth you used to sit in."

"Okay, Daddy," Charlene whispered, then hung up the phone, whirled, and started vomiting in the kitchen sink.

"She's pregnant and hung over," Mercedes explained to the cops. "I'll have to ask you to leave and come back later if you want to talk to her some more."

Outside the cops spotted a red Triumph parked at the far end of the driveway, noted the license number, checked out the Olds, then drove to 2067 Bluebird Lane to talk with Steven Robert Feil. No one was home. As they were driving away, a call came in notifying them that the body of Craig Miller had been found by a hunter, lying in a cow pasture near Bass Lake.

Charlene picked Gerald up at the bar and filled him in on what the cops had said.

"We gotta haul ass," said Gerald, in what was very likely the understatement of his life.

"Maybe we can go to your mother's place in Chico," Charlene suggested. But Gerald rejected the idea, figuring it would be the first place they'd look. (Furthermore, Ed Davies would probably shoot him on sight.)

"How about Oregon?" Charlene asked desperately, hoping Gerald would come up with his usual miracle.

"Nope. Too many enemies up there. We'll just head east, and work our way down to Texas. We'll ditch the Olds in Reno, then take a bus. How much money you got?"

"About a hundred dollars. Where's the fifteen thousand hidden?"

"No place I can get to it now. When we get underground in Texas, I'll have someone bring it to us. But we gotta have more money and some warm clothes. Call your mom and tell her to bring it to us at that bar in Orangevale—you know the one."

At around 7:00 P.M., good old Mom and Dad met Gerald and Charlene at the bar, handed over a few dollars and some warm clothes they'd just bought, begged them not to run, then wished them Godspeed and waved good-bye as they drove off into the foggy night.

At about the same time that Gerald and Charlene were meeting her parents, the cops were running a check on the red Triumph that was registered to Steven Robert Feil. They showed a driver's license photo of Feil to the frat brother who immediately ID'd him as the man in the Olds. The police rushed back to Berrendo Drive, but of course the lovebirds had flown. They spoke to Charlene's parents, and Mr. Williams, hoping it would get his daughter a break, told them that his son-in-law's true name was Gerald Armond Gallego.

When the cops checked that name through the computer and took a look at Gerald's rap sheet, they immediately issued a suspicion of murder and kidnapping APB for both Gallegos, calling them armed and dangerous. The A&D was added to the APB after a search of the Bluebird Lane place, where the police found a .357 Magnum revolver, a .25 semiauto pistol and a .223 AR-15 rifle with twenty rounds in the clip. A fast check with the California Department of Justice showed that the weapons had been purchased by Charlene Adelle Williams at a sporting goods store in North Sacramento. The APB turned out to be completely useless because the sophisticated multimillion-dollar police communications system went down for the afternoon, cutting off all messages to the California Highway Patrol and the sheriff's stations. When it finally came on line again, Gerald and Charlene were long gone.

The next morning, Mr. and Mrs. Williams contacted the police and informed them that their daughter had called home to tell them that neither she or Gerald knew anything about a murder, they fled because of that outstanding warrant on Gerald up in Butte County. The cops weren't buying a dime's worth of that story, especially when the Williams went on to say that they had hired an attorney to represent their daughter, and any further questions would have to go through him. The cops then decided to bring the FBI into the case because the suspects had apparently crossed a state line, making themselves federal fugitives in unlawful flight to avoid prosecution.

Between November 3 and 16, Mr. and Mrs. Williams received several phone calls from their daughter and Gerald, informing them that they would find the Olds in the Circus-Circus Casino parking lot in Reno. The FBI was aware of the calls, probably because the Williams' phone had been tapped after the families of the last two victims spoke to their local senator or congressman, who relayed information to the feds. The facts are that on the morning of Sunday, November 16, Mr. and Mrs. Williams left Berrendo Drive and headed north toward Reno. By the time their car had passed Roseville, twenty miles down the road, two teams of FBI agents were tailing them. The Williams passed Reno and continued on US 40 toward Salt Lake City, Utah. In the small town of Sparks, Nevada, they stopped briefly at a Western Union office, then headed back toward Sacramento. One FBI team continued the surveillance, while the other agents checked with Western Union. It seemed that Mr. and Mrs. Charles Williams had just wired $500 to their daughter, care of the Western Union office at 1818 Dodge Street in Omaha, Nebraska. The agents notified the Omaha FBI, which was to arrest the Gallegos, and because they were considered armed and dangerous, to use deadly force if necessary. The manner in which the Omaha FBI captured Gerald and Charlene would have made the late J. Edgar Hoover smile.

Chapter 21

The Beasts Are In Chains!

While the FBI was watching her parents, Charlene was boarding a bus for Salt Lake City with Gerald. They had one-way tickets and about thirty dollars in their pockets. Charlene wore thick slacks and a heavy, knee-length loose-fitting down jacket that hid her big belly completely. Gerald was dressed in dark wool pants and a nylon windbreaker. They looked exactly like all the other bus passengers—tired, worried, broke, and a little scruffy.

Charlene felt lethargic and sad as she sat staring gloomily out the window, watching the cold desert fly by. As they passed Humboldt Sink, she tried to see the turnoff that led to the spot where they'd buried the two girls in that sandy, lonely grave. Charlene wondered whether the coyotes had eaten them or whether they were still lying in the fetal position, back-to-stomach, under the cold, yellow desert moonlight. It doesn't really matter, she thought, we'll be seeing them pretty soon . . . I wonder if it hurts to die from poison gas? God, I hope not! I can't stand pain. She remembered the movie about Barbara

Graham with Susan Hayward starring. It sure looked awful, watching Hayward die in the gas chamber, choking and gasping for breath. Charlene involuntarily touched her throat and for a half-second, remembered how Helen and Betty had choked to death. But she wasn't really interested in their painful deaths; her thoughts switched quickly back to herself as she wondered what her body would look like when it was carried from the gas chamber. Gerald said that everyone crapped and pissed on themselves. I hope I don't, she thought. Daddy and Mama will bury me in a nice spot, I know that. I'd rather be with Daddy Gerald, but that won't happen. Poor Daddy Gerald will probably end up in Potter's Field alongside all the bums and derelicts, 'cause nobody'll ever claim his body.

By the time they'd reached Salt Lake City, Gerald had figured a way to get another set of IDs for both of them. He explained it to Charlene, and they went through the phone book and picked out twenty names. They called those people, saying they were working for the Republican Party and were trying to clarify some voter registration information—what's your full name and birth date, where were you born, what are your parents' names and birthdays. Within an hour, they had information on a man and woman who were born in Utah and close to their own age. Then they simply went down to the Bureau of Vital Statistics building and bought certified copies of those people's birth certificates. When they walked out of the building, they were both under cover of foolproof aliases—all they needed to do was to get hold of a car and apply for their drivers' licenses. Gerald said they'd do that the minute they got to Texas.

After picking up the 500 dollars from Charlene's parents, just what the couple did in Salt Lake City is anyone's guess. There would be some speculation that they committed a quick abduction-murder, but nothing came of that theory.

On Friday, November 14, Gerald and Charlene arrived in Omaha, Nebraska, at around noon and checked into the Hill Town Inn, nine blocks from the Western Union office at 1818

Dodge Street. Gerald registered them as Mr. and Mrs. Steven Galloway of Chico, California. He paid for a twenty-three-dollar-per-day room with a one-hundred-dollar bill.

"They seemed like nice, pleasant people," desk clerk Susan Urban said later. "They mostly ate at the motel restaurant, except for Sunday night, when they went out for sandwiches and ate them in their room." (The FBI found half-eaten egg salad sandwiches in the waste basket.)

"I didn't talk to the woman. She barely spoke a word the whole time. She'd come in the lobby every night and use the pay phone. I have no idea who she called, but she sure used a lot of quarters. I had to make change for her . . .

"No, I didn't know she was pregnant. She always wore that long baggy coat, and I couldn't tell at all. The man asked me if I knew of any jobs around, and if we had a monthly rate. One time, on Saturday, I think, he asked what kind of car I drove, and did I live around here. I just thought they were a nice young couple who'd moved to Omaha . . ."

What Urban didn't know was that the nice young couple had spent several hours watching her car, hoping to catch her outside long enough to kidnap her, steal the car, and kill her somewhere between Nebraska and Texas. Apparently Gerald didn't consider her as a potential love slave, but with Urban's car and forty-eight hours' headstart before she was missed, Gerald and Charlene could have been in Dallas and safely under cover. Then on Saturday night, November 15, Charlene made her last phone call home, instructing her parents to send $500 the next day so she could pick it up at Western Union on Monday morning.

Gerald liked to sleep late, and the morning of Monday, November 17, 1980, was no exception. By 11:00 A.M., several FBI agents and two interceptor cars had been in position around Dodge Street for three hours. They were waiting for Gerald and Charlene Gallego to pick up the $500 waiting for them at Western Union. At approximately 11:30 A.M., the agent standing at Seventeenth and Dodge saw Gerald and Charlene walking nonchalantly toward Western Union, holding hands and smiling at each other. The agent forgot his frigid feet, numb hands, and dripping nose as he felt a rush of adrenaline at the sight of his prey.

"Coming in," he whispered into the rover radio. "Hold it. They stopped. Male's walking north down the alley. Female's going into the office."

"All units stand by," the soft, whispered order came from his rover. "I'll take the female first when she's inside."

Charlene entered the Western Union office and walked briskly to the window and stated, "I'm Charlene Williams. You have some money for me."

The clerk looked at Charlene and nodded. Then Charlene heard a soft voice behind her ask, "Charlene?"

She turned, smiled and murmured sweetly, "Yes."

"FBI. You're under arrest for unlawful flight to avoid prosecution on a murder warrant. Just stand still, Charlene. I don't want to have to shoot you or the baby."

The man then spoke a two-word command into his rover: "Take him."

Charlene's knees unlocked and her body went limp at the word "FBI." She remembered thinking, I told the dumb Okie prick that the FBIs would get us.

Outside, one interceptor car sped around the block to head Gerald off as another turned into the alley behind him. Gerald saw the car coming toward him, but didn't appear to be aware of the other one behind him. He moved over against a brick wall and kept walking, his hands in the open by his sides. With a sudden burst of speed, the agents behind him slammed their car bumper into the wall six inches from Gerald's knees, blocking him from running forward, then opened the rear door to prevent his running backward. The driver jumped out, adrenaline pumping, shoved his shotgun muzzle against Gerald's nose and screamed, "FBI! FREEZE, COCKSUCKER! DON'T EVEN BLINK!"

"Okay, okay!" Gerald shouted as his hands went up with such speed and force his jacket and shirt ripped under his armpits.

"ONE MOVE AND I'LL BLOW YOUR HEAD OFF, COCK-SUCKER!"

The other interceptor car had arrived now, and six shotguns were pointed at Gerald as two agents threw him facedown on the cold, dirty pavement and cranked the irons on as tight as they could, then searched him very carefully. They clamped leg irons on their prisoner, tossed him bodily into the backseat, told him that he was under arrest for unlawful flight to avoid prosecution on a murder warrant, then meticulously read him his Miranda rights.

"You got the wrong man," Gerald protested. "I'm Steve Galloway!"

"Uh-huh," one agent snorted, "and I'm Prince Valiant."

"Yeah," another agent said, "and I'm J. Edgar Hoover . . . sit up straight, asshole, cause it's showtime and you're going to jail!"

Gerald wasn't sure that Charlene had been arrested until two hours later when US marshals brought him before a US magistrate in the federal building for a bail hearing. He saw her sitting between two female officers. She smiled at him briefly, then hung her head. The US attorney, apparently recognizing a pair of dangerous sociopaths when he saw them, demanded that bail be set at $1 million each.

"Your Honor," he pleaded, "when the FBI searched the defendants' motel room, they found birth certificates that were obtained under fraudulent and false pretenses. These two are, in the government's opinion, extremely dangerous and will run at the first opportunity. Also, there is a matter of another possible murder involvement here."

"Your Honor," one of the US marshals spoke up, "Mr. Gallego has flatly refused to allow us to book him. He won't let us take his prints or photo. He has refused to cooperate in any way, Your Honor."

"Your Honor," Gerald shouted, "I refused to cooperate cause the FBIs viciously jerked me off the street and cuffed me so tight the circulation was cut off!" Gerald held up his hands pleadingly. "On top of that, Your Honor, they verbally abused me—called me a cocksucker twice!"

The judge didn't comment on this accusation, but did set bail at $100,000 for each defendant, then ordered a hearing for the following day to decide if there was sufficient evidence to hold Gerald and Charlene until extradition was arranged.

"I never knew anything about any murder warrants out for me in California, Judge," Gerald told the court, gesticulating for emphasis, "and I'm ready to go back there and get things squared away, cause *I* myself have got nothing to hide."

"Then we aren't likely to have a difference of opinion tomorrow, Mr. Gallego," the judge said, and dismissed the court.

Gerald and Charlene were booked into the Douglas County Correctional Center. Director Joe Vitek said later that "They were real calm and casual. Well dressed, you know, not your hippie types at all. When we separated them, they kinda waved good-bye real sadlike to each other."

Back in California, when Lorraine Davies heard the news, she gushed, "Oh, thank heavens! I'm *so* relieved! Now the poor things can get to clearing themselves of those horrible accusations . . ."

The Williams family refused to say anything—probably because the cops were taking their house apart under a search warrant, looking for anything that might tie Gerald and Charlene to any number of unsolved crimes that the police were anxious to pin on someone. Who knew what those two little bloodthirsty fucks had been up to, or what the authorities might be able to tag them with? The cops believe that everyone is guilty of *something,* and were even looking at Charles and Mercedes Williams with a hopeful glint in their eyes.

The very same investigative reporter who had reported Gerald and Charlene's first murder, the one who'd offered Gerald her love, help, understanding, and everlasting friendship, looked into the camera that night, squinted her steely-blues, and proclaimed to her audience in a voice of biblical doom, "The beasts are in chains."

Chapter 22

The Final Betrayal

The arrest of Gerald and Charlene for the Craig Miller–Mary Beth Sowers kidnap-murder set off a news-gathering frenzy among TV and print media reporters. News teams from Los Angeles, San Francisco, Sacramento and the Midwest swarmed around the old Placerville courthouse like sharks circling a dying whale. When the foreign press arrived, it became frantic.

They screamed and demanded attention, they pushed and shoved and cursed each other. They jealously made obscene gestures behind the backs of top network anchormen and women from New York, who pulled up to the curb in stretch limousines, all dressed alike in imported English Burberry trenchcoats and mink trooper hats that they'd picked up while doing news spots in Moscow. The natives said that while it might be a little cold in Placerville, they didn't think it was necessary for them to dress like it was forty below. Two dozen TV reporters were trying to film their "exclusive" reports at the same time, all standing within ten feet of each other because

248

everyone wanted to use the picturesque old courthouse as back-ground. There were Americans, British, West Germans, French, Italians, Japanese, and assorted other foreigners in the group; most of them were forced to shoot all over again because their microphones picked up the babble of each other's conver-sations and reports loud and clear. One enterprising British chap left the mob and went down to the main street, where he saw a life-size dummy hanging on a rope over the sidewalk with a sign around its stretched neck that read: "Hangtown," which was what Placerville, which is located roughly 35 miles from Sacramento and is the seat of Placer County, had been called in the gold rush days when all the hangings in the area were carried out on that street in front of a cheering crowd. He finished his report with the hanging dummy as background, then spent a pleasant half-hour with a very elderly but spry lady named Ida Webb, who said that she had attended every criminal trial in Placerville since 1900.

"This is the best one since Blacky Lopez was convicted and got lynched on the same day back in 1910," she informed the British lad. "But oh my goodness, I'm really shocked at the way those reporters are carrying on, especially that pretty little Ori-ental girl from New York, well, you'd think she was so sweet and all, but heavens, I heard her tell that Mike something to go . . . well, I can't even *say* it!"

They day before Mary Beth Sowers' body was found, her father personally placed a call to the California attorney gen-eral, George Deukmejian, who would later become governor. Mr. Sowers informed the attorney general in no uncertain terms that due to the possibility that his daughter was still alive and hidden somewhere, the Gallegos had to be made to talk. His daughter's life was at stake, and those two devils had forfeited all rights and privileges when they kidnapped her. If Mr. Sowers meant that Gerald and Charlene should be put on the rack and tortured until they revealed his daughter's location, he probably wasn't the only one who felt exactly the same way. Most cer-

tainly there were many cops and other victims' families who
would have agreed with Mr. Sowers. Even the press didn't fault
him for his "vigilante" attitude. In fact, when the decomposed
body of Mary Sowers was found two days later, the media became even more frenzied. It was an outrage, they screeched,
when a prominent pair of Beautiful People from a wealthy and
socially upscale family were horribly murdered by a couple of
lowlifes like Gerald and Charlene Gallego.

With the media blitz over the Miller-Sowers case exploding,
and powerful politicians' phones starting to ring all over California, it is probable that the friends and relatives of Gerald and
Charlene's other victims found it a bit ironic or even unfair that
a bunch of poor, freeway-running doper kids had been totally
ignored by those same reporters and politicians when they had
been found equally dead. When Gerald and Charlene refused
to say a word to the media, the reporters just intensified their
efforts to get something on the pair. They found out about
Gerald's father's conviction and execution in Mississippi and
began leading with the "sins of the fathers" headlines. The
stories became so wild and inaccurate that many locals wondered if the reporters were attending the same court proceedings they were.

Gerald and Charlene were put in the old Placerville City Jail
to await a bail-and-arraignment hearing before a justice court
judge, and Charlene's high-powered criminal trial lawyer was
already in action. Gerald, having no money, was given a public
defender. Neither Gerald or Charlene would say a word to
anyone, including their attorneys. On Friday, November 21,
1980, Gerald and Charlene were brought into court through a
side door to avoid the two hundred or so reporters standing
elbow-to-elbow, hip-to-hip, in the narrow hallway of the one-
hundred-year-old courthouse. The judged ordered the courtroom door locked against most of the reporters until the hearing was over, but did allow a maximum crowd of spectators,
including the little old lady, Ida Webb, who used her best

straight-arm shove to negotiate the crowd and happily grabbed a front-row seat.

Gerald and Charlene were seated three chairs apart in the empty jury box; several deputy sheriffs took up watchful positions behind them. Gerald wore an orange jumpsuit and Charlene had on a blue denim jailhouse dress that hung on her like a sack. They stared around the courtroom for a few minutes with wide, frightened eyes, then looked at each other. Right then, as if on cue, Charlene suddenly screamed, "Why are you doing this to us?" The room froze into a dead silence.

"Yeah!" Gerald shouted, "we're not animals in a zoo! What happened to a fair trial? When do you bring in the lions?"

"You're treating my husband like a wild beast," Charlene moaned loudly, "putting chains on his legs and everything else." She dropped her head and began to wail.

"Yeah!" Gerald roared, "can't you give this poor girl a break? She can't take no more of this . . . she's about to become a mother!"

Charlene's lawyer rushed over and patted her shoulder. Her parents looked at their beloved daughter with tears in their eyes. When order was restored, the clerk stood and read the charges—one count of kidnapping and one count of first-degree murder against both defendants in that they had taken Craig Miller against his will, then killed him. Charlene's attorney entered a plea of not guilty on all charges. Gerald refused to plead; a plea of not guilty was entered on his behalf by the public defender for the record.

Then the People and the defense rose in turn to begin their verbal dance of life and death that would last almost thirty months.

The defense demanded Charlene's release on reasonable bail, claiming that she desperately needed treatment from her own gynecologist, and arguing that she was not an escape risk at all because she would be staying with her parents, who would put up the bail, and were present in the courtroom. The prosecution objected, claiming that both defendants were equally dangerous and escape-prone, which they had just demonstrated by running off to Omaha. The DA also reminded the court that the defendants were likely also involved in the murder of Mary Beth Sowers—to which the defense strongly objected, asking that the DA show proof of another murder before trying to charge his client with it.

The judge ordered both defendants held without bail, and set December 8 for a preliminary hearing.

The arraignment had been more or less cut-and-dried. But the preliminary hearing was something else again in that the DA would have to produce enough proof to connect the Gallegos directly with the kidnap-murder of Craig Miller. The only evidence the People had was flimsy and marshmallow-soft—a body with three bullet holes, a college kid witness who claimed to have seen Miller and Sowers in a car with the Gallegos, and two defendants who'd run like hell when the police came after them because they claimed to fear prosecution on another totally different charge. A judge might just believe their claim; on the other hand, there wasn't a single shred of hard, admissable evidence connecting either Gallego to that body. All Gerald and Charlene had to do was remain silent. The burden of proof was on the People.

Even after Mary's body was found, the DA wasn't much better off in terms of evidence. He now had six empty .25 pistol shells, three found near Miller and three with Sowers. Ballistics maintained all six were fired from the same gun, but they didn't match the .25 semiautomatic found in the defendants' home on Bluebird Lane. Of course, the DA *knew* they did it, but knowing wasn't worth the proverbial fart in a whirlwind. The DA had a very uncomfortable feeling that unless a miracle suddenly occurred, Gerald and Charlene Gallego were going to walk away from this particular kidnap-murder charge. If he'd known about the other eight victims, the DA might just have had a heart attack.

Another factor that made the DA even more certain that the Gallegos would walk was the local politicians' assertion that Placer County simply couldn't afford a trial of the magnitude that the Gallegos' would be. The state attorney general politely declined the offer to send down a special prosecutor, so the entire state could share in the expense. Instead, he suggested moving the trial over to Sacramento County, which could doubtless afford to pay for the whole thing. But it was unlikely the defendants could receive a fair trial anywhere in the Sacramento area because of massive pretrial publicity. Any judge there probably would be obliged to order a change of venue . . . and so on and so forth.

So, after the first blaze of exuberance and righteous anger, and the promise of career-building publicity, the prospects had faded and reality was setting in. It was all coming down to who could afford to try Gerald and Charlene. This kind of debate was good for the defendants, but it certainly appeared as if both the victims and the cause of justice were about to get the shaft.

Sure enough, at their preliminary hearing, the trial venue was shifted to Sacramento County. Gerald and Charlene were bound over without bail on first-degree-murder indictments in the killings of Craig Miller and Mary Beth Sowers. Even though the local DA felt bad about losing the case, he was happy that the killers were at least going to face trial.

Gerald was immediately transferred to the Sacramento County Jail, while Charlene was taken to the Rio Cosumnes Women's Correctional Center at Elk Grove. Rio Cosumnes was known by one and all who worked or served there as Rio Cunnilingus. It has a reputation among female cons as a very hard-time joint.

Every news reporter and sob sister from Bangkok to Berlin had attempted to obtain an exclusive personal interview with Charlene. All such requests were flatly denied.

When the door had finally slammed shut behind her at Rio Cosumnes, Charlene was relieved and happy that the spotlight was off her, and she could settle down to await the birth of little Gerald Armond Gallego Jr., who was due to arrive any day now.

Just after Christmas, Gerald was sitting in the high-power felony tank on the top floor of the Sacramento County Jail. He celled with a handsome, five-time-convicted bank robber named Amos Katz, who did easy time, was straight, humorous, and entertained Gerald for hours with true stories about his years in the bank-robbery business.

Gerald didn't like Katz very much because Amos was a high-class criminal like Gerald had always wanted to be, and he knew that his cellmate looked down on him as not much more than a petty drunkroller, regardless of all the publicity Gerald had received lately. Amos was a hard man to impress, and Gerald was very uncomfortable with criminals who were willing to put their lives on the line when they forcibly took money from honest citizens.

Gerald lay on his bunk taking stock of his present situation. All in all, things weren't too bad. Now that the intense publicity had subsided for the moment, he was breathing a lot easier. Gerald had been manipulating cops, shrinks, parole boards, and the prison system since he was ten years old, and he wasn't overly worried now. He knew that as long as he and Charlene kept their mouths shut, they'd never go to trial. A dozen motions and writs had been filed on his behalf, demanding he be released, the charges dropped, bail granted, claiming that his rights had been violated by everyone from Ronald Reagan to Jesus, or asking for a change of venue all the way to New York City and points in between.

Charlene had a motion filed demanding she be cut loose from Gerald and given a separate trial: let the state's case against her stand or fall on its own merits. A kindly judge had agreed to consider every single motion and writ that had been filed, and Gerald knew that it would take months until things were settled. Of course there were those other eight murders—and Gerald felt a cold chill flutter down his back when he thought of *that,* knowing only too well that all that stood between him and the gas chamber was Charlene's absolute silence. So far, Charlene seemed to be bearing up extremely well under the ordeal of her first incarceration, and she and Gerald had exchanged a half-dozen kited letters. In her last one, she'd written in a beautiful script, ". . . don't worry about me. I know exactly what to do. Just wanted you to know that the past three years were the happiest of my life and the most exciting . . . I can't wait to see our baby . . . I just know it'll be another beautiful Gerald Armond Gallego . . ."

Little Gerald Armond Gallego Jr. arrived on Saturday, January 17, 1981, and got his first look at the world via a hospital prison ward, where his mother lay exhausted on the narrow bed, chained to the wall by her right wrist. Two weeks later, the baby was picked up by his maternal grandmother and great-grandmother, and unless he has followed the proclivities of his father, paternal grandfather, and his great-grandpa Pullen, he's probably with them today, although no one will admit that the boy exists.

During the next ten months, Gerald and Charlene made numerous court appearances, a dozen motions were filed by both sides, and the two murderers rested comfortably in jail while the bodies of their victims, known and unknown, rotted in their lonely graves. A judge had clamped a gag order over the entire case, effectively cutting off all publicity, which would allow the public to forget about the whole thing by the time it reached a trial—if it ever did. By late October 1981, Gerald could sense that Charlene was slipping out of his control, that he was losing his influence over her. She hardly ever wrote him or sent messages by the visitors who also came to see him. What Gerald didn't know was that Charlene had gotten into some lesbian activities in jail, and that the authorities had replaced her black female lover-cellmate with a paid informer.

One night in late October, Gerald had a nightmare—a vision, really—of the round, malevolent, pale green gas chamber at

San Quentin Prison. He woke up wet with sweat, experiencing a cold terror he'd never known before. His mouth was so dry he couldn't even light a cigarette. It was at that moment Gerald finally realized he'd lost all control of Charlene, that she would turn on him when she felt the time was right, that the big heat was on, that he was going to need a lot of sympathy as well as a lot of luck in order to have even half a chance of beating that double kidnap-murder charge when she did decide to squeal.

Gerald thought of his dear old dad for the first time in many years. Now, if his father really had been an executed triple-murderer . . . and given his own background as an abused, neglected child, one of the poor, unskilled and unwashed—hell, the possibilities of what a few shrinks and a sympathetic judge and jury might do with that were unlimited. Gerald had seen it work countless times for countless cons. What with Charlene as the weak link in the chain that kept the gas chamber locked, Gerald knew he'd better get moving on the sympathy end. So he sat right down and wrote a letter to Mississippi Governor William Winter.

The letter was neatly printed, dated November 2, 1981—one year to the day that Gerald and Charlene had killed Craig Miller and Mary Beth Sowers. It read as follows:

> "*Dear Sir,*
>
> "*I come to you with a very special request. My father, Gerald Albert Gallego, was executed at your Penitentiary on March 3, 1955. It is my understanding he was executed in your gas chamber for killing two police.*
>
> "*I was raised in California by my mother, and while I was growing up, I would ask my mother about my father, and my mother would tell me he was killed in the war. To this day, my mother refuses to tell me anything. What information I received was from other people because my mother wouldn't tell me anything. I never even seen a picture of my father.*
>
> "*This has been on my mind most of my life. I have come to the point where I must understand how my father could take another life. If its true, its beyond my understanding.*
>
> "*I need to know just what kind of man he was. My grandmother has*

told me he was a good man, a kind man, then out of no where he became
a killer.

"Governor, I can not tell you how important this request is for me. I
now have a son, Gerald Armond Gallego Junior. For his sake, I must
have this information. I know your a busy man, but help me out.

> *Thank you. Respectfully, Gerald A. Gallego.*
> *620 H Street, Sacramento, Ca. 95814."*

Gerald didn't mention that this address was the Sacramento
County Jail—or that he was an inmate in it.

The letter was turned over to Christine Huston, chief of records for the Mississippi Prison System, and on January 18, 1982, she wrote the following reply:

"Dear Mister Gallego,

"The inner conflict you have suffered over the years is plainly evident
in your letter, and it is with much difficulty that I attempt to respond to
that need.

"I have personally reviewed your father's file and can offer no information as to background experiences, influences, or pressures that moulded
his behavior patterns. It is impossible to judge the measure of a man from
the two overt acts for which he paid full retribution.

"If we look at nothing but the cold facts, we would find that your
father was tried and convicted in the Circuit Court of Jackson County,
Pascagoula, Mississippi, on June 10, 1954, and was sentenced to death
for the murder of two policemen. At 2:00 P.M. on March 3, 1955, he
was executed in the gas chamber at the Maximum Security Unit, Parchman, Mississippi.

"Our records show that your father was a man of conscience. Before
his death, he professed a belief in God and begged the forgiveness of the
relatives of the slain men.

"This is the most difficult letter I have ever written, and I hope it will
bring you the peace of mind you have been seeking for so long.

"If you find disappointment in the cold facts, may you find comfort in
the thought that your father became a Christian before he died . . ."

"Hot fucking damn!" Gerald marveled aloud as he reread the
letter to the group of murderers and armed robbers with whom
he shared the high-power felony tank, "The stupid bastards fell

for it! She's so overcome with pity for me, you can almost see the tears on her letter! When the jury reads this letter about my poor dad, they're gonna cry their eyes out for me!"

"Sounds as if your dad went out like a real man," said Katz, the bank robber. "How about you, buddy? Can you match your old man's guts when the time comes?"

"They'll never get me nowhere near that gas chamber!" Gerald said, looking at Amos with ferocious eyes. "There's not a court system in the world that I can't beat!"

"Yeah? If you did what I think you did, and your old lady rolls over on you, you're a dead man, partner."

Gerald knew it was true, and while the chills rippled up his spine, he sat down to write the good-hearted woman in Mississippi a thank-you note—he just might need her again. His letter read as follows:

> *"Dear Ms. Huston,*
> *"I just received your letter and I could never tell you just how moved I was. The kindness and compassion of you and your governor is plainly evident.*
> *"I could never find the right words to thank you both. Myself and my son, Gerald Armond Gallego Junior, will always be grateful.*
> *"The words come hard right now. I would like to say I regreat the deeds of my father and I always will feel deep remorse for the two men he killed and there familys. My motives behind my request to you were very strong and real deep, and to explain them would take a livetime.*
> *"Again I thank you from the bottom of my heart and you will always be in my prayers. Your a very nice lady!*
> *Always, Gerald Gallego."*

Back in Rio Cosumnes, Charlene was getting sick and tired of doing endless dead time. Most of all, she was tired of waiting for Gerald to get on his white horse and take her off the hook by saying he'd forced her to help him with the kidnap-rape murders. He had promised to do that many times. She could still hear him saying, "Baby, if we're caught, I'll say I *made* you do it. That the whole thing was my idea . . ."

Daddy Gerald hadn't done that, and Charlene was pretty much convinced that he wasn't going to do it. On Sunday, July 27, 1981, she made a tentative feint at getting out of jail by announcing that she could claim Gerald killed Craig Miller and Mary Beth Sowers if the DA would agree to release her on bail. When her offer reached downtown, it was ignored. Then sometime in late April 1982, after sixteen months of doing dead time, still no closer to trial or freedom than the day she was arrested, with Gerald still stonewalling her by his total silence, Charlene made her move.

One version of the story is that she simply became terrified when she finally realized that Gerald had no intention of saving her by taking all the blame, and that she was going to be convicted right along with him. Even though only eight women had been executed in California over the past century, Charlene wasn't about to take a chance on becoming number nine. Another reason was that she'd heard from a reliable informant that Gerald had been funneling all that spare money to his daughter, including the $15,000 he'd stolen from the Big Swede, as well as the proceeds of the van sale, and that he'd allegedly told someone that he intended to take out a $50,000 double indemnity life insurance policy on Charlene, stage a lethal accident, collect, then go to Texas with his daughter and live happily ever after.

Her version was that ". . . in the loneliness of her cell, the burden of guilt became too heavy to bear and she had to clear her conscience for the sake of her family and baby . . ."

Whatever the real reason, on Tuesday, March 2, 1982, Charlene called in her lawyers and announced that she was ready to make deal for her life and eventual freedom. In exchange for a light prison sentence, she would tell them about not two, but ten murders, how they were carried out, and most importantly, where they had been committed. It was just too much. No one believed her; she was advised to stop babbling such nonsense before she talked her way right into the gas chamber all by herself. But she persisted, and finally Charlene, her lawyers, the

DA, and several police officers from each of the jurisdictions where the ten murders allegedly occurred met for a little talk. Again, everyone thought she was lying. As the talks went on for hours, however, detailing a terrifying, picture-perfect, three-year odyssey of ten brutal killings, the cops and lawyers began to listen. No one, they reasoned, could know that much about ten crimes unless they had witnessed them.

Charlene made a full, detailed confession to her lawyer. In order to preserve the credibility of its own witness, the prosecution extrapolated from that confession what it thought best to use in open court against Gerald. The confession was then sealed so that it couldn't be used against Charlene even if she changed her mind about testifying against Gerald. In essence, she had given up nothing that could be used against her, but had gained immunity from the death penalty—a brilliant legal maneuver by her defense.

There was a good deal of bitter debate among factions in the law enforcement establishment—how could they in good conscience cut a deal with an equally guilty, equally cold-blooded, self-admitted aider, abettor, coconspirator and accomplice to such heinous murders? The answer to that hypothetical question was easy: in order to send one of them to the gas chamber they had to allow the other one to do a flat sixteen years, eight months. It was necessary for the prosecution to adopt the following approach, as allegedly expressed in the words of a DA from another county: ". . . You don't look a gift horse like this in the mouth. You kiss its ass and go for the death penalty on the man. You'd never get a death sentence on the woman, anyway. Not the way the California court system operates. Other than Miller and Sowers, there aren't any important victims to worry about who might stir up public opinion, so you better go with Charlene's deal." Everyone—except, of course, Gerald Armond Gallego—would go away happy.

Some experts were not so sure about the rather ambiguous California law concerning evidence supplied by a coconspirator. Under that statute, if a person is present at the scene of the crime, offering moral support, aiding and abetting, then each conspirator is criminally responsible for all crimes committed by his coconspirators if said crimes are committed to further the objective of the conspiracy. Under the accomplice rule, on the other hand, no defendant can be convicted of any crime on the uncorroborated testimony of an accomplice. The most perverse and at the same time wondrous aspect of criminal law is that while one statute will create an inviting loophole, another will close it. It is here that DAs and criminal trial lawyers earn their keep—trying to find ways to utilize these openings in the law to their best advantage.

The prosecution knew that in the Gallego case, they would also be up against the jury's natural prejudice toward Charlene testifying against her husband. The answer to that, they reasoned, would be to explain, very carefully, that she wasn't really testifying against a husband because their marriage hadn't been a legal one.

The final decision was to go for it. What the hell? Nothing ventured, nothing gained . . . and maybe the DA would get lucky and come up before a judge favorable to the People's case.

The state of Nevada was also eager to prosecute the Gallegos, while Oregon declined. Because California had possession of the defendants, it had dibs on them. Nevada agreed to take seconds, and signed a plea bargain identical to the one California had made with Charlene. In essence, it said that in view of her cooperation being vital to law enforcement, and in the event that she testified truthfully at the trial or trials of Gerald Armond Gallego, the People would not seek the death penalty against her in any of the cases known to law enforcement. In exchange for a plea of guilty to two counts of second-degree murder in the Miller-Sowers case, the People agreed that the maximum sentence would be sixteen years, eight months, without possibility of parole or time off for good behavior or work. The People contended, with a straight face, that this particular amount of flat time was determined because it equalled the number of years a defendant served on a twenty-five-to-life sentence for a second-degree-murder conviction.

By the middle of October 1982, the People of the State of California were as ready to go to trial against Gerald as they would ever be. The trial date was set for November 15. A change of venue had been ordered, and the case would be heard in Martinez, a small coastal town on San Francisco Bay in Contra Costa County.

Chapter 23

A Monster To Die!

The old American Bar Association canon of ethics states that the primary duty of a lawyer engaged in public prosecution is not to convict, but to see that justice is done. Whoever thought that one up would have made a good political speech writer, because in reality the single, tunnel-vision purpose of a prosecutor is to win for the People, and his/her concern for the defendant is about as benevolent as a hungry lion running down an antelope on the African plain. This attitude is also a simple matter of survival—no victory for the DA equals no publicity; no publicity equals not much hope for promotion and certainly no chance of running for public office. Without such prospects, the most a prosecutor has to look forward to is a lousy pension after twenty years, or a private practice defending drunk drivers and suing for dog bites. The defense works on the same principal in reverse. In California, as in numerous other states, the defense has a tremendous advantage over the People because every shred of evidence the DA has must be shared immediately with the defense under the discovery act. On the other hand, the defense is not required to tell the People anything about its strategy. For the most part, though, other than a witness caught red-handed lying on the stand, everyone knows what the defense has in mind. This situation invariably surprises, shocks, and disappoints a generation who grew up on Perry Mason and Hamilton Burger, and who either expect the defendant at some time during the trial to leap up and admit, "Yes! Yes! I did it!" or some guilty-looking party in the audience to start sneaking for the door when the defense has exposed the fact that someone else actually committed the crime with which the defendant has been charged. If the prosecution has been programed to win at all costs, the defense will do anything that won't invite disbarment or arrest in an effort to free the defendant. As for the jurors, almost everyone engaged in criminal law will maintain privately that most jurors have a tendency to be not only downright stupid, but certifiably insane. And that is what makes juries so unpredictable.

On Monday, November 15, 1982, the trial of Gerald Armond Gallego opened in Martinez with a handsome, confident defendant acting as his own attorney. He had a staff of lawyer-advisors and private investigators empowered to issue subpoenas—all hired by the court—backing him up. He'd grown a macho Tom Selleck–style mustache and wore a dark pin-striped suit with a pink shirt and red tie. Gerald had fired his public defender, who had managed to delay his trial for two years. Another attorney was appointed as advisor, but Gerald refused to allow him to sit at the same table, stating that he didn't need a babysitter. Gerald had copies of all police field reports, access to all evidence against him, and a copy of the testimony Charlene was to present from the stand. He faced the court, and after a few nervous seconds, opened the proceedings by stating that he intended to call forty witnesses. He then made his first motion, asking for a dismissal on the grounds that he had been denied the right to a speedy trial. The motion was denied.

Jury selection lasted over a month. At one time, Gerald had the jury stacked with ten women, his theory being that no woman worthy of the name would find him guilty of anything. Eventually, his advisors wisely persuaded him to settle for seven women and five men.

It was observed by one and all that the role of lawyer fitted Gerald. As far as jailhouse lawyers went, he was a good one; he had a remarkable courtroom decorum, and was very adept at addressing the judge, jury, and DA. Unlike the usual criminal defendant, who can't move from his seat, Gerald, acting as his own lawyer, was free to roam about the courtroom at will. That scared the hell out of Charlene's defense but there wasn't anything they could do about it. Gerald was escorted to court each morning from the jail one block away in shackles and chains. He ate lunch alone in a holding cell, making notes and chain-smoking, but he was allowed to roam the courtroom in the role as his own attorney.

The People called some thirty witnesses in an attempt to tie Gerald directly to the Miller-Sowers murders. Gerald handled them well on cross-examination and redirect, and observers said that he did as well as most experienced lawyers could have done.

One of those witnesses was Mercedes Williams, who appeared only under subpoena. She tearfully swore that when she'd visited Gerald in jail, he told her, among other things, that he would mount a diminished-capacity defense by claiming untruthfully that he and Miller got into an argument over a dope deal, which resulted in a fight, that Gerald then killed Miller in self-defense, and that Gerald said during one of her visits, "Hey, Mom, I'd take fifteen years on a diminished-capacity in a minute." Mrs. Williams also claimed that she had willingly notified the FBI about her daughter's calls for money. When Mercedes Williams concluded her testimony on direct, Gerald bit his lip, looked down, and said, "Judge, I don't want to question this witness."

When Charlene was finally escorted into court to testify against Gerald, her hair was neatly done, she wore makeup and a long-sleeved Victorian-style blouse with a long beige skirt—no teenage look for her now. Gerald allowed his advising counsel to take Charlene through some of the cross-examination, hoping to throw her off guard as she was expecting Gerald to tear into her.

". . . Can you tell me anything you did to prevent any of those people from being murdered?" the defense asked.

"I just sat there like a fool," Charlene answered through the tears she would shed during almost all of her time on the stand. "I didn't do a damned thing."

"You don't think that you're responsible for a little, tiny part of those deaths?"

"Yes, I do. I should have taken a gun and shot him, played God, I guess."

"Just tell me . . ."

"All right! My wifely duties were to do his bidding, until death do us part. I had no right to stop him from doing those things, or for me to escape. There are many different sides to Gerald. My life with him was a mixture of love and fear and of pleasure. I wish I were dead. The only good thing to come out of all this is my son, Gerald Junior."

"You say that he told you to get the girls . . . what kind did he want?"

"They had to be very young, very pretty."

"And you went and got them?"

"Yes, I did."

"What did you say to them?"

"Something about a party, or drugs, or both, I think."

"Why did you lure the girls?"

"To fulfill his sex fantasy."

"You had no sex fantasy?"

"No."

"All right. What would happen then?"

"I took them out to the van and Gerald pointed a gun and said they were kidnapped."

"In all the cases involved here, was it always the same?"

"Yes."

"Tell us about it."

"Well, we, Gerald and I, would drive around shopping malls looking for girls—for the kind he liked as sexual partners . . . when we'd see them, I'd lure them over to the van."

"Then you would help your husband, the man you still love, to sexually assault then murder them, is that right?"

"Yes."

"But, didn't you say previously, right here in this court, that you were not involved in the sexual molestations and the actual killing of the victims?"

"I wasn't."

"All right. Then we, this court and the jury, are to assume that you risked your life and freedom, and everything that is precious to a young woman, you risked all that just to help your husband fulfill *his* sexual fantasies?"

"Yes."

"And you got nothing out of it except making *him* happy?"

"No."

"All right, let's go to the woman bartender for a moment. You said that you did not lure her outside, or do anything that would put her at ease when she came out into that dark parking lot?"

"I didn't."

"Do you know why she didn't run or scream?"

"No."

"Did you wipe Gerald's fingerprints off the victim's car after Gerald had put her into your van?"

"Yes."

"Why?"

"I didn't want us to get caught."

"Then *you* drove the van home, with the victim and Gerald more or less right beside you, and sat in the house, petting a cat and rocking in a rocking chair, while Gerald stayed in the van outside and raped and murdered that victim?

"Yes."

"Then when your husband was finished raping and killing the woman, you helped him dispose of the body?"

"Yes."

"In every one of those ten cases that the court has allowed you and the People to talk about in this trial, you admit that you lured the victims, you helped your husband subdue them, you assisted in hiding the bodies, but you're saying here and now that you *did not* participate in any of the sexual assaults and murders?"

"That's what I said. I didn't."

"Oh? You just went along to help your husband so that you could make him happy, is that it?"

"Yes."

"All right. I have nothing else for this. Witness for the State!"

Now Gerald was finally able to talk to Charlene face-to-face for the first time in almost two years. It is likely that he still believed he could influence and/or intimidate her enough to make her change her testimony against him, which many observers believed to be the real reason he insisted upon acting as his own attorney.

"Isn't it a fact, Mrs. Gallego," Gerald asked, starting right off with evidence he thought would discredit and impeach anything she might have said or would say, "isn't it a fact that you are a lesbian, and that you have had lesbian relationships while in jail?"

"Well, I may have had what some would describe as a homosexual affair in jail, but I wouldn't call myself a lesbian," Charlene answered, looking Gerald right in the eye.

"You wouldn't?"

"No."

Everyone in the courtroom leaned forward, hoping Gerald's next question would be what did she call herself if not a lesbian. It wasn't.

"Now Mrs. Gallego," Gerald continued, staring her right in the eye with that old Rasputin gaze, "you came into this court and accused me, your husband, of all sorts of crimes. You lied, didn't you?"

"No," Charlene replied sweetly, staring right back at him.

"Now Mrs. Gallego," Gerald said, taking another tack, "I want you to help me re-create for this jury exactly how you now claim that I shot Craig Miller."

Charlene started to cry again, and between sobs, blubbered, "I heard some shots and saw some flashes of light and then Miller fell down in front of the car."

"He was falling when the flashes went off?"

"Oh, Gerald! For god's sake!" Charlene sobbed, and took a deep, quivering breath.

"Now, Mrs. Gallego, if you think I'm not going to fight for my life just because you start crying . . ."

"Just a moment, Mr. Gallego!" The judge shouted, "You just ask the questions and I'll control the courtroom! Answer the question, Mrs. Gallego."

"It all happened at the same time—the shots, the lights, and him falling."

"All right, Mrs. Gallego, were all the shots fired before he hit the ground?"

"I don't know! I . . . I guess it all happened at the same time."

"But you saw Craig Miller shot by me, correct?"

"Yeah."

"What were your feelings? Were you afraid?"

"I guess it was more of a shock."

"A shock? But were you afraid? What were your feelings at the time? You just seen me kill a man."

"I'd never seen anybody killed before. How do you expect me to feel?"

"That's what I'm asking *you*. That's the question. How did you feel?"

"Sick."

And so it went for six days—an angry husband and wife arguing in the courtroom, the husband asking questions and the wife attempting to outmaneuver him by countering with another question.

On the sixth and final day, Gerald took his best shot at Charlene.

"What did you think—how did you feel when I got in the backseat with Mary Beth Sowers and started fondling her after I'd killed Craig Miller?"

"The whole thing was disgusting—sick. It was just sick. The only thing I could really focus on was that I'd just seen a man killed right in front of me."

"Sure. Then what happened?"

"I drove us home and you took Mary Beth Sowers into our bedroom."

"Where were you?"

"I waited outside in the living room," Charlene said with a faint smile on her lips as she looked him right in the eye without flinching.

"How long did you wait?"

"I don't know exactly, but I told you finally that it was almost morning and we had to find a place to kill her before daylight."

"So Mary was still alive, according to you?"

"Yes. You put her in the backseat and I drove us out to Placer County, out in the country, following your directions. When we got there, you asked me if I wanted to kill her."

"What did you say?"

"I said no, of course, that you'd promised me I'd never have to kill any of them. Then you took her out of the car and walked over to someplace, and I heard some pops."

"How many?"

"Three."

"What did the pops sound like?"

"Like a small-caliber handgun."

Gerald switched directions again and asked, "What was my sobriety at the time Miller was shot?"

"In my opinion? You seemed to know what you were doing."

"Why did you lie to the police when they came to your parents' house to talk to you about Miller and Sowers?" Gerald asked, switching directions once more.

"To protect *you*—us. I was scared and didn't want us to be caught."

"Then you were relieved at seeing them?"

"No, not really."

"Mrs. Gallego, why did you go along with me, drive the van and car, and help me do all those kidnap-killings you say I did?"

"Well, I was afraid for my own life at times—and for the life of our unborn child . . ." Charlene lowered her head and sobbed.

"Uh-huh. Why didn't you take advantage of all those hundreds of chances you had to run away or call the cops and say, 'Holy cow, I just seen people murdered'."

"It would have been nice . . ."

"But you didn't, did you?"

"No."

"Didn't you, Mrs. Gallego, show me where *you* shot and killed Mary Beth Sowers?" Gerald suddenly shouted.

"I did not shoot Mary Beth Sowers!" Charlene shouted back, "*You* of all people should know that!"

"All right. Why did you tell so many lies to the police when we were arrested?"

"I lied to cover up for you! And you know that, Gerald Gallego!"

"Mrs. Gallego, the only one who seems to be covering up today is you."

"I'm not!"

Gerald suddenly wheeled around and faced Charlene, his eyes gleaming. "Mrs. Gallego, isn't it a fact that you entered into this cover-up against me as a willing witness and eager participant . . . BECAUSE YOU ARE IN FACT A *MURDERESS?*"

"NO!"

"YES YOU ARE!"

"I AM NOT! YOU *LIAR!*"

"Mr. Gallego! Mr. Gallego!" the judge leaned forward and shouted right along with them. "Please, Mr. Gallego! I want you to stop improperly commenting on the witness' answers!"

During recess, the spectators gleefully commented the cross-examination was really getting quite interesting; it was just like being present in the bedroom of a battling husband and wife.

"Now Mrs. Gallego," Gerald said, holding a folder in his hand, "I'm going to read some statements you made to the prosecution and I will ask you to comment on some of them. You were asked why you told them your story and you said, 'There were lots of reasons. At first, I didn't want to hurt my husband. That is my husband and I love him very much.' Did you say that?"

"Yes."

"And then you were asked, 'You mean you still do?' And you said, 'I love him, but I have a son to think about now and I can't see why after all this time I'm still in jail for something I didn't do, depriving my son of a mother.' Did you say that?"

"Yes."

"And did you say, '*If* Gerald did this, I don't ever want to be around him. I do have a fear of him, but I still love him.' Did you say that?"

"Yes, I made that statement."

"Mrs. Gallego, are you aware that I was very angry that you would drag our son through your lies and use him as a sentimental backup to sell your story?"

Charlene giggled and covered her mouth, but didn't answer.

"Now Mrs. Gallego, I have here a couple of letters you wrote to me in jail. I want you to read them to the jury."

"Why?" The wife peevishly asked her husband.

"Because they'll prove that you couldn't have been afraid of me at any time. Read 'em!" The husband said firmly to his wife as he shoved the letters into her hand.

"This one is dated January 17, 1982," Charlene began reading. "Well, today is our son's first birthday. You know, we're really lucky to have such a beautiful and healthy boy. I can just look at him and see you. I love our son so very much and I do love you. It doesn't matter what people say or do to us, the fact still remains that we had a beautiful love once and we always will. You're the only man I've ever loved and you're the only one I will ever love. Honey, I miss you and I need you. I just wish we could be together."

Charlene handed the letter to Gerald and picked up the second one.

"This is dated February 5, 1982.

"It was a surprise to hear from you this morning. Thanks for the beautiful kitten and roses. You always did know what I like [smile].

You drew them on the letter," Charlene said, looking up at Gerald with cold eyes, then read on, "I love thinking about where we went camping together and how you played your guitar for me and how much you loved me. Please don't ever leave me. I'll see you in my dreams. Goodnight. Love, your wife, Charlene."

"Did you write those letters?"

"Yes."

"And do you expect the judge and jury in this courtroom to believe that a woman who felt as you did about her husband would be *frightened* of him? That you were helping him kidnap and kill people because you were afraid not to help him?"

"Yes."

Gerald looked at Charlene with a mixture of shock and disbelief, apparently trying to comprehend the fact that he was no longer her sweet daddy, that she had finally and irrevocably turned on him, that she really did intend to do everything she could to send him to the gas chamber.

"Mrs. Gallego," he said slowly, seeming to have problems collecting his thoughts. "Let me ask you this . . . why . . . why did you clean out the car and wash down the walls that morning after Miller and Sowers . . ."

"Because you *told* me to," Charlene answered quickly.

"Yeah . . . I did . . ." Gerald muttered.

The judge flinched, the DA beamed, and the advising counsel clenched his hands so hard the knuckles popped. Gerald had just admitted that he'd ordered Charlene to destroy incriminating evidence, and that would most certainly cause the jury to believe he had committed the crimes as charged, and would crush any credibility he might have built up with the jury during his cross-examination of Charlene.

Gerald was now sworn in and took the stand as his own witness to rebut Charlene's testimony.

"The problem," Gerald told the jury, his face flushed a dark scarlet as if his blood pressure had leaped fifty points, "was that I was loaded on all kinds of drugs and alcohol that night, and what I'm about to tell you was what Charlene Gallego told me the next morning.

"Some of the things I'm gonna tell you, you won't like . . . *I* don't like them, but I've made up my mind they got to be said, in order for you, the jury, to understand what really happened, I got to tell you, because nobody else will, especially Charlene Gallego.

"Now, I think I did shoot Craig Miller. But I'm not sure of what I'm guilty of cause it was self-defense. I'm gonna tell you why as far as I can recall. But—and most of all, I intend to prove beyond any doubt that I did *not* shoot and kill Mary Beth Sowers. I'll prove beyond any doubt that Charlene Gallego did it.

"I'm not trying to slip anything over in this courtroom. I did not come here like Charlene did, to slip and slide in this chair. I have been as honest as I can, and I'm gonna continue to be as honest as I can, and I intend to prove I didn't in fact kill Mary Beth Sowers.

"After we got arrested in Omaha, Charlene, me, and my mother-in-law, Mrs. Williams, started making up stories. We had more stories than we needed, we had made up an oversupply of what our fictitious alibis would be.

"My initial story in Omaha was that I told Charlene if we got arrested, just blame everything on me—you weren't even there. I was going to defend Charlene at any cost. I told her that. I promised her that. And since I now know in my own mind that I *did* shoot Craig Miller, what's the difference in one murder or two? Why not take the blame for Mary Sowers too? Because I didn't kill her, that's why.

"But when Charlene came in here and lied and put the blame all on me, and testified against me with lies, I felt I didn't owe her that promise anymore, and now I'm gonna tell the *real* story . . . as I remember it . . ."

"Me and Charlene went out that night. We were both carrying guns. She had a .25 pistol she bought back in 1977, and I had a .357 Magnum. We stopped at a bar and I got to drinking and using drugs with a guy I knew as Ernie. I got loaded to the point I'm not certain where I was or who I was with. I don't even remember leaving the place. I do have some memories of that night, but I don't know if they're real or if it was what Charlene told me, or something I read in the papers.

"The next thing I remember real clear is that I'm home and it's morning. Charlene is washing me with a wet towel because there's blood on my face. I had cuts on both lips and some bumps on my head.

"I asked Charlene what happened, and she told me this long story. She said we had met Craig Miller someplace and decided to rob him. He had this girl with him, so after we robbed them, we kidnapped them and took them out into the boondocks to drop them off so we'd have time to get away . . ."

"Charlene said that during that process, Miller attacked me, tried to disarm me, knocked me down and beat the hell out of me. Then he turned on Charlene like he was gonna kill her, and then I jumped up and shot him from behind, then passed out again. Charlene said that she tried to wake me up but couldn't, and she then got real scared, and shot Mary Beth Sowers to cover up the whole crime, to protect me—*us*—and our future together. It was all a horrible nightmare to me, you know, and I couldn't believe it. I still shiver when I think about it.

"When I was feeling a little bit better, I made Charlene drive me to where she said we'd dumped the girl's body so I could see it for myself. I said, 'I got to see this.' Now, it's not that I didn't believe her, because at that point in time, I knew Charlene wouldn't lie to me, but I had to see this. She took me out there and I can't find a thing. Then she showed me Mary Beth Sowers. I looked at the body maybe one fourth of a second, and ran back to the car in tears.

"Then I got real mad. I think I even slapped Charlene. It just seemed to me that it was bad enough for one of us to be a murderer and now we both were murderers. That's when we threw the guns away and got rid of all the other evidence and took off for Omaha, where we intended to change our identities and make a new life for ourselves and our unborn child, which was due anyday . . ."

"My diminished-capacity defense because of drugs and alcohol is the actual truth in this matter asserted. I do not remember killing *anyone* in the first degree, and I did *not,* for a believable fact, kill Mary Beth Sowers."

The court recessed for a two-hour lunch break, after which Gerald took the stand again as his own witness.

"The district attorney asked me if Charlene sexually satisfied me," he testified, "and you heard me say no way. Now, I would like to explain that answer to the jury. Charlene Gallego is a *lesbian!*

"Some years ago, I came home from work one day and caught Charlene in bed with another girl. After that, I couldn't get a sexual interest in her. Oh, I wanted to leave her, yes, I did, but I loved her too much. It disgusts me even today to think about it, but I loved her, and she promised she'd never do it no more. *But she lied! To me, her husband!*

"I will now put on a witness who will prove everything I've

said, and will prove beyond a shadow of a doubt that I have impeached Charlene Gallego as to what she has said up here on the stand, and whatever she might say later.''

His witness was Nancy Romero, a former inmate who had served time at Rio Cosumnes with Charlene.

"Did Charlene Gallego ever make any sexual advances to you while you were in jail with her?'' Gerald asked Romero.

"Yes. She tried to seduce me on several occasions. Once she tried to hold my hand, and I rejected her forcibly. She became very angry.''

"What did she say?''

"That she would take care of me, that she had ways.''

"What ways?''

"Well, she had this black lover who was really mean, and I was warned by other inmates that this black lover would be waiting for me in the shower.''

"What was Charlene Gallego known as, there in jail?''

"Well, she was a troublemaker, real foul-mouthed and domineering and a very aggressive lesbian.''

"What did you do after being threatened by her?''

"I asked to be put into protective custody.''

"Were you?''

"Yes.''

Gerald's daughter, Mary Ellen Gallego, was presented to the jury as a witness in absentia. Her testimony was delivered during an hour-long private session in chambers with the defense and the prosecution, then subsequently read into the record by the judge in open court. Gerald emphatically requested that his daughter not appear in open court, and in doing so, he admitted her allegations against him were true. (If he had insisted on attempting to maintain his innocence, he would have allowed her to be called as a witness in court, then cross-examined her. But he figured that her testimony would do him more harm coming from her own mouth than being read by the judge and that any cross-examination or denials on his part could not outweight that effect.) Furthermore, Mary Ellen also requested that she not be forced to testify against her father face-to-face in open court.

Gerald asked to be removed from the court while the testimony was being read to the jury. Meanwhile, nineteen-year-old Mary Ellen was slipped out of the judge's chambers, her head covered by a cop's jacket, so that she could escape the crowd of panting reporters. She was, after all, the witness everyone had been waiting to see and hear.

"The witness was subpoenaed by the prosecution," the judge read. "If left to her own desires, she did not want to testify against her father. She understands that her testimony may be used by the prosecution to argue for her father's death.

"Her father's sexual molestation has left her with ambivalent feelings toward him. At times she hates her father, at times she loves him, and at times, she does not know what her feelings are for her father."

A state investigator leaned over and noted to a colleague that her effectiveness as a state witness against Gallego had just been shot to hell and if she didn't hate him, why did the state bring her there?

"He told her," the judge read on, "that it was natural for her to allow him to commit sexual acts with her. She would protest the sexual contacts sometimes, but would usually oblige. The assaults were committed periodically, sometimes with force, from the time she was six until she was fourteen. Those acts were intercourse, oral copulation, and sodomy. Her father celebrated his thirty-third birthday by committing sodomy and other sexual acts upon her and a minor girlfriend. On occasion, Charlene Gallego was present in the same apartment when she was being abused. The sexual attacks stopped only when the witness reported them to the Butte County authorities, and formal charges were filed against Gerald Gallego on September 25, 1978."

The People may have hoped for a more vehement and effective in-person witness, but had to be satisfied with no more than entering into the record the fact that Gerald Gallego, along with all his other faults, was an incestuous father and child molester.

It was now time for the defense's mandatory psychiatric evaluation of the defendant. A clinical psychologist from a mid-American college took the stand to tell the jury why the defendant did it. He admitted that for four days' work and expenses, his fee would be $5,800.

". . . Gerald has brain damage and will be a danger to society for the rest of his life," the psychologist testified. "No question about that. I can't pinpoint the reason for Gerald's brain damage, but the condition could be responsible for his apparent abnormal sexual preferences, even the grotesque ones. His brain has shrunk to the size normal for a seventy-five-year-old man! He just does not see the world the way the rest of us do."

Just how he had measured Gerald's brain, and what the exact difference was between the size of a thirty-five-year-old's and a seventy-five-year-old-man's brain was never explained, and no one bothered to ask. But probably startling the hell out of the defense, the shrink did say, "This man is not a good man. He has done grotesque crimes. Criminal conduct is not a manifestation of brain damage, nor an excuse to let him go. Brain damage has nothing to do with what this man has done. It was first-degree murder as far as I'm concerned!"

Just why the defense would call on a psychologist who seemed to want to do his level best to convict the defendant would be hard to explain—someone was crazy (either the shrinks with their bizarre testimony, or Gerald's advising counsel for talking him into calling a shrink to testify, or the law for allowing such testimony at all) but it certainly wasn't Gerald Armond Gallego.

A second shrink was sworn in for the defense, and, after stating that his fee was $10,000, gazed at the ceiling and said, "Gerald looks like a grown-up, talks like a grown-up, but has the mind of a little boy. And that little boy has such contrasting feelings of love and rage toward his mother that he both symbolically slept with her and killed her during those very real acts of violence against other women."

Two bailiffs rolled their eyes at each other as if to say "Oh, God! Here comes the old I-hate-my-mama crap!"

". . . My diagnosis of Gerald's problem," the doctor continued, "is a severe disturbance of personality, whose primary feature is the persistence into adulthood of infantile characteristics ordinarily seen in very small children. It is almost impossible to pinpoint the reasons for Gerald's retarded emotional development. I see him as the end result of overlapping genetic development and organic factors, all of which have allowed him to bring into adulthood very poorly repressed infantile wishes, fears, angers, and hatreds.

"Gerald's murders, on the other hand, were the results of displaced feelings of rage against his mother, the victims being seen as pieces of his mother, against whom he could now act in an extraordinarily uninhibited way.

"Being strong is important to Gerald, because he has great concerns about his masculinity—"

At this point, Gerald leaped out of his chair and advising counsel had to grab the defendant's arm to force him back.

"—As a result of that, his need to dominate and control others is pervasive. I see that with all the victims—binding, controlling, inflicting pain . . . on one hand, Charlene is a person he could dominate. On the other hand, she is a dominating person herself, not weak, a strong person against whom he could lean . . . because of his need for a father, he created one out of fantasy. His mother was his father—he wished to possess that very important mother. When Gerald had sex with his daughter, he was treating her as his wife and mother . . . the real wife of his fantasies . . . Gerald feels that he has his father inside him. If Gerald is executed he will have been strong. If he lives he will have been weak. Gerald needs a father beside him and in him."

The overall effect of the doctor's testimony was more-or-less summed up when an elderly gentleman in the front row leaned over to his equally elderly companion and in a loud stage whisper asked, "What was that fellow talking about? Did he say Gallego wanted to have sex with his mother? Or was it with his father?"

There is another procedure in every criminal trial known as TMA—Typical Mother's Appeal—where the defendant's mother takes the stand and tearfully tells the jury that *her* boy couldn't have done the things he is accused of because he had always been a good boy, that he didn't steal money out of her purse very often, that he'd always been such a gentle little fellow who wouldn't harm a fly, much less a human being. No one pays much attention to a TMA, but it makes mama feel better, makes the DA look more human by allowing it in the record, and gives the defense something to do as a last resort. The procedure is always followed, and Gerald's trial was no exception.

Lorraine Davies, age fifty-six, claimed to be in a Chico hospital on her deathbed after exploratory cancer surgery and couldn't appear in person to make her TMA. She was allowed to make a sworn statement via a tape recording that was played for the jury.

"I don't want my son to die. The boy you have down there isn't the boy I knew because my boy couldn't even butcher a chicken.

"He had such a terrible life because he was abandoned, neglected, and there was forbidden love and physical and mental abuse. He was a mama's boy. He always cried when I had to go to work. He wanted me to hold him all the time." Davies went on to tell about her teenage marriages to George Bennet and Harold Hunt, then to Gerald's father.

"Gerald's dad was really dumb. If someone told him there was a million dollars at the end of the rainbow, he's go look for it. I never told Gerald about his dad being a killer or how he died. Gerald wanted a father real bad, and I thought I'd solved the problem when I married George Bulgar.

"Little Gerald was just six then, and George treated him like his little boy until George's own son was born. After that, he wouldn't pay any attention to Gerald. Gerald couldn't sit on his lap or hug him. It was like Gerald didn't exist anymore.

"George Bulgar was *very* jealous of my other kids, including little Gerald. George wouldn't allow them to hug me or sit on my lap. At one time he accused me of having sex with my two sons.

"George was a drunk and beat me and the kids all the time. It sounds so stupid now, but at the time . . . well, now, as a woman, I could have done things about it, but then, it was different."

Davies said that she had left Bulgar and married Ed Davies about eighteen years ago, and that Bulgar had died but she didn't know exactly when.

"From the age of ten, Gerald got locked up a lot. Once for having sex with a little girl. I made lots of mistakes. Instead of trying to buy Gerald's love, I should have made him earn it a little more, but it was easier to buy him a bike than it was to spend time with him.

"The last time I saw Gerald was the night we all found out about him having sex with his daughter. We sat under a walnut tree and talked, and I held him close and told him that he needed help. He cried and said he knew that now, and that he wanted to explain to me, you know, what happened. He promised to get help right away, and that he realized now that what he'd done was really unforgivable, but he loved her so much he just forgot what kind of love he was supposed to show a daughter. Then we hugged and kissed, and he took off in the van with that Charlene.

"If he'd never met that woman, all this wouldn't have happened. She is and was a liar, but I thought she loved him, and I wanted someone to love him the way he needed to be loved.

"My feelings for Gerald are very mixed. I can't believe he's capable of the things he's being tried for. I love him, and yet I don't understand him. But I don't want him to die . . . God puts everybody on this earth for some reason, and He must have had *some* reason for putting Gerald here . . ."

Lorraine didn't mention that she and her sister had been sexually molested by her father, or the fact that she had raised Gerald's daughter. She didn't say whether Mary Ellen had ever told her about Gerald's molestation prior to having told Ed Davies.

The five man–seven woman jury was out fourteen hours. They returned on Wednesday June 22, 1983, three years and seven months after the deaths of Craig Miller and Mary Beth Sowers. Gerald's face was a doughy, pasty white, and he clinched his hands as he listened to clerk Laura Sherwood read the verdict:

"We the jury in this case, having found the defendant, Gerald Armond Gallego, guilty of violation of California penal code section 187, murder in the first degree as charged in counts three and four of the information, and having further found the special circumstances to be true, fix the penalty at death . . ."

Gerald allowed one of the attorneys he had fired to make a final appeal to the judge before sentence was pronounced. The defense quoted Clarence Darrow's famous argument against the death penalty from his closing statement in the Loeb and Leopold Case in 1927:

"The shedding of blood must stop here. Hatred and cruelty should not control the hearts of men. I beg that you temper justice with mercy and love. I wish you, Judge, the wisdom and courage to do the right thing."

The People stood and countered with, "Gallego's acts are the most monstrous of crimes. The People have had *enough* of Gerald Armond Gallego . . ."

The judge then reviewed the aggravating circumstances of Gerald's crimes, and read from the report of Deputy Probation Officer Mary Frey:

"Gerald Armond Gallego's deviance is so thoroughly ingrained," Frey wrote, "and of such long standing, that it would be utter foolishness, at best, and probably criminal, to even suggest that Gallego be released into society again.

"Gerald Armond Gallego is a veritable monster, cunning and devious, virtually devoid of all feelings and emotions such as empathy and compassion, and he is not fit to live in a free society.

"He has committed one of the most monstrous series of crimes that can be imagined. And his victims are forever dead because they were available when Gerald Armond Gallego felt the urge to act out his aberrant fantasies.

"Counsel," the judge said in reply to the defense appeal, "while it is true that Mr. Gallego appears to have had a hard life, it is also true that many men have had a life far more difficult than Mr. Gallego, but they did not commit the gruesome crimes he has been convicted of. The jury has found him guilty of those crimes, and without mercy, recommended the death penalty. I have no intention of tampering with that recommendation by considering mercy . . . and I guarantee that 'I have the courage to do the right thing' by sending Mr. Gallego to the gas chamber. He is another glaring example of our failed justice system, but that system did give him every chance to make good, and he refused each and every one of those chances . . . I see nothing in his background that forced him to kill Mary Beth Sowers and Craig Miller . . ."

The judge then ordered Gerald to be remanded to the Contra Costa County Sheriff, who would take him to San Quentin Prison, where he would be put to death by the administration of lethal gas. By nightfall, Gerald was on his way to San Quentin to join 134 inmates on death row. His stay there would be brief.

At about the same time Gerald was being processed at the Big Q, Gerald's favorite female TV reporter aimed her steely-blues at the camera again, narrowed them, and notified her audience that as per the judge's instructions, the monster would die.

The trial had lasted six months and ten days, and had cost taxpayers approximately $2 million. California justice is, if nothing else, expensive. The Nazi War Crimes Trial in Nürnberg took eight months, but it did result in a number of mass murderers bouncing on the end of a rope. In the case of Gerald Armond Gallego, there wasn't a single person in that Martinez courtroom who believed he would really die in the California gas chamber.

A cop from Oregon who had come down to witness the trial stood in the hallway, shook his head and told a reporter, "If we aren't going to execute the sentence of death, or send murderers to prison with a life sentence we know they'll actually serve, we may as well sell them a license to kill, and stop going through the motions . . ."

Everyone was thinking about the fact that the chief justice of the California State Supreme Court, Rose Bird, and her four colleagues had thrown out every death sentence that came before them for review—over sixty cases—including that of a repeat child molester and torture-murderer who had not only confessed to skinning alive a three-year-old girl and then inserting his penis in her mouth while holding her nose until she choked to death, but had written it all down and taken photos of the victim to enjoy later. Chief Justice Bird ruled that the police should not have used the defendant's private notes against him just because they conveniently found them, along with the photos, in his car. She ruled that the man deserved a new trial, and that she was throwing out the confession and photos as evidence.

The angry father of Mary Beth Sowers wrote to the Woodland judge who had approved Charlene's plea bargain," With a sentence of sixteen years, justice has not been served for her admitted part in the murders, which were so heinous, atrocious, cruel, and which manifested exceptional depravity. Her sentence is menial and grossly unfair to the victims."

Mary Beth Sowers' grandmother, Sara Marsh, said, ". . . I don't think we could have stood it if the verdict had been different . . . it's been a horribly tragedy . . . it seems like yesterday she died . . . everyone thinks it happens to someone else . . . but in 1981, twenty thousand teenagers were murdered just like our Mary Beth . . .''

Jerry Sowers, brother of Mary Beth, said, ''. . . I've never believed in the death penalty until now. I want Gallego DEAD! Someone should kill him. If not me, then the state of California or Nevada. He should have been killed long ago.

"But my biggest reaction to Gallego's death sentence is that it doesn't mean a whole lot in California. To be perfectly honest, I don't think they'll ever execute him in this state. I want to see Nevada get him. I think that state will kill him.''

The state of Nevada did want to kill Gerald Armond Gallego, and that state immediately began maneuvering to have Gerald extradited into their hands.

Chapter **24**

Shanghaied And Tried Again

The Nevada authorities were ready and willing to try Gerald for kidnapping and killing two girls inside their state, but first, they had to get him out of California. The gates of the Big Q had barely slammed shut behind Gerald when the Nevada boys made their move by filing extradition papers with the governor's office in Sacramento. Like everyone else, Gerald believed that if he could stay on San Quentin's death row he would, ironically, be safe from execution. So he prepared to fight extradition any way he could. California Governor George Deukmejian stated that he had signed the extradition papers the moment they landed on his desk, and said that, ". . . the death sentence Gallego has may never be carried out in this state due to the Rose Bird supreme court . . ."

Gerald's court-appointed attorneys in San Francisco filed motions to prevent their client's extradition, and when the Nevada authorities arrived at San Quentin, they were forced to leave without their prize prisoner. The crafty Nevada boys then filed

an objection to Gerald's motion, deputized a Sacramento cop
as a special agent of the Nevada State Police—and waited.

Their luck held, and the California Appellate Court over-
turned the motion to keep Gerald in San Quentin. There would
be several hours when Gerald was in limbo, no longer under the
orders of any court, until his attorneys filed another motion.
Nevada was notified that, during those few hours, Gerald could
be snatched out of San Quentin. The recently deputized special
agent for Nevada and several other cops rushed to the prison,
showed their court order for Gerald's release on the extradition
warrant, loaded Gerald into a car, then drove at top-speed
ninety miles to the Sacramento Metropolitan Airport, where a
twin-engine Nevada sheriff's plane was waiting. Gerald was hustled aboard and the planeload of happy cops and their shang-
haied prisoner were on their way to Nevada.

A very happy Nevada cop said, "It was real close getting him
out of there ahead of another court stay, but we done it."

A very angry and surprised Gallego lawyer bellowed, "I
didn't even know he was gone! It is our position that it was an
unlawful extradition . . ."

Now that they had Gerald, Pershing County discovered a
major problem—how could they pay the estimated $60,000 cost
of Gerald's trial in a county with less than 4,000 people?

Then one prominent Sacramento columnist wrote a piece
about the lack of funds, suggesting readers send in a dollar each
to help try Gerald. Mail poured in from all over the world. Craig
Miller's mother sent $25. One letter read, "Here's a dollar to
make America safe from bums like him." From Sacramento a
citizen wrote, "Here's 100 dollars. When justice has been carried out, another check will be sent for the bastard's burial
expenses." Another letter from Sacramento read, "I'm sending
five dollars. When you find Gallego guilty, and he starts claiming to be a born-again Christian, burn him alive." An Ohio man
wrote, "I'm sending a check for ten bucks. When he's put to
death, it'll make my day." A Texas lady said, "Here is two

dollars from my social security check. You can buy the rope with it."

The mail turned into a deluge, and Pershing County took in close to $30,000 in donations toward Gerald's trial. A fund drive to conduct the trial was a real first in legal circles, but it worked.

Ironically, Gerald and Charlene's county jail cells in Lovelock, Nevada, were less than sixty feet apart. Until his trial started, Gerald would walk the floor all night and sleep all day. According to her jailers, Charlene read all day and played her violin most of the evening.

Whether Gerald's extradition to Nevada was totally legal was never tested in any court, and his trial was set for May 23, 1984. His attorney did file a motion to have him returned to California, but the motion was denied and they did not appeal. Had they done so, they very likely would have won. Apparently, once he arrived in Lovelock, Gerald had had enough of trying to defend himself, and allowed the court to appoint an excellent attorney to handle his defense there.

On May 24, 1984, Charlene, who volunteered to return to Nevada as part of her plea bargain, once more took the stand against her husband. The first motion from the defense was to take immediate issue with the husband-wife confidentiality law. But as they had in California, the People pointed out that Gerald and Charlene were never really legally married in the first place. The judge agreed, and the trial began.

Once she had been sworn in as their star witness, Charlene was instructed by the People of Nevada to explain what happened on that fateful morning.

"Well, Gerald woke up that morning and said, 'I want a girl.'"

"What did he mean by that?"

"I took it to mean he wanted to kidnap, rape, and kill another girl who fitted his sexual fantasy."

"What did you do or say?"

"Nothing. We got dressed and drove around in the van looking for girls who fit his fantasy."

"Let's back up a little, Charlene. Tell the jury how you can
remember so clearly, after all those years, just how everything
was at the time."

"There's a—photograph thing that develops in my mind. It's
like I can hear and see the things with my eyes open."

"Now, do you lapse into a hypnotic trance or anything like
that?"

"No, I do not."

"All right. Tell us what happened next."

"We sat around the shopping mall until we saw the girls
Gerald liked. He told me to go get them."

"And did you?"

"Yes."

"How did you go about it?"

"I went up to them and offered them some dope. I said me
and my old man were having a birthday party and did they want
to join."

"And they said yes."

"Un-hunh. We went to the van, where Gerald was waiting.
When we got in, Gerald pointed a pistol at them and said they
were being kidnapped. He said to them, 'Are you two really
worth anything to anyone?'."

"Were the girls frightened?"

"I guess they thought it was a joke. Gerald told them they
wouldn't be hurt."

"Go on."

"I helped him tape them. Then I drove and Gerald was in
back with them. He was talking real nice and friendly and they
were laughing. When we got to Reno, Gerald said stop, and he
went into a store and bought a hammer."

"For what purpose, did he say?"

"No. It was understood between us—to kill them with."

"Okay, go on."

"We drove to a place where we'd camped, way out in the desert . . ."

"You and Gerald and the two victims?"

"Yeah. I parked the van. It was real cold, but I got out and listened to Gerald having sex with them. Then because of the cold, I got back in and watched them having sex and—and after a while, he asked me if I wanted to have sex with them, too."

"What did you say?"

"I said no."

For the first time in the Lovelock courtroom, Gerald showed some emotion. He gripped the arms of his chair and stared at Charlene. If looks could kill, Charlene would have fallen over dead.

"Then what happened?"

"Gerald told the girls that we were going to stay the night and he was going to fix up a place down the hill where we'd camp. He went down there and dug the grave in the dark. I couldn't see, but I knew what he was doing."

"Were you frightened?"

"Yes. I wasn't sure Gerald wouldn't kill me, too."

"How about the girls, were they frightened?"

"No, they never did seem to be scared during the whole time. Gerald took them down the hill one by one in the dark and killed them with the hammer. One of the girls said she was cold and he put his jacket around her shoulders before taking her down there."

"You're saying now that he killed both victims with the hammer he'd bought just for that purpose?"

"Yes, sir."

"Go on."

"After he killed them, he called me to come down, but I was afraid—afraid of what he might do to me. Then he came back up the hill and said he wanted to show me the grave. I didn't want to. He said that they were already dead, and led me down there anyway, where they were buried . . ."

"He said to you at that time that he had killed the girls and buried them there?"

"Yes, he did."

"What happened next?"

"Not much. We drove back toward Winnemucca and camped for the rest of the night. Then we went to Lake Tahoe and stayed at a nice hotel and partied for two days. When we got back home, we got rid of all the evidence, their purses and all, and I washed and vacuumed the van, inside and out."

"Why?"

"Because Gerald told me to do it."

"Did he help you?"

"No. He just sat there and watched."

The court called a thirty-minute recess. Everyone went out for coffee and a smoke except the defendant. Gerald sat at the table, seeming to be in a trance, his face a grayish white, eyes staring unblinking into space. A bailiff became concerned and touched his shoulder. The bailiff said later that Gerald seemed he had died, but couldn't fall over.

Charlene took the stand again after recess, and the People asked her to tell the court what her life with Gerald had been like.

"I don't fully understand," she said.

"Well, let's start with how he treated you."

"Oh, at first he was considerate, polite, and fun to be with. Then he started getting mean and domineering, wanting to control me all the time, saying I had to do what I was told to do. I was just a servant to him."

"A real chauvinist, eh?" A male voice gruff-groffed from the audience. The judge frowned and called for order.

"I was working and paying all the bills. I never did know what he did with his money. Then he ordered me to start wearing my hair in bangs and pigtails, and made me dress in tight jeans and T-shirts, and once, he made me cut my hair real short and—and . . ." Charlene stopped to sob and wipe away a few tears, ". . . he said that I was too old for him, and that he wanted me

Marci Hunt poses with her two young grandsons, David Hunt, left, and
Gerald Gallego, right. *(Author's collection/Phoenix Enterprises, Inc.)*

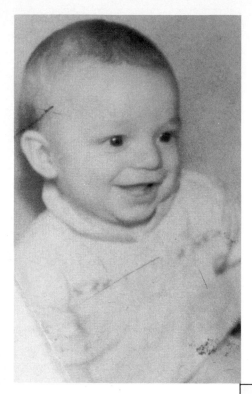

David Raymond Hunt, age eight
months. *(Author's collection/
Phoenix Enterprises, Inc.)*

David Hunt, age five, left, and
Gerald Gallego, age four, right.
*(Author's collection/Phoenix
Enterprises, Inc.)*

Lorriane Bennett Hunt Gallego
Bulgar Davies, age 21, in 1948;
mother of David Hunt and Gerald
Gallego, she was murdered in
August, 1989 at her home in Chico,
California. *(Author's collection/
Phoenix Enterprises, Inc.)*

Sue Ellen Hunt, aka Rayette, age
14, and Gerald Gallego, age 11,
relaxing on the sofa at home; note
that Gerald is gleefully pretending
to hack at Sue Ellen with a knife.
*(Author's collection/Phoenix
Enterprises, Inc.)*

Gerald Gallego about to be transported back to California for
arraignment after his arrest by
the FBI in Omaha, Nebraska,
1980. *(Associated Press/
Wide World Photo)*

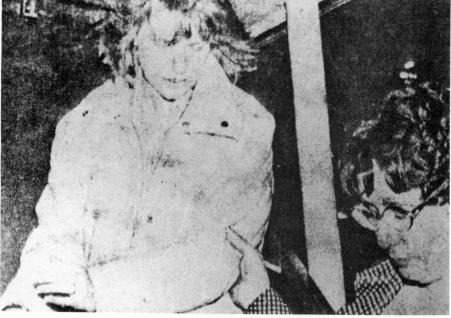

Charlene Gallego is escorted onto the airplane in Omaha for the trip
back to California and arraignment for murder. *(Associated Press/
Wide World Photo)*

Charlene being taken into court during Gerald's California trial. *(Associated Press/Wide World Photo)*

Gerald Gallego during this trial in Nevada, the result of which was a death sentence. *(Associated Press/Wide World Photo)*

STATE OF CALIFORNIA
DEPARTMENT OF HEALTH SERVICES

CERTIFICATE OF DEATH
STATE OF CALIFORNIA

001121

LOCAL REGISTRATION DISTRICT AND CERTIFICATE NUMBER

DECEDENT PERSONAL DATA	1A. NAME OF DECEDENT—First: LORRAINE	1B. Middle: EVELYN	1C. Last: DAVIES

2A. DATE OF DEATH (MONTH, DAY, YEAR): August 15, 1989 — 2B. HOUR: 0100

3. SEX: female — 4. RACE/ETHNICITY: white — 5. SPANISH/HISPANIC: No — 6. DATE OF BIRTH: February 20, 1927 — 7. AGE: 59

8. BIRTHPLACE OF DECEDENT (STATE OR FOREIGN COUNTRY): California

9. NAME AND BIRTHPLACE OF FATHER: Clifford Pullin – Oregon

10. BIRTH NAME AND BIRTHPLACE OF MOTHER: Hazel Sloan – Missouri

11A. CITIZEN OF WHAT COUNTRY: USA — 11B. IF DECEASED WAS EVER IN MILITARY, GIVE DATES OF SERVICE: 19 n/a TO 19 n/a

12. SOCIAL SECURITY NUMBER: 555-36-0359 — 13. MARITAL STATUS: married — 14. NAME OF SURVIVING SPOUSE IF WIFE, ENTER MAIDEN NAME: Edward Davies

15. PRIMARY OCCUPATION: Housewife — 16. NUMBER OF YEARS IN THIS OCCUPATION: Adult Life — 17. EMPLOYER (IF SELF-EMPLOYED, SO STATE): Self — 18. KIND OF INDUSTRY OR BUSINESS: Homemaking

USUAL RESIDENCE

19A. USUAL RESIDENCE—STREET ADDRESS (STREET AND NUMBER OR LOCATION): 1785 Dayton Road — CITY OR TOWN: Chico

19D. COUNTY: Butte — 19E. STATE: California

20. NAME AND ADDRESS OF INFORMANT—RELATIONSHIP: Ed Davies – husband, 1785 Dayton Road, Chico, Ca 95928

PLACE OF DEATH

21A. PLACE OF DEATH: Residence — 21B. COUNTY: Butte

21C. STREET ADDRESS (STREET AND NUMBER OR LOCATION): 1785 Dayton Road — 21D. CITY OR TOWN: Chico

CAUSE OF DEATH

22. DEATH WAS CAUSED BY: ENTER ONLY ONE CAUSE PER LINE FOR A, B, AND C

IMMEDIATE CAUSE (A) Gunshot Wound to Head

DUE TO, OR AS A CONSEQUENCE OF (B) Brain

DUE TO, OR AS A CONSEQUENCE OF (C)

23. OTHER SIGNIFICANT CONDITIONS—CONTRIBUTING TO DEATH BUT NOT RELATED TO CAUSE GIVEN IN 22A

24. WAS DEATH REPORTED TO CORONER?: Yes

25. WAS BIOPSY PERFORMED?: No

26. WAS AUTOPSY PERFORMED?: yes

APPROXIMATE INTERVAL BETWEEN ONSET AND DEATH

27. WAS OPERATION PERFORMED FOR ANY CONDITION IN ITEMS 22 OR 23? TYPE OF OPERATION: No — DATE

PHYSICIAN'S CERTIFICATION

28A. I CERTIFY THAT DEATH OCCURRED AT THE HOUR, DATE AND PLACE STATED FROM THE CAUSES STATED. I ATTENDED DECEDENT SINCE (ENTER MO. DA. YR.) — I LAST SAW DECEDENT ALIVE (ENTER MO. DA. YR.)

28B. PHYSICIAN—SIGNATURE AND DEGREE OR TITLE — 28C. DATE SIGNED: 8/15/89 — 28D. PHYSICIAN'S LICENSE NUMBER: G 31380

28E. TYPE PHYSICIAN'S NAME AND ADDRESS: Gwen Hall, M.D., P. O. Box 1188, Oroville, Ca

INJURY INFORMATION

29. SPECIFY ACCIDENT, SUICIDE, ETC.: Unk. — 30. PLACE OF INJURY: Residence — 31. INJURY AT WORK: No — 32A. DATE OF INJURY (MONTH, DAY, YEAR): August 15, 1989 — 32B. HOUR: 0100

33. LOCATION (STREET AND NUMBER OR LOCATION AND CITY OR TOWN): 1785 Dayton Road, Chico, Ca — 34. DESCRIBE HOW INJURY OCCURRED (EVENTS WHICH RESULTED IN INJURY): Gun shot wound to the head

CORONER'S USE ONLY

38A. I CERTIFY THAT DEATH OCCURRED AT THE HOUR, DATE AND PLACE STATED FROM THE CAUSES STATED, AS REQUIRED BY LAW I HAVE HELD AN INQUEST-INVESTIGATION: Investigation — 38B. CORONER—SIGNATURE AND DEGREE OR TITLE: Hal T. Brooks, Coroner — 38C. DATE SIGNED: 8/15/89

EMBALMER'S LICENSE NUMBER AND SIGNATURE

39. DISPOSITION: Burial — 40. DATE (MONTH, DAY, YEAR): Aug., 19, 1989 — NAME AND ADDRESS OF CEMETERY OR CREMATORY: Chico Cemetery – Chico, Ca — 6760

40A. NAME OF FUNERAL DIRECTOR (OR PERSON ACTING AS SUCH): Brusie Funeral Home — 40B. LICENSE NO.: 371 — 41. LOCAL REGISTRAR—SIGNATURE: Chester L. Ward, R.E.D. — 42. DATE ACCEPTED BY LOCAL REGISTRAR: AUG 1 9 1989

STATE REGISTRAR A. 7 — B. X — C. — D. — E.

This is to certify that this document is a true copy of the official record filed with the Office of State Registrar.

Kenneth W. Kizer, MD, MPH, Director and State Registrar of Vital Statistics

by: David W. Mitchell

DAVID MITCHELL, CHIEF
OFFICE OF STATE REGISTRAR

DATE ISSUED

275516

This copy not valid unless prepared on engraved border displaying seal and signature of Registrar.

Lorriane Davies' death certificate; note the misspelling of her first name (she always spelled it "Lorriane" although it was pronounced "Lorraine") as well as item 29 ("Specify accident, suicide, etc.") which is listed as "Unk." or unknown.

David Raymond Hunt awaiting
arraignment in Woodland after he
was returned from Lewisburg Federal Pennsylvania. *(Barbara Cheney/
The Davis Enterprise)*

Richard Harold Thompson in court
in Woodland awaiting arraignment. *(Alison Portello/The Davis
Enterprise)*

Sue Ellen Hunt in custody of Yolo
County police officers as she, her
husband David and his associate
Richard Thompson were being
charged with multiple counts
of murder. *(Alison Portello/
The Davis Enterprise)*

DAVID C. HENDERSON
District Attorney of Yolo County
P. O. Box 1247
725 Court Street (308 Courthouse)
Woodland, California 95695
Telephone: (916) 666-8180
D.A. File No: tmf

Attorney for The People

Muni. Ct. No. 2-35701

FILED
YOLO COUNTY

NOV 2 9 1989

by Yolene Durad

YOLO COUNTY SUPERIOR COURT

COUNTY OF YOLO, STATE OF CALIFORNIA

THE PEOPLE OF THE STATE
OF CALIFORNIA,

                    Plaintiff,

        vs.

DAVID RAYMOND HUNT, aka
ARTHUR McKAY DURAND, JR.,

                    Defendant.

)
)
)
)
)
)
)
)
)
)
)
)
)

No. 1 1 1 0 4

APPLICATION AND ORDER FOR
WRIT OF HABEAS CORPUS
AD PROSEQUENDUM

COMES NOW the plaintiff herein represented by the District
Attorney of Yolo County, and represents and shows:

That there is now confined in the Federal Prison at
Lewisburg, Pennsylvania, one DAVID RAYMOND HUNT, aka ARTHUR
McKAY DURAND, JR., who is in the custody of the Warden,
Sheriff, or Jailor thereof; that said prisoner is presently
charged in the Yolo County Municipal Court with two violations
of Penal Code section 187, MURDER, and Penal Code section
190.2(3), SPECIAL CIRCUMSTANCE MORE THAN ONE MURDER; and that
said prisoner must appear to answer said charges on
December 8, 1989; and that in Order to secure the attendance of
said prisoner it is necessary that a Writ of Habeas Corpus ad
Prosequendum be issued commanding said Warden to produce said
prisoner to the Yolo County Municipal Court, Department D,
725 Court Street, Woodland, California, on December 8, 1989, at
1:30 p.m.

WHEREFORE, your petitioner prays for an order directing
the issuance of a Writ of Habeas Corpus ad Prosequendum, out
and under the seal of the Court, commanding said Warden to have
and produce said prisoner in Department D of the Yolo County
Municipal Court on said date, then and there to respond to and
answer the charges made against the prisoner, and at the
termination of said case to house him in a local facility.

IF IS FURTHER PRAYED that the United States Marshall be
reimbursed for his services and costs in the transportation and
custody of said prisoner.

DATED: November 28, 1989.

David C. Henderson
DAVID C. HENDERSON
DISTRICT ATTORNEY

The Yolo County application for writ of *habeas corpus* for David Raymond
Hunt to be transferred from Lewisburg Penitentiary.

to dress like a kid, you know, like a teenager. He wanted me to look like his fourteen-year-old daughter. He was always belittling me, and said I was stupid and ugly."

"What was your sex life like with him?"

"It was a problem all the time. He was always trying different kinds of sex, things that hurt me and I didn't want to do it that way, but if it hurt *me* that was too bad. He did it anyway."

"Are you talking about anal sex—sodomy?"

"Yes," Charlene whispered, then sobbed for a few minutes, but told the judge she didn't need a recess.

"Go on, please."

"He couldn't get an erection most of the time. He always said it was my fault . . . everything that went wrong in the bedroom was *always* my fault!" Charlene cried again as the People waited patiently, the judge looked at the ceiling, the defense sneered, the spectators rolled their eyes upward, and Gerald glared at Charlene with that old hardened stare.

"Then . . . then—he—when he *could* do something, he couldn't have a climax," Charlene sobbed, wiping away tears and looking at the DA, "it was always *something* with him . . ."

"You're saying that everything was bad in the bedroom all the time, and Gerald was never satisfied with you, is that right?"

"Uh-hunh."

"And that was the reason he wanted to have what you call 'love slaves'?"

"Yes."

"And you helped him fulfill his fantasies about love slaves because you loved him and believed he'd leave you if you didn't help him, is that what you're telling us?"

"Yes."

"All right. Charlene, don't you think that for your part in those murders, you too deserve the death penalty?"

"Yes! Yes!" Charlene screamed, then quickly added, "But that wouldn't bring those children back to their loved ones! I do know what I did . . ."

"Has anyone in law enforcement, me, or anyone else, *ever*

suggested that you deserve anything less than execution for what you have done?"

"No," Charlene gasped, then dropped her head and cried and hiccupped as the judge called an adjournment until the next day.

The next morning, the defense got up and tore into Charlene with the only real rebuttal it had—impeachment of her credibility as a witness.

"Charlene, isn't it a fact that you have made a plea bargain with the district attorney's office in which you pleaded guilty to two counts of second-degree murder, and given a sixteen-year sentence because of your cooperation in testifying against Gerald Gallego, your husband?"

"Yes, that's true," Charlene replied sweetly.

"Aren't those stories a bunch of lies—to save your own life?"

"No. I have nothing to live for, nothing to save my life for. I know what I did, know what I've been a party to, and I know what I *didn't* do. I didn't try to stop the killing. The only thing on my mind was pleasing Gerald Gallego—my husband, as you said."

"Uh-hunh. You think you're a lot smarter than Gerald, don't you? You didn't have any trouble making a fool out of him at the California trial, did you? When he asked something you didn't want to answer, you'd start laughing or crying, wouldn't you?"

"I can't answer the way you're asking those questions . . ."

"You think, you *know,* that if you start crying maybe us mean old strong men will back off, don't you? Right?"

"No sir."

A woman spectator muttered loud enough to be heard across the small oval courtroom, "She's been turning the tears off and on like a faucet. She and her man should be buried out in the desert with people looking for *their* bodies—not that anyone would want to . . ."

The judge called for order and said that if there was one more interruption in his court, someone would be going to jail.

"Charlene," the defense said, smiling, "I've been dying to ask you this question all day . . . I'd like for you to try to explain to me and this court and this jury, just why you spent almost three years helping your husband fulfill *his* sex fantasies. I, and I'm sure everyone else, will listen with the greatest of interest."

"All right. When I first met Gerald, it was a time in my life that I was trying to make it on my own." Charlene paused for a moment to wipe away more tears. "An independent woman, you know. I didn't want to need anyone, a husband, a boyfriend. I didn't even want to need my parents. Other divorced women could make it on their own, and so could I. I'd already failed in two marriages . . . and when I met Gerald . . ." Now Charlene exploded into a fit of loud, gurgling sobs, hiccups, and wailing. After a short recess, Charlene was able to take the stand again. She was now composed but red-eyed and shaky. Gerald glared at her with venom in his unblinking eyes.

"You may continue," the judge told her after the reporter had read back her previous testimony.

"As I was trying to say, I just wanted to make it on my own, but I had been a failure in everything, and when I met Gerald, I no longer wanted to be alone—or fail again.

"He really made me feel as if I was wanted, that he really wanted to be with me. I wanted to spend the rest of my life with this man, and I would do anything to please him. I would be anything he wanted me to be, accept any role. I knew I'd never find anyone else who would want me. He was security. I didn't want to fail again. That is my explanation of my relationship with Gerald Gallego, the best way I can explain it. That's why I stayed with him, why I went along with all this. I hope you understood my answer when I said Gerald filled a desperate need in my life. I know that's not an excuse for what I did, but that's *why* it happened."

"That's all really very interesting, Charlene, but you didn't have any trouble getting rid of two other husbands, did you?"

"No."

"It didn't bother you at all, did it?"

"No, but I was also afraid of Gerald. He'd beat me up. I was afraid he would kill me if I didn't—if I made him mad enough, if I wouldn't go along. Deep in my heart, I knew the only way we'd ever end our relationship was when he killed me because I knew too much."

"Uh-hunh. Now Charlene, aren't you making up all this, just accumulating all the bad parts of Gerald, making him look so bad the jury won't take a chance on letting him go, whether there's enough real evidence to convict him on these charges or not?"

"I'm just trying to answer your question."

"Sure. Charlene, here's another question I've been dying to ask you—if, as you claim, you were forced by Gerald to help him do those killings, why didn't you shoot him? You had lots of chances, you know how to use a gun, don't you?"

"I can't answer that. I loved Gerald. I didn't want to be alone again. I was trying to please him."

Charlene broke down into sobs, hiccups, and wailing once again and the judge once again recessed the court for the rest of the day.

A female clinical psychologist took the stand to present the mandatory "why he did it, and why he isn't responsible for his actions" aspect of the defense.

". . . Emotionally, Gerald has the level of control of a five- or six-year old child," the psychologist testified, "Gerald has extreme problems with emotion control, and a very low sense of self-esteem. This trial has also given him a feeling that there is some negative assessment of him in this community. Gerald suffers from some kind of brain damage that makes him feel *incredibly* passive and dependent upon others.

"On the other hand, Charlene, the woman he was with for

several years, has an IQ of one hundred and sixty, an intelligence quotient that puts her in the top one percent of the population, and from a psychologist's point of view, she would have had far more control over their relationship than Gerald did.

"As we all know," the shrink plodded on, "the best prediction of future behavior is past behavior . . ."

The defense quickly objected to its own witness in order to prevent the People from gleefully cross-examining her. Gerald simply did not have a great deal of luck with shrink witnesses. Objection or not, the jury had heard that his past behavior would repeat itself, and that was the only thing the jury would remember from her testimony.

" The People's case rests upon tales from an admitted liar," the defense said in its summation to the jury. "Mr. Gallego's wife made up the sex-fantasy story from whole cloth. No one should be convicted anywhere on this kind of evidence. If it were a burglary case, you'd walk him out the door in ten minutes.

"What little physical evidence there is may link Charlene to the crimes, but not Gerald. She's capable. She could have done it. She knows how to handle a gun, she can swing a hammer as well as Gerald can, and she's much more intelligent than he is. If you think he is guilty, well, what is the difference between his culpability and hers? We know someone has to answer for those killings—but surely not an innocent man. I'm going to ask you to do something that's going to take a lot of courage—I want you to find him not guilty."

The prosecution then stood up and showed the jury pictures of the victims' head wounds.

"You want horror?" The DA said, "Well, *that's* horror!"

"I've been waiting for the defense to tell us how Charlene was able to put semen into those girls. She may be pretty intelligent, but she couldn't do that. Now, the judge will instruct you by law to be leery of Charlene's testimony because she was an accomplice. She helped see that those crimes were carried out. I believe you will have mixed emotions as to what she told you, and about her personally."

The defense's rebuttal consisted of the assertion that Charlene was testifying against Gerald Gallego for self-preservation, pure and simple—and that was the best reason for her to lie."

The People stood up again and said, "Simply put, do your duty and find him guilty. Anything else would be a travesty of justice."

The six-man, six-woman jury was out three hours and forty minutes. It was June 7, 1984. A verdict of guilty on two counts of murder in the first degree was returned with a recommendation of death on each count. They also found Gerald guilty on two counts of kidnapping and set the penalty at two life sentences without parole. All that remained was for the judge to approve the jury's recommendations and pronounce sentence.

Gerald stood now, and for the first time during his trial, spoke openly to the court and jury.

"Judge, what this court has done to me is wrong. It made a very serious mistake. With the help of the media, all that power of the press, you can convict any man on anything—on any matter.

"I've been quiet during this whole trial and it hasn't been easy. But I'm a very quiet man really, and let my lawyer do the talking. I can see that was a real bad mistake. I was guilty even before I got here, and somebody's got to pay the price, and anybody who can't see that is a fool. I didn't kill those girls and you don't have a damned thing that says I did. The *only* evidence against me was from the prosecution's hired gun, Charlene Gallego. His paid assassin is all she is. She got paid with her life back. If I'd had a fair trial I'd been found not guilty. What you people done to me is wrong.

"I don't see how the district attorney could put on a case like this. Was he there? The only thing he knows is what Charlene Gallego told him, and the only thing she told him was what she wanted him to know. Charlene's deal was made in the back room of the district attorney office."

The judge then asked if that was all Gerald had to say. When Gerald nodded, the judge sentenced him to death by lethal injection, to be carried out within the walls of the Nevada State Prison at Carson City, Nevada.

Chapter 25

Epilogus Atque Sententias

As of the time of this writing, Gerald Armond Gallego has been waiting five years on Nevada's death row for his death sentence to be carried out. He has exhausted his first round of federal and state appeals and is starting over through state channels again. In September 1989 his final state appeal, on file at that time, was rejected by the Nevada State Supreme Court, which stated that Charlene's plea bargain was not illegal and did not jeopardize Gerald's right to a fair trial in Lovelock.

Gerald has gotten along fairly well on death row, except for a fight with another inmate in 1987 in which Gerald bit off a section of the man's ear.

No matter what direction the appeals process may take for Gerald, he will never set foot outside prison as a free man. Another death sentence awaits him in California. The Rose Bird court was voted out of office in 1987, and supreme court justices were voted in who have approved ninety percent of all capital cases reviewed. If and when Gerald is finally executed by the people of Nevada, his death will be far less painful, far more

300

dignified, and much faster than the sentences of death he carried out on his and Charlene's victims.

Death by lethal injection means that the prisoner is strapped to a hospital gurney about fifteen minutes before the time set to carry out his execution. He is wheeled into the death chamber and two IV needles are inserted into the main arteries of his left and right arms. The IVs are connected to a small pumplike machine concealed behind a screen, where a doctor or medical technician waits for orders to start the IVs. After the formalities and last words, the warden nods and the IVs are started. Fifty milligrams of Thiopental is pumped into the right arm, and the prisoner lapses into an immediate coma. Then a mixture of Oradauan, Lorazepan, and potassium chloride are released into the left arm, causing the heart to stop within one to three minutes.

It is almost exactly the same mixture of chemicals used by pounds to kill dogs and cats.

A Texas cop who witnessed the execution of a particularly vile torturer-murderer at Huntsville said that death came much too easily: "The guy just went to sleep, like you'd turn out a light. He didn't know or feel a damned thing. Where's the punishment in that kind of execution?"

Charlene is currently serving her sixteen years and eight months in the women's section of the same prison where Gerald is waiting. As of this writing, she is in solitary confinement for assaulting a guard who broke up a fight between Charlene and another prisoner, also an aggressive lesbian, while the two were battling over a recently arrived prisoner who they thought was cute. Providing she isn't killed by another inmate, or her legal team can't find a way to break the plea bargain, Charlene will probably be released in August of 1997 at age forty-one, with many good years ahead of her. She will likely inherit her parents' money and property, and will be able to live a comfortable life without a concern in the world.

Gerald Armond Gallego, Jr., will be sixteen when his mother

comes home. It is anyone's guess what kind of life they will have together. At worst, it will be far better than anything faced by the victims who lost their lives at the hands of Gerald and Charlene Gallego.

And now, even after three generations of a family filled with murder, armed robbery, rape, kidnapping, incest, and almost every other offense known to civil and criminal jurisprudence, the Gallego story just seems to continue on a path of senseless, bloody violence and destruction without an end in sight.

Two major and sensational developments occurred in the continuing saga of the Gallego sex-killing case during the months immediately prior to this writing. In mid-August 1989, Lorraine Davies, Gerald Gallego's beloved mother and the chief source for much of the information in this book, died of a gunshot wound to her head. She was found in the living room of her home, a converted barn in the mountain town of Chico, California, with a hole in the middle of her forehead. And three months later, in mid-November 1989, almost exactly nine years to the day from Gerald and Charlene's arrests, Gerald's half-brother, David Hunt, who is allegedly Lorraine's son by the tall Texican, Harold Hunt, was arrested and charged with kidnapping and murder in the first degree. There is little doubt that these killings are connected in some way to the Gallego's spree—just how deeply intertwined they are is, at least officially, a matter of conjecture at this point. In the following pages, I'll attempt to illuminate some of the chilling theories that are beginning to come to light and that will very likely be proven in Hunt's trial during the months to come.

On November 13, 1989, Hunt, age 45, and his wife, Sue Ellen, age 44, were arrested and charged with two counts of kidnap-murder, which occurred on December 20, 1980, near the University of California at Davis, some twenty miles from Sacramento. It is alleged by the Woodland, California, police department that Hunt and his wife committed those crimes as copycat killings in order to draw suspicion away from Gerald and Charlene, who were in jail awaiting trial for the murders of Craig Miller and Mary Beth Sowers. If the same type of murders were still being committed, they reasoned, then the real murderer(s) must have still been free, and when they locked up Gerald and Charlene they must have locked up the wrong couple. This type of scam is obvious even to the most slick-sleeved rookie cop, but it is a beloved pipe dream of the conscienceless sociopath, who will use any means available, no matter how desperate or heinous, in an attempt to clear himself. The fact that innocent people must die a horrible death in order for his alibi to appear credible means absolutely nothing to him.

Another lifelong hard-line convict named Richard Harold Thompson, age fifty-one, was also arrested as a conspirator and/or participant in those kidnap-murders.

Thompson and Hunt were cellmates at San Quentin for many years, and their friendship goes back to the middle sixties. California authorities have alleged that while on parole from an armed robbery conviction, Hunt helped Thompson escape from a medical clinic in Marin County on October 11, 1980. On that foggy morning, as Thompson and two guards exited a prison vehicle, a man wearing a ski mask stood up from behind a car, pointed a shotgun and ordered the guards to remove the cuffs and leg iron from Thompson, then forced them to lie down on the pavement. Thompson ran to his rescuer and both men disappeared into the heavy fog. Thompson was captured a few months later, but being a true-blue, hard-line convict, refused to name the person who had risked life and liberty to help him escape. And by that time, the two kidnap-murders had already taken place. The guards could only say for certain that the man with the shotgun was tall and skinny, a description that fit Hunt, at the time.

David Raymond Hunt was born in Sacramento on September 13, 1944. David is the middle name of his alleged father, while Raymond comes from his maternal grandfather, Pullin, who molested his and Gerald's mother, Lorraine, when she was a young girl. If his half brother Gerald's life was terrible, then Hunt's must have been even worse. He was more or less raised by everyone *but* his mother—grandparents, aunts, cousins, whore friends of his mom, and an endless parade of babysitters.

His alleged paternal grandmother—though she couldn't be sure that David was her grandson—tried to lend a helping hand by buying David and Gerald clothes and feeding them whenever she had the opportunity. She took a number of pictures of David and Gerald when they were children, and did her best to make them feel some kind of love. She tried to make life a little easier for the boys whenever Lorraine would let them visit or stay with her. She was not a wealthy woman, but offered to adopt both boys. Lorraine refused, however, and continued to allow her kids to float willy-nilly from one cockroach-infested Okie shack to another. She pawned them off on good-hearted grandparents or indifferent babysitters—or, if there were none available, she just flat left the boys to fend for themselves while she was out doing her thing, whatever that might be.

By the time David was fourteen, Lorraine had already married George Bulgar, who had lost his skid row bar and gone into pimping. He couldn't seem to get the hang of it, even though he had two attractive, hardworking girls in his stable. One of those girls was a pretty, slim, natural redhead who had a fourteen-year-old daughter with reddish blond hair. The daughter was then known as Rayette. During the harvest season, George and Lorraine would take their girls out to farm labor camps around Sacramento and rent them out to Filipino laborers at a flat rate of two hundred dollars per night.

Bulgar was arrested several times on pimping charges, did a few months in the county jail, was released, and then went right back to hustling his girls. He was, by then, a falling-down, slobbering, vicious alcoholic, who beat the hell out of Lorraine and her two sons, David and Gerald, along with his hardworking whores. When Bulgar was arrested for contributing to the delinquency of a (female) minor by soliciting her for immoral purposes, and faced some real jail time, Lorraine finally decided that it was time to hit the road. Both David and Gerald were in reform school at the time, so she rented the Okie shanty on Heraldsburg Street in Chico and tried to get undercover. But she took the pretty, fourteen-year-old Rayette with her, possibly as seed money because she hoped to do a bit of pimping herself. Whatever the real reason, Lorraine made a virtual slave out of the girl.

Rayette spent twenty-four hours per day doing Lorraine's cooking, housecleaning, laundry, ironing, and acting as a body servant to her self-appointed benefactress. David was home only between prison sentences, but he and the pretty little modern-day Cinderella got along like a house on fire. What little spare time Rayette had was spent reading, improving her knowledge, grammar and manners. Lorraine had two small kids by Bulgar. Rayette was kept hopping, taking care of the kids, the house, and tending to Lorraine's personal needs by helping her get dressed and bathed, and giving her soothing massages.

When they all went to the movies, Rayette usually stayed in the lobby with the noisy, spoiled kids and missed the film so that Lorraine could enjoy it without being distracted. Rayette was under orders to check with Lorraine occasionally to see if she needed popcorn, candy or maybe a Coke.

Lorraine denied ever putting the girl on the street or bringing men home for her to service. Given Lorraine's background, her life with George Bulgar, and her powerful desire for cash, one can easily imagine this scenario.

During this time in Lorraine's life, David Raymond Hunt was in and out of reform schools for numerous crimes, but was generally released after a few months by psychiatrists who pronounced him cured of all criminal proclivities.

In 1961, when he was seventeen, David held up the Stagecoach Stop bar on Folsom Boulevard just north of Sacramento. When he pulled his gun and demanded the money, the proprietor took one look at the skinny, scruffy bandit and laughed. David didn't take kindly to being laughed at, and the bar owner went down in a hail of bullets, barely surviving three rounds in the chest. David was caught in a matter of hours. He was tried as an adult, and this time took a real bad fall—five to life in San Quentin for armed robbery and attempted murder. But not to worry. Exactly twenty-three months later, a prison psychiatrist recommended to the parole board that David be set free. He was deemed no longer a danger to society and found to have rehabilitated himself by attending group therapy sessions and high school equivalency classes. He had regained his self-esteem, and admitted he'd done wrong, had seen the light and wouldn't ever do it again. The parole board must have had some qualms about the shrink's recommendation, because when they released David in 1963, they left him dragging a very long tail—ten years on parole.

Parole meant nothing to David Raymond Hunt—no more than it had meant to his half brother, Gerald Armond Gallego. Within a matter of days, he was back in the armed robbery business, a career path he would follow until he finally made the fatal mistake of delving into federal crime and bumping heads with the FBI—the same law enforcement agency that brought down Gerald and Charlene. Information from the FBI would eventually land David in a federal penitentiary that wasn't run by naive psychiatrists and social workers.

Hunt was paroled from San Quentin, where he had been serving a sentence for armed robbery, in early October 1980. He and his cellmate, Richard Thompson, had plenty of time there to plan Thompson's escape. Thompson feigned illness on a prearranged schedule and was transported to a medical clinic where San Quentin inmates were regularly treated. It was there that Hunt stepped in and sprung his old friend, at which point the two were ready and willing to engage in whatever activities suited their needs and/or those of their loved ones.

It is alleged by the chief informant in the Hunt-Thompson case in secret conversations with investigators, that sometime in November 1980, shortly after his arrest for the Miller-Sowers kidnap-rape murders, Gerald Armond Gallego sent word to his

mother that he wanted to see her. During that meeting, it is
alleged that Gerald requested that Lorraine arrange with someone to carry out a couple of copycat killings of a young man and
woman in order to draw suspicion away from him and Charlene
in the Miller-Sowers case.

Lorraine then supposedly contacted David and suggested
that he fulfill his brother's request. As it was a family matter,
there may have been others involved. Numerous family members and associates are classified as "being under suspicion."
David did have a ready-made helper in Richard Harold Thompson, as well as his own wife, Sue Ellen. And Lorraine, if these
allegations are true, was an accessory to the murders.

At around 10:00 P.M., Saturday, December 20, 1980, John
Harold Riggin and Sabrina Marie Gonsalves, both eighteen-
year-old students at the University of California at Davis, left a
fast-food restaurant near the campus and headed north toward
Sacramento, some twenty miles away. Just past the Yolo Cause-
way, they were allegedly flagged down by a woman standing
beside a van, who claimed she was having engine trouble and
asked Riggin to take a look. When he went to the van, Riggin
was allegedly taken prisoner by two men and placed inside.
Gonsalves apparently didn't try to run, and was also put in the
van.

Riggin's and Gonsalves' bodies were found the next afternoon by a highway patrol unit lying just off the road in some
bushes. There had been no attempt to hide the bodies as they
could be seen from any passing car, but the heavy fog concealed
them from view most of the day. Their heads had been smashed
in, and their throats cut. According to coroner's records, neither corpse showed any indications of sexual abuse. One must
assume that the Hunts and Thompson knew the details of Gerald and Charlene's sex killings and would have inflicted similar
atrocities upon their victims for a better replica of the Gallego
killings, but that it was simply not in their nature. If they could
have brought themselves to rape and sodomize their victims
they probably would have done just that, but they couldn't, so

they didn't. With Gerald's history of molesting his daughter, the sexual aspect of the kidnap-murders was a natural extrapolation. Not with Hunt and Thompson.

On Monday, December 22, 1980, some fifty miles north of Davis in a sparsely populated area in the wooded foothills between Lincoln and Marysville, California, a teenage boy and girl were braving the afternoon chill while fishing for catfish in a small creek about five hundred yards from a seldom traveled, paved country road.

It is alleged that the couple were approached by a tall, slim, red-haired woman who claimed she was having trouble with her van, and said she'd give the teenage boy twenty dollars if he would drive her to a garage so she could hire a tow truck. The boy agreed, and the three of them walked back to the road. A passing motorist saw two men, one tall and skinny, a red-haired woman, and two "teenage kids" standing beside a blue van, apparently arguing about something. Not wanting to get involved in a roadside scuffle, the motorist drove on.

At around 6:00 P.M. that same day, the teenage boy and girl were found by a couple who were hiking through the area. The bodies were lying in plain sight some ten feet from the road. Their heads had been bashed in and their throats cut from ear to ear. Again, the coroner did not report any signs of sexual abuse.

Back in Sacramento, newspaper headlines were screaming "SERIAL KILLERS STRIKE AGAIN!" And Gerald Gallego's old nemesis, the local female TV reporter, again narrowed her steely-blues, glared at the monitor and inveighed, "Have our police jailed the guilty ones? Or is this another group of serial killers crying out for help in a wilderness of uncaring people who refuse to hear their pitiful pleas for love and attention?"

People were listening all right, but they didn't like what they were hearing—particularly the cops working the Gallego case. Just a copycat killing, pure and simple, claimed nervous police spokespersons to the TV cameras. Nothing whatever to do with Gerald and Charlene Gallego . . . Of course we're investigating, but there isn't a thing to connect these killings with the Gallegos . . . (The last thing they wanted to do was connect the killings to the Gallego case and then possibly come to the next logical conclusion—that they had gone to all this trouble to lock up the wrong people, that the real killer(s) were still roaming the shopping malls and country roads.)

And so the official version held together for eight long years. Gerald and Charlene had their days in court, were convicted and sentenced. (Interestingly, during his trial for the Miller-Sowers killings, Gerald's attorney subpoenaed documents relating to the copycat murders in the hope he would show enough similarities that the real killer could be assumed to be on the loose. Ultimately, of course, this strategy did not work.)

Lorraine Evelyn Davies lived with her husband in their converted Okie barn at 1785 Dayton Road, Chico, California. Whenever she received a phone call or visitor she didn't know, she claimed to be the cleaning woman. She continued to plan complex and often unworkable con jobs. And she arranged dozens of secret meetings with an ex-cop and a writer from Southern California to whom she bared her tortured soul and exposed the life history of her entire family, including her own sordid, miserable, fifty-odd years of existence in a world she made for herself.

The copycat victims rotted in their lonely graves and their bones began that long, cold journey back to dust.

In 1984, David Raymond Hunt allegedly kidnapped a woman and made a ransom demand upon her family. Hunt was captured when he tried to collect the ransom, and the victim was released unharmed. Knowing that it was pointless to try for the death penalty, the feds asked for and got a thirty-two years-to-life sentence for Hunt. They were sent to the Lewisburg Federal Correctional Facility in Lewisburg, Pennsylvania.

There are a number of federal pens, financed by the taxpayers and known as government Club Meds, where white-collar criminals serve out their time. These facilities are complete with swimming pools, tennis courts, jogging paths, catered meals, cable TV, individual rooms minus locks, gyms with the latest and most expensive body-building equipment, first-run movies, libraries that seem to be as well stocked as the Smithsonian Institution, and comfortable mobile homes where monthly con-jugal weekend visits from wives are allowed for the white-collar criminals so that they won't become too tense and testy and maybe think of escaping, or turn gay and embarrass the hell out of the government by appearing on the "Geraldo Rivera Show" and claiming the prison system spun them around.

But Lewisburg is no Club Med. Next to the Marion Federal Penitentiary in Illinois, it is the toughest government slammer in the US prison system.

David had been at Lewisburg only a few weeks when a woman who claimed to be his wife applied for visiting privileges, claim-ing that her name was Sue Ellen Hunt. She was a tall, slim, very pretty natural redhead. Tired of being taken to court by cons very time one of their requests is turned down, the feds allowed Sue Ellen to go on record as Hunt's wife. She moved into an apartment in Lewisburg and got a job as a "counselor" with a state-financed program, in which she was supposed to find jobs for ex-cons and what are laughingly referred to by those in the know as "*former* dope addicts." Whether she had any other source of income is not known, but she seemed to be quite well-to-do, considering her $1,000-per-month job as a coun-selor.

Meanwhile, back in California, Lorraine Davies got to think-ing about money. Money was one thing, perhaps the *only* thing, that Lorraine truly loved. She was greedy for it and sometimes her greed was enough to cause her to turn on her friends in a vicious way. Back in 1958, for example, while she was still mar-ried to George Bulgar, she and George knew a nice married couple who were several cuts above them on the social scale. These folks took a liking to Lorraine for whatever reason— probably because they felt sorry for her. But they would learn, as everyone else eventually did, that feeling sorry for Lorraine

Evelyn Davies was about as safe as petting a pissed-off rattle-snake. Lorraine and George showed up on their friends' door-step one summer evening about 10:00 P.M.. Lorraine was screaming accusations at the couple that they had bought whis-key for her sixteen-year-old son, David, who was lying dead puking drunk in the backseat of their car. (George was showing some pretty obvious signs of drink himself.) Lorraine de-manded $200 in cash reparations. She threatened to report the couple to the sheriff and have them arrested on charges of obtaining liquor for a minor if they didn't pay up. The couple quickly called Lorraine's bluff, at which point anyone else trying to float a scam as blatant as this one would have been happy to back off and run for it. It was obvious it wasn't going to work. But not Lorraine. She played it right out to the end by actually calling the sheriff and making a formal complaint to a deputy while still standing in her friend's driveway.

The deputy was rather embarrassed at the whole situation, knowing as he did that George Bulgar had a vice rap sheet as long as his leg and that David Hunt's record for holdups already rivaled that of John Dillinger. But he was obligated to go through the motions. He checked with the liquor store clerk who was alleged to have sold the couple the liquor they sup-posedly then gave to Hunt. The clerk would not back up Lor-raine's story, however, and the affair was ended as was Lor-raine's friendship with one pair of law-abiding citizens.

It's not hard to imagine how Lorraine's endless scams of this nature might annoy her numerous acquaintances or how such a relatively insignificant caper, magnified a few times, might really piss somebody off badly enough to want to do serious bodily harm to her.

Sure enough, checking back through Lorraine's past, one finds it scattered with as many deadly enemies as corpses on a World War I battlefield. But deadly or not, very few were willing to talk openly about her. Harold Hunt, her second husband, was not exactly an enemy, though he was well aware of her many shortcomings. He knew her terrible greed for money, which she tried to obtain in any way possible, and her above-average intelligence, which she never exercises in any fashion other than to think up more scams than a family of roving Gypsies.

Hunt recalled that a few months after their bogus marriage back in the forties, Lorraine, who was only sixteen at the time, and under the legal age of consent, did her level best to talk him into kidnapping a woman her mother worked for, collecting a "big" ransom, then killing the woman and hiding the body. Harold Hunt said that he may have been young at the time, but he wasn't stupid. He refused to have anything to do with the scheme. Lorraine also tried to get him involved in the old hugger-mugger con where she would lure servicemen out of bars into dark alleys, then Hunt could coldcock them with a club so the two of them could rob their victims at their leisure. Fortunately, Hunt said, he also refused that offer.

Almost any psychiatrist would agree that Lorraine had some real sexual hangups. But Hunt claimed this wasn't remotely true—that Lorraine sometimes gave the outward appearance of being prudish and somewhat shy, but in actual fact she was a happy, eager lovemaker, willing to try anything that might be pleasurable to her or her sex partner. Hunt said that a few minutes after their first sexual encounter in the back seat of a car, she told him that, yes, she had liked it, but wasn't sure a woman was supposed to, and didn't know if she should lie and say no, or tell him the truth. But when he assured her the truth was better, Lorraine never had any question about sex until many years later when she went into the whore business and asked him to teach her how to perform fellatio.

Lorraine and Harold Hunt split up and fell out of touch for years. They met up again by chance when Hunt walked into the establishment owned by Lorraine's future husband, George Bulgar, one night. Lorraine was bartending there, and she and Hunt resumed their relationship but on a much looser, less regular basis.

"I remember one time I was supposed to meet her after she got off work at Bulgar's skid row bar," Hunt recalled, "but she told me she'd be about two hours late because something came up. Now, to this day, over forty years later, I still don't know why I decided to follow her. She was picked up by Chubby, the guy she later told me was her pimp. He drove a Greyhound taxi. They went out to a crappy little mobile home park in West Sacramento. I sat in my car and watched Lorraine go up to a trailer, knock on the door, then go in. But that time, I knew of course what she was doing, and just drove off. It really wasn't any of my business what she did . . . we were just friends by that time, but had no real love for each other anymore . . . at least I didn't.

"I started meeting her less and less, and the last time I saw Lorraine was in late forty-nine or early fifty. I remember she was sitting on the motel bed and took off her bra . . . she must have had thirty dollars in change stuffed in there. Coins fell all over the bed like a broken piggy bank. We both laughed like hell because she had such big tits and the coins made her look lumpy. She said it was her nightly take in tips from the bar."

It was probably shortly after this that Lorraine and George Bulgar went into the pimping and whore business full-time. If they were financially successful at it, they had nothing tangible to show for their efforts. They never had a new car, and there is no record of Lorraine ever owning property until she was married to Ed Davies. And even then, it was no more than a run down converted barn that any self-respecting Okie wouldn't even have lived in. Ed Davies probably made a good lower-middle-class living, but that would never have satisfied Lorraine. Again, her greed must have taken over her good sense, and she made the final, fatal mistake of hustling the wrong person.

In 1986, one particular female member of Lorraine's family said to an ex-cop in Beverly Hills, "If you have any influence over that dumb-assed Lorraine, tell her she's fucking with the undertaker. Why? Because she's trying to collect some money from someone who's gonna kill her if she doesn't back off."

The ex-cop had no idea who Lorraine might be demanding money from, or for what reason, and he didn't want to know. He did, however, feel obligated to pass that warning along, only to be told by its recipient, "I appreciate your concern, but I'm not doing anything dangerous. I mean, who'd want to kill an old broad like me?" The answer to that question was three years down the road . . . At around 1:00 A.M. on Friday, August 15, 1989, Lorraine was found, most likely by her husband Ed, on the floor of her house, a gunshot wound in her head, with brains, blood and pieces of skull plastered to the wall behind her. An autopsy was performed on the body, and she was buried four days later at a cemetery in Chico. Her funeral was sparsely attended by family members. She was sixty-two years old, apparently in good health (which belied her claim during Gerald's trial six years back that she was dying of cancer). Still a handsome woman, no would have guessed her age at more than forty-five. Her death certificate indicated the cause as a "gunshot wound to the head and brain" with specifics unknown.

Chico is a small mountain town. Its ordinary citizens and the bureaucrats who run the place are a tightly knit, closemouthed group. Other than a very short obituary notice, not a word of the death appeared in the press. And some weeks later when a request was made for a copy of the coroner's report, it was promised several times. As of this writing, the report remains in bureaucratic limbo, not refused officially, still promised "as soon as we can get to it." All of which would indicate to anyone familiar with the bureaucracy that someone has orders to stonewall the Lorraine Evelyn Davies case.

The fact is that the local Chico police as well as the Butte County authorities never seemed to take much notice of Lorraine's premature demise, that despite the clear indication on her death certificate, which is signed and dated August 15, 1989, that the fatal shot, which entered in the center of her forehead and exited in the rear of her skull before lodging somewhere in the wall behind her, was from an "unknown" source, there seemed to have been absolutely no investigation to speak of. In fact, Lorraine seemed to have been considered just as much of a nonentity in death as she was in life.

Rather than face assertions on the part of some intrepid reporter that they dropped the ball entirely, the local authorities very likely elected to clamp a tight hold on any information about Lorraine's death. The other possibility is that Butte County investigators have indeed been in contact with their counterparts in Woodland, that they have put two and two together and drawn the connection with the Hunt-Thompson and Gallego cases. Whether or not this has occurred, by all appearances, everyone connected with the Hunt-Thompson case has proceeded, until the time of this writing, as if they were completely unaware of Lorraine's death. (Newspaper articles on the Hunt-Thompson pretrial proceedings, dated as late of December 24, 1989, continued to refer to Lorraine in the present tense even though she had been dead for more than four months.)

Was Lorraine's death murder? Suicide? An accident? At this point, those questions remain officially unanswered. But according to certain law enforcement agents familiar with the case, shortly after Lorraine's funeral, a "very, very reliable informant came forward" claiming to know why she was killed, and who may have done it.

Who that informant might be is, at the time of this writing, a matter of speculation. Was it one of Lorraine's immediate blood relatives? Her sister Ramona? Was it Ed Davies? Davies is certainly the most likely candidate to be this all-important informant, and his motive for blowing the whistle is crystal clear: to avenge the death of his wife.

The informant claimed that Lorraine was blackmailing a certain dope dealer back East in exchange for keeping her mouth shut about four murders that had taken place in California some eight years before. Her demands were made off and on over a period of two or three years. Supposedly her blackmailing victim got sick and tired of the threats, or became frightened, and either killed Lorraine or hired a hitman to do it.

Who was she blackmailing? Well, the informant is alleged to have replied, the wife of some guy in the federal pen in Lewisburg, Pennsylvania. And for which murders? You know, those copycat killings that took place back in 1980 after the Gallegos were arrested for their sex-killing spree.

Is it possible that, were this crucial informant indeed Ed Davies, he would know so little about his wife's family's twisted doings that he wouldn't immediately jump to the obvious conclusion that it was Sue Ellen Hunt whom Lorraine was blackmailing, that Sue Ellen and David were responsible for the Gallego copycat killings? Absolutely, yes. Davies is a modest, retiring, physically unassuming man who would have no reason to inquire actively into his dominant wife's complicated and often brutal family history. After all, what good could possibly come of asking nosy questions about the likes of Gerald Gallego and David Hunt, if indeed Davies was even aware of their connection to his wife?

The authorities, on the other hand, probably did jump to some such conclusion and so they were off and running—right smack in the direction of David Raymond Hunt, his wife, Sue Ellen, and Richard Harold Thompson, the prime suspects in the killings of John Riggin and Sabrina Gonsalves on December 20, 1980.

It should be kept in mind that the police and the prosecutors, like anybody else, follow the path of least resistance. When it comes to investigating a murder case, the authorities are free to pick and choose which particular murders to prosecute, invariably selecting the one that can lead to conviction with the least effort and expense. In this instance, they've chosen the Riggin-Gonsalves killings. Lorraine has not been mentioned and neither have the teenage boy and girl found beside the road up in Marysville on December 22, 1980. One would imagine—and hope—that the authorities are simply holding the three other killings in abeyance, in the event that the Riggin-Gonsalves case falls through.

On November 13, 1989, David Raymond Hunt was arrested by the FBI in his cell at the Lewisburg correctional facility. Sue Ellen Hunt was picked up at her job the same day. All three were charged with two counts of murder in the first degree and two counts of kidnapping with intent to do great bodily harm, both capital offenses.

Apparently the three suspects waived extradition. Sue Ellen was flown immediately to Sacramento and placed in the Sacramento County Jail, even though the trial would be held in Woodland, California, a small farming town some twenty miles away in Yolo County. It was a different matter when it came to deciding where to hold Hunt and Thompson to await trial. Both men were experienced escape artists; both were considered extremely dangerous and both had plenty of friends on the outside who owed them long-standing favors.

Thompson was flown to California and placed in a solitary confinement cell at the old hard-time, escape-proof Folsom Prison some twenty miles north of Sacramento. Hunt was brought to town in total secrecy. Upon arrival by plane, he was taken to the Sacramento County Jail and put in a holding cell in the basement that was usually reserved for prisoners awaiting transport to death row.

On December 4, 1989, Sue Ellen was brought into superior court for arraignment on two counts of first-degree murder and kidnapping. She pleaded not guilty, was bound over for a preliminary hearing without bail, and then transferred to the Yolo County Jail in Woodland.

At 9:00 A.M., on December 21, 1989, police units sealed off a four-square-block area around the old courthouse in downtown Sacramento, refusing to allow anyone in or out. Motorcycle cops cruised slowly up and down the empty streets, checking parked cars, pedestrians' IDs, and staring up at windows. (One man almost got himself arrested when he angrily challenged a cop's authority to keep him confined in the four-block area. He later told news reporters that he missed an appointment with his hairdresser, which he would be forced to pay for anyway, and was thinking of suing the city.)

At around 10:00 A.M., a blacked-out van literally surrounded by police units came flying down the street and screeched to a stop in front of the courthouse. Doors flew open, cops poured out with shotguns aimed in all directions, then Hunt and Thompson were helped out of the van. Each man wore two sets of leg irons. They were chained together and each wore a heavy brown leather belt to which their handcuffed wrists were shackled; another set of handcuffs had been cranked on each man's forearm, keeping them almost shoulder-to-shoulder. The prisoners were carrying at least fifty pounds of steel, and it took them almost ten minutes to walk up the forty or so courthouse steps.

The Sacramento police hadn't put on such a tight security show since they'd jailed Charlie Manson's main mama, Annette (Squeaky) Fromm, for the Secret Service after she tried to shoot President Gerald Ford in a midtown Sacramento park because, Squeaky claimed, Ford wasn't doing enough to protect the redwood trees. All in all, it was a good show that morning, complete with a little hedge-hopping helicopter that buzzed around overhead. Everyone enjoyed it—with the possible exception of the guy who missed his hairdressing appointment.

Hunt and Thompson were taken into a courtroom that had been prepared in advance for the high-risk prisoners. They met their attorneys, public defenders, and were seated at a table with the attorneys between them. They talked to each other for a few minutes, smiled and nodded, then the arraignment was called to order.

Hunt suddenly stood, and looking like an Inquisition heretic before the Papal Bar in his clanking chains, informed the startled judge, "Your Honor, in order to save the court's time, I wish to say that on the day this crime was committed, December 20, 1980, I, and Sue Ellen Hunt, were in Carson City, Nevada, getting married. I believe that Your Honor will find ample proof of that on file with the bureau of vital statistics in Carson City, complete with irrefutable times and places." Hunt sat down, looked around the courtroom, and then smiled at what he saw.

The judge was staring incredulously at the DA, the DA was staring open-mouthed at Hunt, the defense looked as if they'd just won the state lottery, and four ashen-faced police investigators on the case looked as if *they* had just been indicted for first-degree murder. It was one of those occasions that is known colloquially in the lawyer business as tight-asshole time, in that an accused has suddenly presented evidence unknown to anyone else, which could throw the case against him into total disarray and make the DA and his minions look like a bunch of total idiots.

The DA turned to glare at the cops who'd brought the case to his office—and had assured him that the evidence was cleaner than a hound's fangs, and *ab so lutely* foolproof.

The judge seemed to recover first, and asked what the People had to say—to which the People replied that they wanted a sidebar. When the defense, the People, and the investigating team were all hanging onto the edge of the judge's bench, excitedly stage-whispering, waving their hands and spraying the judge with coffee and tobacco-flavored saliva, the DA demanded that His Honor order the defense to tell why they hadn't mentioned Hunt's alibi. To which the defense snarled that they weren't required to mention a damn thing, and on top of that, they didn't even know what Hunt was going to say when he stood up . . . after all, they had only met their clients ten minutes before . . . but now they were asking that all charges against both defendants be dismissed.

The People asked for and were granted a thirty-minute recess in order to phone the vital statistics folks in Carson City, Nevada, to make sure there was such a marriage license on file. The defense, having nothing better to do, went along to listen in on the call. Sure enough, a David Raymond Hunt and a Sue Ellen "Wilson" had taken out a marriage license at 1:15 P.M. on December 20, 1989, and were married by a justice of the peace at 2:30 P.M..

It was now time for some hallway justice, that time-honored method whereby eighty percent of criminal cases are settled— with or without the immediate knowledge of the plaintiff or defendant. To those familiar with court proceedings, the Hallowed Halls of Justice are just that—the courthouse hallways, where lawyers and DAs argue, threaten, beg, bluff, and act their way to the best deal they can get from their opponent.

The scenario between the People and defense in the Riggin-Gonsalves case probably went something like this:

"That marriage license doesn't mean a thing! Anyone could have gone through the motions for Hunt and his girl."

"Yeah? Well, you're gonna hafta *prove* it!"

"Yeah? Well, I damn well *will* prove it! I'm going back and ask for a thirty-day continuance in order to get an exemplar done on that so-called marriage license!"

"Yeah? Well, we're gonna ask for a dismissal because these are Mickey Mouse charges! Whatta you think of *that?*"

"I think you must be out of your mind and I'm going in there and get the go-ahead to totally destroy that little murderer's alibi!"

And so on and so forth . . .

The facts are that the judge refused the defense motion for a dismissal, granted a continuance for the People until January 16, 1990, allowed the charges of two counts of first-degree murder and kidnapping against the two defendants to stand until the next hearing, entered into the record that the People were asking for the death penalty for Hunt and Thompson, life without parole for Sue Ellen, and approved the People's request that the defendants be held without bond.

Hunt's surprise alibi claim that he was getting married on the day he is accused of helping kill two people was a good ploy, one that all state-raised convicts like Hunt and his half brother Gerald love to spring out of the blue. It was an excellent delaying tactic, and delay is the name of the game for criminals in the US justice system. What the hell, they'll be doing the time anyway, and the longer a trial is put off on whatever pretext, the better the chance that the DAs quit or retire and are replaced by someone who has no interest in a time-consuming rehash of a no-publicity, long-forgotten crime; that witnesses die, disappear, or just flat refuse to have their private lives disrupted for the umpteenth time.

It is an ironic fact that many condemned murderers outlive the judge, DA, the witnesses, and their defenders. Of course, anyone who has ever wasted their time by watching "who-done-it" TV programs will instantly point out that if Hunt and Sue Ellen were married at 2:30 P.M. in Carson City, they could have easily driven the sixty-odd smiles back to Yolo County by 10:00 P.M. on December 20, 1980, and then killed Riggin and Gonsalves at their leisure. But the People will have to prove that to a jury somewhere down the road.

The People of Woodland in Yolo County, California, have adamantly declared that they, and they alone, will try the Hunts and Thompson for the kidnap-murder of John Riggin and Sabrina Gonsalves. All information about the case, the defendants, the victims, the evidence—has been cut off from the public by court order in an effort to prevent a change of venue. After all, the Yolo County prosecutors would not want to miss out on all that career-building publicity that will attend the eventual conviction of Gerald Armond Gallego's half brother and sister-in-law.

As for Richard Harold Thompson, one cop said, "I don't really know where that Thompson guy fits in this deal, but even if he just went along for the ride, he's gonna take a real hard fall by letting himself get mixed up with the Hunts."

As for publicity, Yolo County could use some—good, for a change. The elected high sheriff of the county has been indicted by a federal grand jury for bribery, conspiracy, racketeering, and other high crimes and misdemeanors. And the ten-year delay in any positive developments on the Riggin-Gonsalves case didn't exactly endear the local police to the citizenry. When all is said and done, when all the posturing in front of TV cameras is completed, when all the platitudes have been mouthed to the press, one should remember the old police axiom, "In a stranger-killing-stranger homicide, you can keep the clues, just give me a good, reliable informant anytime . . ." And fortunately for all concerned, they apparently stumbled over one.

So far in the Gallego-Hunt case, there are at least fifteen victims who were slaughtered without any cause excusable or acceptable under the law. Why are there hundreds upon hundreds of known and unknown serial killer homicide victims in America? Are they nonentities going in harm's way? In the wrong place at the wrong time? Just bad luck on the victims' parts? To even attempt an answer to those rhetorical questions would seem to put the *victims* at fault for getting themselves killed. One thing would appear to be absolutely certain—without Gerald Armond Gallego, David Raymond Hunt, Richard Harold Thompson, and their female associates, it is almost inconceivable that any of those fifteen young people would be rotting in their graves.